ROUTLEDGE LIBRARY EDITION:
SYNTAX

Volume 2

STUDIES IN THE SYNTAX OF RELATIVE AND COMPARATIVE CAUSES

STUDIES IN THE SYNTAX OF RELATIVE AND COMPARATIVE CAUSES

AVERY D. ANDREWS III

LONDON AND NEW YORK

First published in 1985 by Garland Publishing, Inc.

This edition first published in 2017
by Routledge
2 Park Square, Milton Park, Abingdon, Oxon OX14 4RN

and by Routledge
711 Third Avenue, New York, NY 10017

Routledge is an imprint of the Taylor & Francis Group, an informa business

© 1985 Avery D. Andrews III

All rights reserved. No part of this book may be reprinted or reproduced or utilised in any form or by any electronic, mechanical, or other means, now known or hereafter invented, including photocopying and recording, or in any information storage or retrieval system, without permission in writing from the publishers.

Trademark notice: Product or corporate names may be trademarks or registered trademarks, and are used only for identification and explanation without intent to infringe.

British Library Cataloguing in Publication Data
A catalogue record for this book is available from the British Library

ISBN: 978-1-138-21859-8 (Set)
ISBN: 978-1-315-43729-3 (Set) (ebk)
ISBN: 978-1-138-20776-9 (Volume 2) (hbk)
ISBN: 978-1-138-20777-6 (Volume 2) (pbk)
ISBN: 978-1-315-46117-5 (Volume 2) (ebk)

Publisher's Note
The publisher has gone to great lengths to ensure the quality of this reprint but points out that some imperfections in the original copies may be apparent.

Disclaimer
The publisher has made every effort to trace copyright holders and would welcome correspondence from those they have been unable to trace.

Studies in the Syntax of Relative and Comparative Clauses

Avery D. Andrews III

Garland Publishing, Inc. ■ New York & London
1985

Library of Congress Cataloging-in-Publication Data

Andrews, Avery D. (Avery Delano), 1949–
  Studies in the syntax of relative and comparative clauses.

  (Outstanding dissertations in linguistics)
  Originally presented as the author's thesis (Ph.D.—Massachusetts Institute of Technology), 1975.
  Bibliography: p.
  1. Grammar, Comparative and general—Relative Clauses.   2. Grammar, Comparative and general—Comparative clauses.   3. English language—Comparative clauses.   I. Title.   II. Series.
P297.A53   1985   415   85-15903
ISBN 0-8240-5419-9 (alk. paper)

© 1985 by Avery D. Andrews III
All rights reserved

The volumes in this series are printed on acid-free, 250-year-life paper.

Printed in the United States of America

To Cindy

Meditatio

When I carefully consider the curious habits of dogs
I am compelled to conclude
That man is the superior animal.

When I consider the curious habits of man
I confess, my friend, I am puzzled.

-- Ezra Pound

Acknowledgements

I am indebted to many people in the preparation of this thesis. Susumo Kuno, David Perlmutter and Stephen Anderson brought me into linguistics, and started me working on many of the topics that now concern me, and have helped me with discussions on a variety of specific problems connected with this work.

Ken Hale and Paul Kiparsky, who understand everything that has to do with language, have helped me continually throughout my time at MIT. Hu Matthews has also greatly aided my development. Morris Halle and Noam Chomsky, *che discernono della vera cittade almen la torre*, have helped with their teaching, advice and encouragement, and have by example set the highest intellectual standards. What conception I have of serious work derives largely from them. Finally, my advisor, Haj Ross, has long listened to my stories, corrected my papers, and curbed my excesses. His and Professor Chomsky's extensive remarks on earlier drafts of this thesis have been enormously valuable.

I have also benefitted from contact with George Lakoff, Paul Postal and Jim McCawley, who have influenced my thinking on a variety of topics. I am especially grateful to Joan Bresnan, whose work has provided a basis for much of my own, and whose advice and encouragement has been very helpful. Howard Lasnik, J.R. Vergnaud, and Wayles Browne have also stirred and provoked me with useful stimulation and criticism.

Among past and present fellow students, I would especially like to thank Mark Liberman, Cindy Allen, Sandy Chung and Michael Szamosi; and also Arlene Berman, Fred Katz, Ivan Sag, Dorothy Siegel, Edwin Williams, Bob Fiengo, Bob May and Jane Grimshaw. Claudia Corum, Polly Jacobson and Larry Martin deserve a wave of the hand as well.

Needless to say, I, rather than these scholars, am responsible for the many faults of this work.

I owe a debt to a succession of roommates and friends who have tolerated more household negligence than they should have had to, and especially Bob and Michael, who had to put up with the special chaos of dissertation year.

I would like to thank my parents and family, whose confidence that I would actually get through it all has supported me in many moments of doubt, and also Carey and Edith Welch for their friendship in Cambridge.

I am grateful again to Cindy, for help other than intellectual.

And last, a word for Fran, who as we all know, really runs the department.

* * *

I would like to thank Ellalene Seymour for typing this version of the manuscript and Rose Butt for checking it. This was made possible by the support of the Department of Linguistics, The Faculties, The Australian National University.

Contents

Introduction... 1
Chapter 1. A Typology of Relative Clauses.......... 4
   1.1 Constituent Structure Relations............ 10
   1.2 The Treatment of NP_{rel}..................... 83
   1.3 The Extraction Analysis.................... 108
   Footnotes to Chapter 1......................... 114
   Appendix to Chapter 1.......................... 116

Chapter 2. Comparative Clauses in English.......... 117
   2.1 The Head, Revisited........................ 118
   2.2 Comparative Clauses in the Base............ 156
   2.3 Global Relations........................... 172
   Footnotes to Chapter 2......................... 196

Bibliography.. 197

INTRODUCTION

Bresnan (1972) suggested that much of the grammar of sentence-embedding could be divided into two areas: the 'predicate complement' system and the 'determiner complement' system. Predicate complements serve in syntactic structure as complements to nouns, verbs and adjectives, and correspond in logical structure to the arguments of predicates. Determiner complements are the relative and comparative clauses. They appear to bear some sort of relationship to determiners, and in logical structure, they restrict the variables bound by the operators corresponding to these determiners. In this study, I will pursue two different approaches towards the syntax of the determiner complement system.

In chapter one, I conduct a typological survey of relative clauses in the languages of the world. I direct most of my attention to determining the varieties of constituent structure relations between relative clauses and their heads. I ultimately discern three major types: headless relatives, which have no head embedded relatives, which may occur either attached to their head or extraposed; and adjoined relatives, which appear at the beginning or the end of the matrix. The distinction between extraposed relatives and adjoined relatives that follow their matrix will not emerge until the discussion of adjoined relatives in section 1.1.3., and will be further developed in chapter two.

One major finding is that the various types have underlying structures that are largely identical to their surface structures. Headless relatives lack heads in underlying structure, and extraposed and adjoined relatives are not generated as underlying constituents with their heads, but in their surface positions. I propose that headless relatives are introduced by a rule NP → $\bar{S}$, embedded relatives on heads are introduced by NP → NP $\bar{S}$ and NP → $\bar{S}$ NP, extraposed relatives are introduced by S → S $\bar{S}$, and adjoined relatives are introduced by $\bar{S}$ → COMP ($\bar{S}$) S ($\bar{S}$). The principal evidence for the claim that extraposed and adjoined relatives are generated in the base in their surface positions is that they both may have multiple heads.

I also examine various things that happen to the "relative" NP (wh Marking, Deletion, etc.) in the relative clause, and discuss some possible evidence that the heads of relative clauses are extracted from within them as a copy of the relative NP.

In the course of the chapter I discuss numerous theoretical issues, but the primary focus is descriptive and suggestive rather than theoretical. There are obviously great limitations on the depth and breadth of the coverage of individual languages. Furthermore, reduced relatives will not be treated, and the structures most closely related to relative clauses, interrogative and focus constructions, will be ignored. Despite these limitations, I believe that the chapter provides a valid and useful picture of the relative clause construction in universal grammar.

In chapter 2, I examine comparative clauses in English, integrating the material with selected aspects of the work in chapter one, and taking a considerably more theoretical standpoint. I first examine Bresnan's (1973) analysis of the head constituents of comparative clauses, such constituents as *as good a linguist* in *he is as good a linguist as she is*. I modify the analysis in certain respects, and formulate the crucial rule of 'QP Raising' that Bresnan leaves unformulated. I also extend the analysis to accomodate the 'indefinite comparative' construction of *the more you study, the less you know*.

In the course of these efforts, I motivate certain

theoretical principles on the basis that they reduce the
range of data needed to determine the correct analysis of
grammatical phenomena. Some are principles of rule-appli-
cation to ensure that rules motivated by simple paradigms
apply correctly in more complex cases. There is also a
convention rendering certain potential derived constituent
structures ungrammatical. This rules out an analysis which
the evaluation measure prefers for a small data set in
favor of a more complex analysis that is in fact the correct one when more data is considered.

The identification of certain analyses as minimal is
based on possibly erroneous inspection rather than rigorous
proof, and is aided by the assumption, perhaps too strong,
that the data which determines the selection of grammars
specifies certain strings as ungrammatical, and provides
the deep structures for those that are grammatical. Despite
the lack of rigour and the overly strong nature of the
assumptions, the discussion shows that it is possible to
argue from explanatory adequacy with a considerable higher
degree of explicitness than is usually attempted (with
certain exceptions, such as some recent work by Hamburger,
Culicover and Wexler).

Further implications are that Bach's universal rule
hypothesis, suggested by Peters (1972) as a solution to the
projection problem (the problem of getting linguistic data
to determine grammars and thereby project the given data to
predictions of more data) may be an unnecessarily violent
step. One can get substantial results from imposing highly
substantive restrictions on linguistic structure without
dictating an inventory of rules. One might, for example,
consider a restriction requiring that an S (a) be coordinate
(b) be a predicate nominal or adjective construction (c) or
otherwise have exactly one verb.

I next show that the traditional assumption that comparative clauses in English are generated in the determiners of the QP they modify cannot be maintained. I show that
ordinary comparatives correspond to embedded relatives,
being introduced by a rule $X^3 \rightarrow X^3 \bar{S}$ (N^3 being, for example,

an X-bar notation for NP) when they appear attached to a
head, and by S → S S̄ when they appear extraposed. I then
show that the indefinite comparative mentioned above corresponds to the adjoined relative clause.

I finally develop, in rather tentative and incomplete
form, a solution to the classical problem of the selection
restrictions between degree particles and complementizers
of comparative and result clauses, and of similar restrictions involving relative clauses and their heads. The
solution takes the form of a system of extra-constituent
structure 'global relations' between degree particles and
NP determiners and the complementizers of relative and
comparative clauses. As much of the theory of this system
as I formulate is common to both comparative and relative
clauses, thus supporting Bresnan's claim that they constitute a unified system, the determiner complement system.

I close by using the mechanisms developed to formulate
some principles that have the effect of reducing the database needed to determine correct analyses for relative
clauses, thus returning to the problem of projection taken
up at the beginning of the chapter.

1. THE TYPOLOGY OF RELATIVE CLAUSES:[1]

In this chapter I offer a typological survey of relative
clauses in the languages of the world. The genesis of this
work is the observation of Bach (1965) that relative clauses
differ less between languages than one might expect. It
appears that a limited number of options are being put together in a limited number of ways. The goal of this study
is then to present a broad picture of what relative clauses
are like in the languages of the world.

What is a relative clause? For the purposes of this
chapter, a relative clause is any clause with approximately
the semantic structure and function of a relative clause
(restrictive or nonrestrictive) in English. I shall sharpen
this rough criterion somewhat by saying that a relative
clause is a subordinate clause that modifies a constituent
external to it by virtue of containing a constituent that is

in some sense semantically equivalent to the modified constituent. I shall call the modified constituent the head constituent, and the equivalent constituent within the relative clause the relative constituent. In the case where both are NP, I shall designate them as NP_{hd} and NP_{rel}. The relative clause and its matrix clause I shall designate as S_{rel} and S_{mat}. In addition to being vague, this account is also too narrow: we shall find in section 1.1.2 a kind of relative clause that has no head constituent. But in spite of its deficiencies, this account permits work to begin.

To improve on my intuitive description of the semantic structure and function of relative clauses, it would be necessary to adopt some particular theory of the semantics of natural languages. I shall not do so here, but refer the reader to (Keenan 1972), (Montague 1974) and (Hintikka 1974) for some interesting alternatives. On the basis of the theoretical discussion of relative clauses that I will offer in chapter two, I will provide a syntactic definition of the notion 'relative clause.

Once one has made the initial observation that there do not seem to be terribly many types of relative clause constructions, an attempt to construct a systematic inventory of relative clause types is immediately justified. To the extent that there is inexplicably little variation in the syntactic structures used to express some kind of logical form, there is a possibility for narrowing linguistic theory, and therefore for achieving a better explanation of the possibility of learning languages.

This consideration is strengthened by the fact that the relative clause is a structure with extremely rich connections elsewhere in the theory of grammar. Some of the more prominent syntactic contributors are the determiner system of NP, the grammar of subordinate clauses, pronominalization, syntactic variables, and functional sentence perspective. On the semantic side, relativization is no less involved with other aspects of grammar, for example with variables, scope and binding; with coreference, and with presupposition. Hence, restrictions on relativization are likely to be reflections of more general restrictions of broad explanatory potency.

The primary purpose of this survey is to provide a background of information about diverse languages in order to convey a sense of what relativization is like in the languages of the world. I also wish, however, to suggest a general theory, which I develop gradually and informally in this chapter, and present more formally in the text.

The principal results of the survey are that some relative clauses do not have heads in underlying structure, and that others do not at any level of structure form constituents with their heads, but rather may be separated from them by an unbounded stretch of material. Most theories of relative clauses make crucial use of constituent structure relations between relative clauses and their heads in stating various rules and restrictions. For example, wh-Preposing rules for relative clauses are often given a form like (1):

(1) $W_1 - [_{NP} \text{ NP} - [_S W_2 - \text{NP} - W_3]] - W_2,\quad 2 = 4$

$\quad\;\; 1 \qquad\;\; 2 \qquad\;\; 3 \quad\; 4 \quad\; 5 \qquad 6 \quad\Longrightarrow$

$\quad\;\; 1 \qquad\;\; 2 \qquad 4+3 \;\;\emptyset\quad\; 5 \qquad 6$

To preserve an account of the rules and restrictions involving relative clauses in the face of the breakdown of constant constituent structure relations between relative clauses and their heads, I propose a theory of extra-constituent structure relations that identify the relative and modified constituents of relative clauses. These relations may be represented as systems of directed arrows connecting the nodes of a tree. A more formal treatment will be given in chapter 2.

I develop the theory as an extension of Bresnan's theory of complementizers (Bresnan 1970, 1972, 1974a). Bresnan hypothesizes that clauses are introduced by a rule $\bar{S} \rightarrow \text{COMP S}$ (or by its trivial variant $\bar{S} \rightarrow \text{S COMP}$) where COMP is the category of the clause-introductory particles that Bresnan calls complementizers. These complementizers then determine important aspects of the semantic interpretation of main and subordinate clauses. Important among the complementizers recognized by Bresnan are the *that* that introduces many finite clauses, the *for* that introduces infinitives, the abstract 'Q' that Baker (1968, 1970) proposes to introduce questions and indirect questions, and the *than* and *as* that introduce comparative (and some relative) clauses.

I propose that universal grammar provides a feature of COMP, 'R', that is specified as [+R] on the COMP of relative clauses. A preterminal that is [+COMP +R] I shall call a relative complementizer. 'R' guides semantic interpretation of relative clauses in a language universal fashion, and is also involved in language particular grammar in various ways. For example, many languages have special morphemes that precede or follow relative clauses. These may be regarded as elements that are lexically inserted for relative complementizers.

I shall extend Bresnan's theory by claiming that there are two extra-constituent structure relations in which relative complementizers participate. First, there is the trigger-target relation, which holds between the COMP of a relative clause and its relative constituent. Second, there is the head-trigger relation that holds between the COMP of a relative clause and its head constituent. In cases where these constituents have determiners, it seems best to relate the COMP with the determiners rather than with the containing constituents. The reasons for this will be seen in chapter 2.

Assuming English relative clauses to be introduced by an NP → NP $\bar{S}$ rule, we then get the following representation for *the boy who Zack gave a joint to*:

(2)

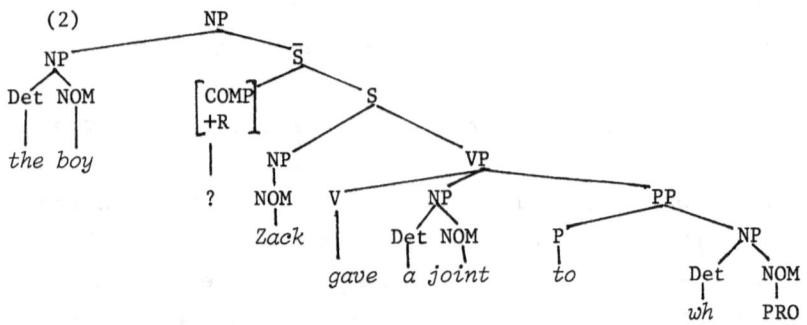

The extra-constituent structure relations are crucially used in explaining the properties of examples in which the relative clause cannot be associated with the head by a simple constituent structure relation. Such an example is Ross and Perlmutter's (1970) *a man came in and a woman went out who were similar*:

(3)

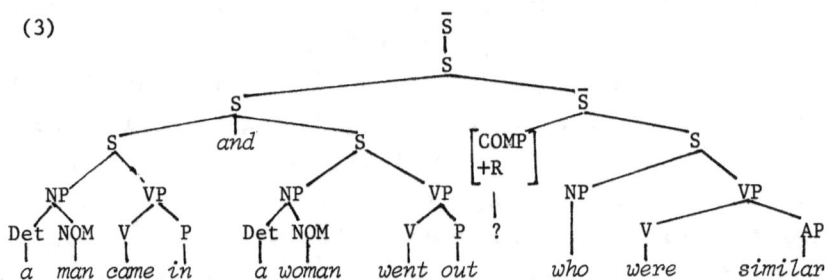

Observe that the nature of the predicate in the relative clause makes it impossible to derive this example by extraposing the relative clause within each conjunct and then applying Right Node Raising.

The reasons for formulating the system along the lines given here instead of in other ways that one might imagine will be primarily developed in chapter 2. Observe for the present, however, that Baker's (1968, 1969) work on questions (attacked by (Kuno and Robinson 1972) and re-supported by (Hankamer 1974)) shows that there are connections between complementizers and 'target' constituents within their clauses in cases where there is nothing like a head constituent. Furthermore, the properties of result clauses associated with (sometimes multiple) occurrences of *so* in examples like *Bill drank so much beer in so little time that he threw up* (see Liberman 1974)) show that there are connections between clauses and head constituents that are separated from them even when there is no constituent in the clause other than the complementizer that can be connected to the head. Our treatment thus minimizes the variety of extra-constituent structure relations utilized.

I shall conduct the study under several limitations of scope. First, I shall for the most part be restricted to describing the more obvious formal properties of relative clauses: what morphemes mark them, whether anything moves or deletes, where it goes, etc.. Subtler topics, such as accessibility (see (Keenan 1972), (Keenan and Comrie 1972)), will sometimes be treated, but only sporadically.

Second, I shall not attempt to consistently draw fine distinctions between types of relative clauses. It is obvious that the category 'relative clause' in English alone covers a wide range of different constructions, and in universal grammar the range can only be wider. There are for example restrictive relatives, ordinary nonrestrictives on NP, nonrestrictives in both *which* and *as* on constituents other than NP (*Max squealed, for which he'll die; Mary is pregnant, as you know*), *whatever*-clausal NP (*I'll take whatever items I find to my superiors*) and pseudo-relative comparatives (*he's not the linguist he used to be*). These types are surely only a beginning. I believe that a thorough investigation of the variety of types of relative clauses in English alone would yield many more species than I discern in this study for language as a whole.

Amongst all these types, the restrictive relative clause on a definite head, which has the semantic effect of forming a definite description from a clause, seems to be the core relative clause. Almost all languages (Jakobson reports Gilyak as an exception) have some equivalent to this construction, while the representation of the other types is more sparse. Portguguese, for example, lacks nonrestrictives that modify S (personal communication of Carlos Quicoli), while Navajo lacks nonrestrictives entirely. Japanese and Turkish, on the other hand, make no syntactic distinction between restrictive and nonrestrictive, using the same structure indifferently for both. It is interesting to observe that speakers of these languages seem to have difficulty in seeing the difference between the two usages. Inasmuch as the restrictive clause on a definite head NP seems to be the most prominent and universally represented variety of relative clause, I shall concentrate on it and mention other types less consistently.

Finally, I shall restrict my attention to relatives that are clauses in surface structure. I shall ignore reduced relatives.

The varieties of relative clause construction submit to classification under a unified scheme. On the other hand, languages seem to select their particular inventory of relative constructions in accordance with no obvious principle. I will therefore organize the typology around the kinds of construction rather than around some classification of the languages.

I will introduce a language at the first point in the discussion where it has something especially significant to offer, at that time giving the necessary background information to render the examples comprehensible. I will then return to any given language as often as necessary in the sequel. In an appendix to this chapter, I provide an index of languages that specifies where in the chapter I give substantial discussion of a language, and what my sources of information on it are.

In section 1.1 I discuss the constituent structure relations obtaining between relative clauses and their heads, in section 1.2 I investigate the fate of the relative constituent, and in section 1.3 I review some phenomena that suggest that some relative clauses have their heads extracted from within them.

1.1 Constituent Structure Relations: In surface structure, relative clauses may appear dominated by an NP within their matrix S, or they may appear at the beginning or the end of the matrix, separated from their head by a stretch of material that is in the general case unbounded. The former kind

I call embedded relatives, the latter, adjoined. Embedded relatives may appear with a head or without one. If they have a head, they may precede or follow it. We thus have three varieties of embedded relative clause. There are then two types of adjoined relative: anticipatory relatives, which precede their matrix and trailing relatives which follow. I shall also suggest that there are extraposed relatives in addition to trailing relatives.

These five surface structure types seem to divide naturally into three major families: the headed embedded relatives, comprising pre- and post-relatives, the headless relatives, and the adjoined relatives. We will find that the types within each family, which differ from each other only in relations of linear order, are closely related. Nevertheless, it will also become apparent that each position has some peculiarities of its own. Hence the existence of transformational relations between paired linear order types is possible, but not entirely unproblematic. We will however, find arguments that the three major families are not transformationally derived one from another, but rather that the deep structures for each family are of roughly the same form as the surface structures.

In section 1.1.1 I will discuss headed embedded relatives, in section 1.1.2 I will discuss headless relatives, and in 1.1.3 I will discuss adjoined relatives. Finally, in 1.1.4 I will make some general remarks.

1.1.1 Embedded Relatives with Heads: These are the most familiar, although perhaps not the most common, types of relative clauses. All of the types studied in (Bach 1965), for example, are in this family. Since embedded relatives with heads have been studied for so long, there are a great many proposals in circulation as to what their underlying structures and derivations are. The majority of these are conveniently summarized and evaluated in (Stockwell, Schachter and Partee 1973).

If we take (4) as representing the constituent structure of the English NP,

(4)
```
            NP
          /    \
        Det    NOM
         |    /    \
         a   N      PP
             |     /  \
          picture P    NP
                  |    |
                  of  Lilly
```

then the most conservative alternatives for the structure of the restrictive relative in English are given by letting it be introduced by one of the rules Det → Art $\bar{S}$, NOM → NOM $\bar{S}$, N → N $\bar{S}$ or NP → NP $\bar{S}$. Of these, my personal favorite is NP → NP $\bar{S}$, and I will assume this rule and its mirror-image NP → $\bar{S}$ NP when I give structures for pre- and post- relative clauses.

(Brame 1968) proposes another analysis in which the head of the relative clause is extracted from within it as a copy of the relative constituent, of which a pronominal copy may be left behind in the form of a relative pronoun. This analysis is proposed in order to explain the grammaticality of such examples as *the headway (that) we made pleased our advisor.* *headway* is a noun which is characteristically restricted to being an underlying object of *make*. Brame's analysis explains the grammaticality of the above example by providing it with an underlying structure in which this condition is met.

(Vergnaud 1974) works out for French a version of Brame's analysis in considerable detail. He gives (pp.81-84) an argument which shows that if there is an extraction of the head from the clause, then the extracted constituent must be an NP, and that if there is not such an extraction, then the NP → NP $\bar{S}$ analysis must be chosen over the three alternatives given above.

The argument may be easily adapted to English. Consider examples such as the following:

(5) a. The man and the woman who were related got married.
    b. An electron and a positron that collided produced a shower of gamma rays.
    c. Any boy and any girl who love each other will buy this device.

These examples share with Ross and Perlmutter's extraposed relative (example 3) the property that the nature of the predicate prevents the relative clause from reaching its surface position by being generated in each conjunct and then being fused and attached to the entire coordinate structure by Right Node Raising. It is immediate that if one extracts, one must extract NP rather than a sub-constituent of NP; and that the NP → NP $\bar{S}$ analysis can generate the constituent structure of these examples while the Det → Art $\bar{S}$, NOM → NOM $\bar{S}$ and N → N $\bar{S}$ analyses cannot. Although I will not adopt the extraction analysis in the following pages, in section 1.3 I will discuss a variety of phenomena which could probably be made to support it.

Although I adopt the NP → NP $\bar{S}$ analysis for postrelative restrictives and its mirror image for pre-relatives, we shall in the following pages find some difficulties with these rules. One such problem is provided by examples like *the motion that we made to expel Harry* or *the proof that I gave in class that pi is irrational* (pointed out to me by Mark Baltin). If one believes that complement clauses are introduced by a NOM → N $\bar{S}$ rule, then these examples suggest that at least some relative clauses are introduced by an N → N $\bar{S}$ rule. We shall find other such problems below.

One matter deserving discussion is the constituent structure of nonrestrictive relatives in English. Unlike restrictive clauses, nonrestrictives cannot stack:

(6) a. the man who was laughing who you pointed out
to me was arrested.
b. *Bill, who was laughing, who you pointed out
to me, was arrested.

We also observe that a nonrestrictive can be attached to an NP modified by a restrictive:

(7) the man who was laughing, who you pointed out to me,
to me, was arrested.

For a restrictive to modify an NP + nonrestrictive combination is, of course, impossible.

Martin (1972), in an extensive study of the restrictive-nonrestrictive distinction in English, proposes that there should be as little structural differentiation between the types as possible, with the major burden of explanation for the distinctions resting upon the differing logical form of the types. But we shall see that in Japanese semantically nonrestrictive clauses seem to be indistinguishable from restrictives, even having the power to stack. This suggests that the special features of nonrestrictives in English should receive an explanation in terms of syntactic structure.

A traditional proposal for the derivation of nonrestrictive relatives is to get them from underlying coordinate structures: a rule called Swooping would produce (8b) from (8a), then nonrestrictive clause formation would yield (8c) from (8b):

(8) a. Clarence is a swinger and he is wearing mauve socks.
    b. Clarence, and he is a swinger, is wearing mauve socks.
    c. Clarence, who is a swinger, is wearing mauve socks.

(Ross 1967: section 6.2.4.2) notes a difficulty with this derivation:

(9) Is even Clarence, who is a swinger, wearing mauve socks?

Of course we can also embed nonrestrictives in imperatives, and (Martin 1972) notes that imperatives can serve as nonrestrictives within declaratives. Likewise even interrogatives have a marginal capacity to be nonrestrictive relatives. These points are illustrated in the following:

(10) a. Get Bill, who is in charge of this operation.
     b. I have included a CV, which find enclosed.
     c. I want to talk to that man, who the hell is he, anyway?
     d. Thoughts, which how found they harbour in thy breast, / Adam, misthought of her to thee so dear? (Paradise Lost IX 288-289)

Since imperative and interrogative clauses cannot be conjoined with declaratives, the coordinate structure source for nonrestrictive relatives has a problem.

It is interesting to note that 'Swooped' coordinate structures are restricted in the same way that ordinary coordinate structures are:

(11) a. *Is Clarence, and he is a swinger, wearing mauve socks?

b. *Buy Clarence, and he is a swinger, a new gas furnace.

This observation reinforces Ross' counterargument to the Swooping derivation for nonrestrictive relatives.

Ross unenthusiastically proposes to analyse nonrestrictives by resurrecting the concept of 'generalized transformation,' having nonrestrictives derived by a transformation that combines two main clauses. Hence (9) would be derived from (12):

   (12) Clarence is a swinger. Is even Clarence wearing
        white socks?

(I have reversed the order of clauses from Ross' in order to make the discourse sound better).

But even this proposal, which Lakoff (1974) has recently advocated generalizing into a theory of 'syntactic amalgams' falls in the face of the following example:[2]

   (13) everybody got a pen, with which he wrote a letter.

The relative clause here has the superficial appearance of a nonrestrictive, and seems to the intuition to be nonrestrictive in force. Nevertheless, it manages to be within the scope of the universal quantifier in its matrix, as is betrayed by the fact that *he* is bound by that quantifier. Such binding is of course impossible between conjuncts or between main clauses in a discourse:

   (14) a. *Everybody got a pen (,) and he wrote a letter
           with it.
        b. *Everybody got a pen. he wrote a letter with it.

The subordinate clause of (13) also has deeper properties of nonrestrictives. For example, Martin (1972) notes that the relative pronoun of a nonrestrictive, but not of a restrictive, can be the object of *of* in a partitive quantificational construction:

   (15) a. The boys, some of whom were rich kids, were arrested.
        b. *The boys some of whom were rich kids were arrested.

Now observe (16):

   (16) everybody got three pens, with one of which he wrote a
        letter.

Ross' proposal likewise seems doomed.

Chomsky has proposed (class lectures, Spring 1973) to introduce nonrestrictive relatives by a 'three-dimensional' rule NP $\cdots\rightarrow$ $\bar{S}$. This notation means that the relative clause is in the sentence structure and somehow related to the NP it modifies, but does not bear linear order or dominance relations to it. Late linearization rules are then supposed to put the clause in the position where we see it on the surface. This proposal could probably be made to avoid the difficulties we have posted against the others, but it possesses the theoretical demerit of requiring an unworked out and ad-hoc modification in our conception of what a sentence structure is. A proposal within the bounds of ordinary notions of constituent structure would be preferable.

Work by Siegel (1974) suggests an answer. Siegel proposes that NP in English (and in languages generally) are introduced by a rule CP → NP CASE (or, of course, its mirror image). She identifies CP as $\bar{\bar{N}}$ and NP as $\bar{N}$, but this is irrelevant here. We may explain the facts that nonrestrictives do not stack and that they follow restrictives by introducing them as sisters of NP under CP. The following examples show that nonrestrictives cannot follow the genitive case-marker:

(17) a. *Bill's, who is a swinger, house is too cold.
 b. *I gave a picture of Bill's, who is a swinger, to Maurice.

I therefore propose to introduce nonrestrictive relatives by revising Siegel's rule to CP → NP ($\bar{S}$) CASE.

We may also observe that nonrestrictives do not sound very good before the genitive case-marker:

(18) a. ? *Bill, who is a swinger, 's house is too cold.
 b. ? *I gave a picture of Bill, who is a swinger, 's to Maurice.

This may be explained by the observation that the genitive case-marker 's is an element which must be a phonological word with the material immediately preceding it. The pause that follows nonrestrictives makes this impossible.

I shall return to the subject of nonrestrictive relatives and Swooping in chapter 2. For the present, I shall end by calling attention to two of the most obvious questions of universal grammar that are raised by my proposal. First, is the association of NP → NP S̄ with restrictive and CP → NP (S̄) CASE with nonrestrictive relativization an accident of English? Second, what linear order variants does the CP → NP (S̄) CASE rule have? I do not have answers to these questions, though I will venture a speculation in section 1.1.1.4.

Now, at last, on to the long-awaited languages! In section 1.1.1.1 I will look at post-relative clauses, in 1.1.1.2 I will look at pre-relatives and in 1.1.1.3 I will examine a number of languages in which the two constructions cooccur. The main result to emerge will be that these relative clauses are the same as adjectives in their external constituent structure relations. Finally, in 1.1.1.4 I will summarize the results and speculate on some tendencies associated with linear order of head and relative clause.

1.1.1.1 Post-Relatives: I have proposed two underlying structures for post-relative clauses in English, (19) for restrictives, and (20) for nonrestrictives:

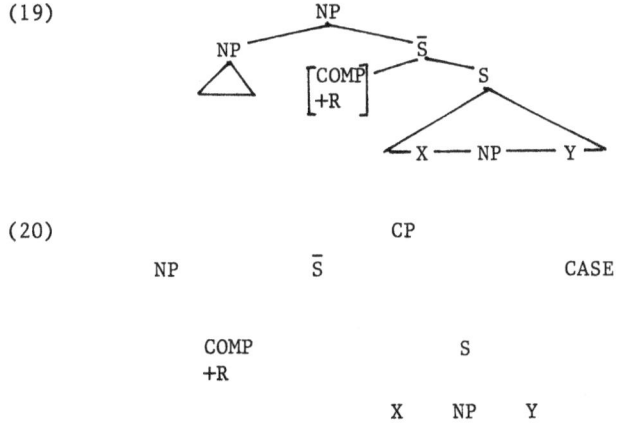

Some languages with a post-relative clause construction that are genetically unrelated are the following:

(21) Languages having Post-relative Clauses:

English	Samoan
Hungarian	Maasai
Hebrew	Micmac
Georgian	Eskimo
Swahili	Shan
Nuer	Vietnamese
Crow	Dyirbal
Papago	Dagbani
Hottentot	

It requires subtle work to choose between (19) and (20), or to argue for them against alternatives. I shall not, therefore so decide for the languages I examine. We will find the evidence consistent with either of the alternatives.

I shall look first at Samoan, then at Faroese, and finally at Eskimo.

1.1.1.1.1 *Samoan*[3]: Samoan is a VSO language. Naturally then, most modifiers of NP follow the head: adjectives, non-pronominal possessive phrases, prepositional phrases and relative clauses. S_{rel} may have NP_{rel} present in surface structure as a pronoun, or, in subject or object position, the pronoun may be deleted by regular processes of anaphoric pronoun deletion.

Here we see adjectives and possessives following the head N:

(22) a. 'o   le teine puta
         Prt. the girl fat
         "the fat girl"

   b. 'o   va'a lapopo'a
         Prt. boats big
         "big boats"

   c. 'o le paopao o Tavita
          the canoe of David
         "the canoe of David"

   d. 'o le naifi a le taule'ale'a
          the knife of the young man
         "the knife of the young man"

The particle *'o* precedes NP in a variety of environments which I do not understand. One of them is when the NP is being cited. The choice between *a* and *o* is made on semantic grounds which are quite obscure, even to student of Polynesian.

These examples show relative clauses that follow the head:

(23) a. 'ua nofo mai i le malō   le tupu fou na te   le'i
         PERF come to the throne the king new he PAST not
         iloa 'Iosefa
         know Joseph
         "There came to the throne a new king who did not know Joseph."

   b. 'o i   tangata toa   'ua āva   'iate 'ilātou
       there are men valiant PERF do honor to   them
       lea tupulanga ma lea tupulanga
       generation after generation
       "There are valiant men to whom generation after generation do honor."

   c. 'o le mea   lenei 'ua   'ou 'aumaia 'iate 'oe
       Prt. the thing this PERF I   bring   to   you
       "This is the thing which I bring to you."
       (Note that extraposition applies here.)

   d. 'ua fa'apea   le tangata 'ua fai masani
       PERF is the same with the man   PERF does habits
       leanga
       bad
       "It is the same with the man who indulges in bad habits."

In all of these examples, NP_{rel} vanishes from the surface form of the relative clause. (24) shows that this can be effected by a rule applying to ordinary anaphoric pronouns:

(24) a. 'ua 'ou 'aumai 'iate 'oe
         PERF I   bring to   you
         "I have brought it to you."

   b. 'ua fai masani leanga
       PERF does habits bad
       "He indulges in bad habits."

In (25) I give relative clauses in which the relative constituent is a pronominal adverbs, and in (26) I give the corresponding main clauses. The pronominal adverbs are ai and $a'i$, which always migrate to behind the verb:

(25) a. 'o tupe 'ua lātou fa'atau a'i   le fanua
         Prt. money PERF they buy   with it the field
         "the money with which they bought the field"

   b. 'o le fale 'u tupu   ai Moses
       Prt. the house PAST grow up in it Moses
       "the house which Moses grew up in"

(26) a. 'ua lātou fa'atau a'i   le fanua
       PERF they buy   with it the field
       "They bought the field with it."

   b. 'ua tupu   ai
       PAST grew up in it

Grinder (19) has observed that Samoan is quite lax in its observance of Island Constraints. Perlmutter (1972) has proposed to explain this on the basis that there is in Samoan no special rule deleting NP_{rel}. Rather, the effacement, when accomplished at all, is accomplished by Pronoun-Drop rules that apply generally to anaphoric pronouns. Pronoun Drop would involve no variables and hence would not set off Island Constraints.

We may also observe that relative clauses occupy roughly the same position as adjectives, except that they may appear extraposed (23c).

1.1.1.1.2 *Faroese*: Faroese is a close relative of Icelandic spoken in the Faroe Islands. Its conventional orthography, which I use here, maximizes the resemblance to Icelandic and minimizes the relation to the surface phonetic form.

Faroese relative clauses are introduced by ∅, the particle *sum*, or sometimes by *ið*, and NP_{rel} is deleted. Like Icelandic, Faroese often suffixes the definite article of an NP to the head. When a Faroese definite NP (usually with the definite article suffixed) has either a relative clause or an adjective, the demonstrative pronoun *tann* 'that' is usually put before the NP as well. Hence we find the following:

(27) a. tann svarti kettlingur-inn
       that black kitten-the
       "the black kitten"

   b. ta   góða korn-i
       that good corn-the
       "the good corn"

   c. tey høgstu fjøll-ini
       those highest mountains-the
       "the highest mountains"

(28) a. tann maður-inn, sum gjørdi hettar
       that man-the that did this
       "the man who did this"

   b. tað er tað ljótasta   djór, eg nakranti havi soeð
      that is that most loathsome animal I ever   have seen
      "That is the most loathsome animal that I ever have seen."

   c. tær   konur-nar heima   skuldu verða, eru burtursaddar
      those women-the at home should be   are away
      "the women who should be at home are away."

Note that in (28b) the suffixed article is omitted. I do not know when this can happen.

These examples show the relative clause acting like an adjective in a more subtle way than merely being in approximately the same place: in fact, the adjective and the relative clause are in different places in the surface structure. We shall in 1.1.1.4 adduce a consideration that suggests that if there is a transformational relationship, then the position of the relative clause after the head is the basic one, with adjectives being transformationally preposed.

1.1.1.3 *Eskimo*[4]: In Eskimo, the relative clause again has much the same external constituent structure as does the adjective, and can in addition be seen to occupy a position between CASE and the head N.

To render the examples more intelligible, I will present a thumbnail sketch of Eskimo morphology and syntax. Eskimo verbs and nouns are built up from a base morph by adding first derivational suffixes and then inflectional endings. The derivational suffixes are many, and the derivational processes are astonishingly productive, and recursive. Suffixes have the semantic effect of modifying adjectives or adverbs, of higher verbs or nouns, or of many other things.

For example, given a form X we may add the suffix *liur* 'to construct,' to get a verb stem meaning 'to construct an X.' To this may be added another suffix *vig* to get a noun-stem X-*liur*-*vig* 'a place in which to construct an X.' After some more suffixes have been added, perhaps, we may add *liur* again in order to get a verb meaning 'to construct a place in which to construct an X.'.

Nouns are inflected for number and case, and have in addition an agreement suffix showing the person and number of the possessor, if there is one. The numbers are singular, dual and plural. The cases divide naturally into 'syntactic' and 'adverbial.' The syntactic cases are the relative and the absolutive. The relative case is used on possessors of NP and on subjects of transitive verbs. It is thus a genitive-ergative (a great deal of Eskimo scholarship has been devoted to trying to make this dual function of the relative follow from something). It is marked with a suffix that is underlyingly a labial, appearing on the surface mostly as *p* or *m*. The absolutive case is used on the subjects of intransitive verbs and the objects of transitives, and is not marked by any formative. Thus it consists of the stem alone. The adverbial cases are Instrumental, Locative, Allative, etc., and appear to be marked by suffixes that are attached to the relative case-form of the noun.

The basic order of elements of the NP is *(Possessor)* Head ($\begin{smallmatrix}Adjective\\Relative\ Clause\end{smallmatrix}$). Adjectives are morphologically indistinguishable from nouns. It is not clear that they are even a separate class of stems. They agree with the head in number and case. Adjectives must be distinguished from a class of adjectival suffixes that may be added to any nominal stem.

Verbs have a mood suffix followed by subject and object agreement suffixes. Furthermore, stems (which are structures of the form *Base + one or more Derivational Suffixes*) are almost always inherently transitive or intransitive, with inherently transitive stems being understood as reflexive when they appear with intransitive inflection. The moods are various, including an indicative, which is used in declarative main clauses, which has the mood suffix *-va* when transitive and *-vu* when intransitive, an interrogative for questions, transitive and intransitive participial moods, which appear to be nominalization forms of verbs, and various others.

The syntax of relative clauses with transitive verbs is exceedingly complex and difficult to discern, owing to the paucity of examples and multiplicity of structures that they seem to exhibit. But relative clauses with intransitive verbs are comparatively straightforward. They are formed by putting the main verb of S_{rel} into the intransitive participial mood and deleting NP_{rel}.

The intransitive participial appears to be the form which nominalized intransitive verbs normally take. Hence we have (29):

(29) passi-ssa-v-r-put   ... kalaaliy-u-šu-gut
     realize-FUT.TR.IND-it-we   Greenlander-be-INT.PRT-we
     "We shall realize that we are Greenlanders."
     (Bergsland 29.4, pg. 46)

(All examples are from (Bergsland 1955), and the transcription used is his). TR.IND is the hieratic symbol for the transitive indicative mood marker, and INT.PRT is that for the intransitive participial. Here *kalaaliušugut* 'we being Greenlanders' is the object of *paasissavarput* 'we shall realize it.' r in the main verb is the agreement suffix referencing the nominalized S.

In relative clauses, if NP_{rel} is the subject of S_{rel}, then it is deleted, and the intransitive participial acts pretty much like an ordinary adjective. An example of this is (30):

(30) iglu-ni   tammar-tu-q   uyar-i-ni
     cousin$_j$-his$_i$ be lost-INT.PRT-he$_j$ see-TR.PRT-him$_j$-he$_i$
     his$_i$ cousin$_j$ who$_j$ was lost   he$_i$ seeking him$_j$
     unnir-lu-gu
     say-CONT-him$_j$
     saying of him$_j$
     "Saying that he$_i$ was looking for his$_i$ cousin$_j$ who$_j$ was lost
     (Bergsland 29.5.2, pg. 46)

CONT is the symbol for one of the subordinate verbal moods which is used mostly when the time of the subordinate clause is roughly the same as that of the matrix clause, and the subjects of both are identical. If the CONT verb is transitive, as it is here, then its own subject is deleted and leaves no agreement marker on the verb.

ni in *igluni* 'his cousin' and *uyarini* 'he seeking him' is the agreement suffix of the so-called fourth person. This is really a kind of reflexive pronoun, used when the antecedent asymmetrically commands (with respect to both S and NP nodes) the pronoun, and the antecedent is a subject. This reflexivization process is not clause-bounded. The pronoun is virtually always deleted by normal anaphoric processes, leaving the fourth person suffix as a remnant. In *uyarini*, the TR.PRT ending is phonologically reduced and the object agreement suffix is destroyed.

More interesting are some examples in which NP_{rel} is the possessor of the subject of S_{rel}. The verbal character of the intransitive participial verb of S_{rel} is shown by its taking a subject in the absolutive case, regardless of the case of NP_{hd}. Bergsland claims that the participial agrees in number with its subject and in case with the NP_{hd}. Unfortunately, in the examples he gives, the head and the subject of S_{rel} are identical in number.

(31) a. natsir-niq   miqquw-i
    seal skin-PL.INSTR hair-PL their
    with seal skins   their hairs
      qummu-kar-tu-nik
      upwards-go-INT.PRT-PL.INSTR
      they going upwards
    "with seal skins whose hairs go upwards"
    (Bergsland 19.3, pg.45)

b. ukiyuliguni   nanu-ršu-up
                           bear-big-REL(case)
    when winter comes big bear
      kiina-a miqqu-qu-ŋŋitšur-su-up
      face-its hair-have-not-INTR.PRT-it REL(case)
      its face it having no hair (the face)
        tikiraa-qqip-pa-si
        come (visiting)-again-IRREAL-it you
        it comes visiting you again
    "When winter comes, when the big polar bear whose
      face has no hair again comes to you."
    (Bergsland 1971.2, pg.49)

IRREAL is the symbol for the Irrealis mood, used in various subordinate clauses referring to things that haven't happened yet. In each example there is a subject of S_{rel}, and this subject is absolutive in case. The verb is S_{rel}, which is an intransitive participial, sports the case ending of NP_{hd}, just as an adjective would. In these examples, as well as in the previous ones, NP_{rel} disappears. It is clear that in the above examples it is not NP_{hd} which is disappearing, because if NP_{rel} were to survive it would be absolutive in case. This disappearance can be taken as a consequence of the Eskimo Pronoun Drop rule: there is no need to postulate a special rule which deletes NP_{rel}.

There are two arguments afforded by Eskimo concerning the constituent structure of relative clauses. First, since the verb of S_{rel} is nominalized, S_{rel} must be dominated by NP, and, second, since it agrees with NP_{hd} in case, it is in the same NP as NP_{hd} and is furthermore roughly the same kind of modifier that an adjective is. This paralellism is reinforced by the fact that relative clauses and adjectives are similar in following the head N, whereas possessors precede it. We may finally observe that if the adjectives and relative clauses precede CASE in underlying structure, the rule case-marking the elements of the NP (or CP) will be a rule copying case to the left, rather than a rule spreading it in both directions. One might take the NP → NP $\bar{S}$ analysis as being slightly favored, because the rule could then be taken as copying the CASE onto all the major constituents of the NP that follow the head N except possessives. These considerations, of course, are highly tenuous.

1.1.1.2 Pre-Relatives: For pre-relatives I propose underlying structures of the form given in (32):

(32)
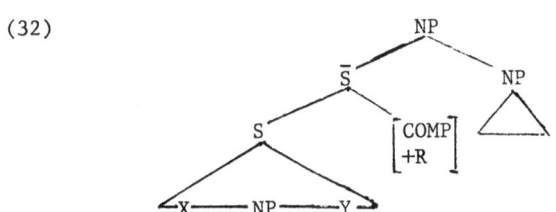

I have found no reason to propose a pre-relative counterpart to (2), the structure produced by the CP → NP ($\bar{S}$) CASE rule. But I do not believe that my research has been sufficent to settle the point.

Below I list some genetically unrelated languages having a pre-relative construction:

(33) Japanese   Korean
     Hottentot   Mongolian
     Turkish   Telugu
     Ainu   Basque
     Navajo   Chinese
     Papago   Classical Tibetan

As representatives of these languages I will discuss Japanese and Turkish.

Before discussing these languages, however, I wish to venture a brief remark on the structure (32). The reader will observe that I have placed the COMP after its S, rather than before. This is because I am aware of no pre-relative clause constructions with introductory particles. Another fact, however, renders the analysis or clause-final relative clause markers (such as we shall see in Turkish, section 1.1.1.2.1.) slightly problematical in individual languages. Kuno (1974) has observed that pre-relatives are characteristic of SOV languages and post-relatives of SVO and VSO languages. Therefore, the COMP at the end of a relative clause may either be a COMP or something inside the S: an AUX or an affix on the verb. I believe that both situations arise.

1.1.1.2.2 *Japanese*:[4] The general form of relativization in Japanese is familiar to linguistics. See, for example, the general discussions in (Kuno 1973) and (McCawley 1972), and the references cited in these works. In this discussion I intend to make an assortment of points connected with theoretical issues in this paper: the constituent structure of relative clauses, the restrictive/nonrestrictive distinction, and the general treatment of NP_{rel}.

Japanese is an SOV language with postpositions, conjunctions that follow their sentences, and modifiers, including relative clauses, that precede what they modify. Grammatical relations are marked by particles that follow the NP.

There is a thematic construction in which an NP is placed initial to the S and followed by the particle *wa*, which sometimes follows, and sometimes replaces the particle appropriate to the grammatical relation of the theme NP to the sentence. This construction bears an intimate relation to the grammar of relativization, which is discussed in the above-mentioned work and will also be treated in section 1.3.1 of the present paper. Case-marking and Thematization are discussed in considerable detail in (Kuno 1973), so there is no need to discuss them here.

A relative clause precedes its head, and in the usual construction NP_{rel} vanishes, taking along its postnominal particles. These points I illustrate in (34-35). (34) is a clause embedded in (35a) by relativizing on the object, and in (35b) by relativizing on the subject:

(34) ano hito ga hon o kai-ta
 that person SUBJ book OBJ write-PAST
 "That person wrote a book."

(35) a. kore wa ano hito ga kai-ta hon desu
 this THEME that person SUBJ write-PAST book is
 "This is a/the book which that person has written."

 b. kore wa o kai-ta hito desu
 this THEME book OBJ write-PAST person is
 "This is a/the person who has written a book."

The subject of a relative clause (or other subordinate clause immediately dominated by NP) may be marked with *no*, the possessive or genitive marker, instead of *ga*. Hence (35a) may be rendered *kore wa ano hito no kaita hon desu*.

The first question I will address is the possibility of replicating in a pre-relative structure the argument of Vergnaud (1974) (discussed above in section 1.1.1.) that English and French have a $[_{NP}\ NP\ \bar{S}]$ surface structure for relative clauses.

While Japanese lacks definite or indefinite articles, it does have the demonstrative pronouns and adjectives *kono* 'this,' *sono* 'that (by you),' and *ano* 'that (yonder).' If we assume that Japanese introduces the demonstratives under the Det produced by an NP → Det NOM rule, then the following example serves to yield a counterpart to Vergnaud's argument.

(36) otagaini   ai   site iru ano otoko to ano onna ga
    each other love doing be that man   and that woman SUBJ
       kekon   si-ta
       marriage do-PAST
    "The man and the woman who loved each other got married."

Unfortunately the claim that relative clauses are introduced by NP → S̄ NP and demonstratives by NP → Det NOM cannot be accepted without further scrutiny. Relative clauses are perhaps best when they precede the demonstrative, but may also come between a demonstrative and its head. These possibilities are shown in (37):

(37) a. boku ga   sonkeisite iru kono hito ga Tokyo ni
       I   SUBJ respecting be this person SUBJ Tokyo in
         sunde iru
         living is

    b. kono, boku ga sonkeisite iru hito ga Tokyo ni sunde iru
       "That person who I respect lives in Tokyo."

These two possibilities are not quite in free variation, but I do not understand the factors that condition them.

One way to accommodate (36-37) would be to claim that the demonstratives were introduced by a rule NP → Dem NP parallel to the rule introducing relatives. This would require finding some further mechanism to block *ano kono hito*, *kono kono hito*, etc.

I leave the resolution of the questions raised by this discussion to scholars of Japanese. It suffices to point out that a clarification of the constituent structure relations of demonstrative adjectives in Japanese would shed light on the constituent structure relations of relative clauses.

It has often been observed that Japanese does not mark a distinction between restrictive and nonrestrictive relatives. Kuno (1973 pg. 235) cites the following pairings of restrictive and nonrestrictive clauses in order to show the formal indistinctness of the two types:

(38) a. watakusi ni eigo   o   osiete   iru Mary
       I   to English OBJ teaching be Mary
       "Mary, who is teaching me English" (nonrestrictive)

b. watakusi ga   sitte   iru Mary
      I   SUBJ knowing be Mary
      "the Mary that I know" (restrictive)

(39) a. honyuu-doobutu de aru kuzira
        mammal   is   whale
        "the whale, which is a mammal" (nonrestrictive)

   b. nihon-kai ni sunde   iru kuzira
      Japan-sea in living be whale
      "the whales that live in the Japan sea" (nonrestrictive)

Similarly, Japanese speakers report considerable difficulty in distinguishing between the two types of clauses, which suggests more strongly that Japanese has no syntactic differentiation between the two types.

To confirm these impressions, we find that Japanese nonrestrictive clauses can stack, just as restrictives can:

(40) kinoo   Mary ga at-ta,   ringo ga suki   na   John
     yesterday Mary SUBJ meet-PAST apples SUBJ liking being John
     "*John, who Mary met yesterday, who likes apples"

These clauses in (40) cannot be conjoined, because Japanese does not conjoin clauses by juxtaposition, but requires special final particles on the initial clause.

The fact that Japanese has nonrestrictives that are essentially indistinguishable from restrictives provides the major motivation for providing the two clause types with different syntactic structures in English, inasmuch as this is the most straightforward way to connect the syntactic differences to the semantic.

The final topic I wish to discuss is the treatment of NP_{rel}. Kuno (1973) shows that Japanese is quite lax in its obedience to island constraints, as is Samoan. Likewise, Japanese has a very general rule deleting pronouns, even first and second person pronouns. Hence there is no need to postulate for Japanese any special processes deleting NP_{rel}: a pronominal NP_{rel} will delete of its own accord by the general rule. To strengthen the plausibility of this explanation, we may observe that Japanese needn't in general delete NP_{rel}: it may attain the surface as a pronoun, a demonstrative, or even as a full NP. Kuno (1973 pg. 237) cites the following examples:

(41) watakusi ga   so   kare   sono hito   no   namae o
     I   SUBJ (that /   he   / that person) POSS   name   OBJ
     wasurete-simat-ta okyaku-san
     forget-PAST   guest
     "the guest whose name I have forgotten"

I shall later develop the notion that the presence of such structures with overt NP_{rel} is related to laxity of island constraints in languages with very general pronoun deletion processes.

I here end my discussion of Japanese.

1.1.1.2.2 *Turkish*: Turkish has both pre- and post-relatives. The post-relatives were borrowed from Persian, and are apparently frowned upon and disappearing from the language. The pre-relatives are the native construction. Here I shall consider only the pre-relatives, deferring the post-relatives for 1.1.1.3.1.

Turkish is an SOV language with considerable scrambling of major constituents in main clauses. In the noun phrase, modifiers typically precede the head, with the exception of the post-relative clause borrowed from Persian. Turkish has postpositions and case-markers that follow the head, marking nominative, accusative, genitive, locative, dative and ablative cases. Verbs and nouns have agreement suffixes referring to their subjects and possessors, respectively. The suffixes manifest person and number. Subject and possessor pronouns are freely deletable. There is considerable syntactic paralellism between the subject of an S and the possessor of an NP, since when an S is nominalized, its subject becomes genitive, and possessor-agreement suffixes are attached to the nominalized verb. The subject and possessor agreement suffixes are morphologically similar, and were originally identical.

The relative clauses (both pre- and post-) are closely related to nominalizations corresponding to the English *that* clauses used as the objects of verbs meaning 'think,' 'say,' etc. The post-relative clause is related to a nominal clause that was borrowed from the Persian along with the relative. The pre-relative is related to a native nominalization.

I shall first describe the native nominalization. This is formed with the aid of the 'personal participle' endings. These endings come in two forms: *acak/ecek* (varying by vowel harmony) for the future, and *dig/dig/dug/düg* (again varying by vowel harmony) for the non-future (present and past). These endings replace endings marking a post-non-past distinction in 'finite' clauses, and do not have the possibilities for aspectual elaboration that verbs in finite clauses have. To the personal participle endings are attached possessor agreement suffixes which show the person and number of the subject, which appears in the genitive case. If the nominalized sentence is being used as a direct object, an accusative case marker appears after the agreement suffix, in accordance with the normal rule.

Hence we have examples such as the following:

(42) a. Halil Orhan-in Istambul-a git-tĭg-i-ni düsün-üyor
Halil Orhan-GEN Istambul-DAT go-NOM-his-ACC think-PROG
"Halil thinks that Orhan went (or is going) to Istambul."

b. Hasan, Fatma-nin o-nu öl-dür-eceğ-i-ni düsün-üyor
Hasan Fatma-GEN he-ACC die-cause-FUT-his-ACC think-PROG
"Hasan thinks that Fatma will kill him."

A likely explanation for the properties of these nominalizations is that they lack an S node to dominate them in the later stages of the derivation, due to some sort of pruning, or that their S nodes are heavily infused with nominal features. The resulting structure would then be roughly like (43):

(43)

Since the subject NP bears the same structural relation the dominating NP as would a possessor NP, it gets the genitive case. Since the NP and the VP are related in the same way as are a possessor and a possessed NOM, possessor agreement suffixes get copied onto the latter. I assume the VP to be a VP because it has the full range of internal structure of a VP; the full set of complements, adverbs, etc. Siegel (1974) gives a fairly similar analysis of the gerund in English. It is worth pointing out one fact, however, which is that there is a general dearth of evidence for a VP node in Turkish. Hankamer (1971) cites the absence of any pronominal VP comparable to the English *do so*, and various other sorts of missing possible evidence as well.

There are two kinds of nonfinite relative clauses: one where NP_{rel} is within the subject, either as the subject itself or as its possessor, or even as the possessor of the possessor, etc.; and the other when NP_{rel} is outside the subject (that is, in the VP). This latter construction has the same internal syntax and morphology as do the nominalizations described above, except that NP_{rel} is always deleted (although agreement markers cross-referencing it may survive). Below are examples:

(44) a. Halil-in (*o-nu) öldür-düğ-ü adam
   Halil-GEN (him-ACC kill-NOM-his man
   "the man whom Halil killed"

b. gel-dik-leri vapur
   come-NOM-their steamer
   "the steamer on which they came"

c. baba-si-nin ev-i-ni al-diğ-imiz adam
   father-his-GEN house-his-ACC buy-NOM-our man
   "the man whose father's house we bought"

d. iç-in-den cik-tiğimiz ev
   interior-its-ABL emerge-NOM-our house
   "the house from which we emerged"

That there is a deletion rule is demonstrated by (40a-b) where a pronoun for NP_{rel} results in unacceptability (contrast with (42)). In (44c-d) it could be that NP_{rel} was being deleted by the rule that deletes unemphatic subject and possessor pronouns. Object pronouns, however, do not freely delete, so this account does not extend to (44a-b).

The other nonfinite construction is used when NP_{rel} is within the subject. For this form a participle ending *en/an* is used for nonfuture tense, and the future tense and a past tense for events not known through personal observation may be expressed with the periphrastic forms *ecek (olan)* and *miş (olan)* respectively. *olan* in these forms is the *en*-

participial form of the verb *ol* 'to be, become.' The subject of S_{rel} is nominative, and there are no agreement suffixes on the verb. Some examples are:

(45) a. dün gel-miş ol-an mektup
 yesterday come-PAST be-PRT letter
 "the letter which came yesterday"

 b. baba-s şimdi konuş-an adam
 father-his now speak-PRT man
 "the man whose father is now speaking"

 c. oğl-u-nun kedi-si et-i yiy-en adam
 son-his-GEN cat-his meat-ACC eat-PRT man
 "the man whose son's cat ate the meat"

The *en/an* formative might be introduced by a transformation or a base-rule. If a transformation is used, then (46) shows that the rule is cyclic or post-cyclic:

(46) dün Hasanin tarafindan öldür-ül-en çocuk
 yesterday Hasan-GEN by kill-PASS-PRT child
 "the child who was killed by Hasan yesterday"

On the reasonable assumption that in Turkish passive sentences the surface subject is derived by promotion of an underlying object, (46) shows that the marking of the participle must follow Passive, since it is not until Passive has applied that NP_{rel} is within the subject. (46) also shows that if the *en/an* participle is to be introduced by a base-rule, there will have to be some sort of interpretive principle constraining its distribution that applies during or after the cycle.

We may further note that the *en/an* participle has the effect of preventing the subject from taking the genitive case. Given a transformational account of *en*-attachment, we could accommodate this by having *en*-attachment precede and bleed the nominalization rule. There would need to be an additional process to delete NP_{rel}. As in Eskimo, the nominalization of the verb evidences that S_{rel} is dominated by an NP node.

I shall now turn to some languages in which pre- and post relative clauses coexist.

1.1.1.3 *Languages with both Pre- and Post- Relatives:*
Some languages with both types of headed embedded relative

clauses are listed below:

(47) Classical Tibetan
Hottentot
Quechua
Papago
Turkish

I shall discuss Turkish, Classical Tibetan and Hottentot.

1.1.1.3.1 *Turkish:* The other Turkish construction consists merely of a clause identical in internal syntax to a main clause which is introduced by a particle *ki* (derived from the Persian *ke*). Clauses introduced by *ki* are also used as subjects and objects of verbs, as are the *ke*-clauses of Persian. In both the Turkish and Persian relative clauses with *ki/ke*, the clause is a post-relative and NP_{rel} is deleted. Persian relativization will be discussed later in this chapter.

Below are some examples of *ki*-clauses in Turkish:

(48) a. düşünüyorum ki   Hasan gelecek
        I think   that Hasan will come
        "I think that Hasan will come."

   b. şüphe-siz   ki gelecek
      doubt-without that he will come
      "It is without doubt that he will come."

   c. bir çocuk ki   kapıyı   kapamaz
      a   child that the door does not close

We note that once again we have a relative clause with the same form as a nominalization. In this case, of course, it is fundamentally a fact about Persian, rather than about Turkish.

Inasmuch as the two relative clause constructions of Turkish are quite distinct in their internal syntactic constructure, I believe that it would be reasonable to derive them by two distinct base-rules, one generating the pre-relatives and the other the post-relatives.

1.1.1.3.2 *Classical Tibetan:* This obscure language has basically SOV word-order. It uses a wide variety of postpositions, and modifiers of nouns can occur on either side of the head. When modifiers precede the head, they are followed by a particle whose underlying phonological shape is *kyi*. Furthermore, the verbs of relative clauses are nonfinite and take a suffix *pa*, which is of extremely common use in Tibetan, forming an agent-nominalization, among other things. Whether *pa* is a relativization marker or just a general nominalizer I do not know. In a relative clause, NP_{rel} is somehow deleted.

(49) a. bla-ma'i gos
       lama:GEN vestments
   "lama's vestments" (*'i* is a reduced form of *kyi*, and, following the conventional usage, I shall label it the genitive. The hyphens in Tibetan transcriptions separate syllables, not formatives.)

   b. skam-pi'i sa
      dry:GEN   earth
   "dry earth"

   c. čhu   ni bsil-ba-yis
      water cold with
   "with cold water"

   d. sans-rgyas-kyi čhös thams-cad yan-dag-par
      Buddha-GEN   law   all   completely
        thob-pa'i   blo
      obtain-REL:GEN intelligence
   "intelligence which completely attains the entire law of the Buddha"

   e. [$_{NP}$ ne-togs dan 'bras-bu'i çin-ljon-pa [$_S$ sna-chogs
              flowers and fruits:GEN trees $_{rel}$ diverse
         dus   tha-dad-par dbyun-ba]]
      times different:LOC bear fruit:REL
   "flowers and fruit trees which at diverse times bear different fruit"

(49d) is a relative clause that precedes the head, and (49e) is one that follows, and we thus find in (49e) no *kyi* following the verb. Note in (49e) the NP *dus tha-dad-par* 'at different times', which has the syntactic pattern HEAD-ADJ-CASE.

These examples show that adjectives and relative clauses share some of the same syntax in Tibetan. There is still a question as to what is responsible for the two possible orders: either two base orders, as in Turkish, or one base order and a process of permutation. It is also worth noting that *kyi* could not be easily analysed as a Complementizer, since it appears on adjectives.

1.1.1.3.3 *Hottentot:* In addition to being entertaining in its own right, the evidence from Hottentot provides further argument that embedded relative clauses are constituents with their head, and that they are a category related to adjectives and other nominal modifiers. I shall discuss the Nama dialect.

The basic Hottentot sentence structure is Subject-Verb Phrase. I have not yet untangled the syntax of the verb phrase with its rules for the placement of verb, objects and tense and aspect particles. These rules are quite complex. There is a curious rule which extraposes the subject into the VP and provides it with an accusative case-marker if it is non-initial due to there being an introductory particle or topicalized NP at the front of the S. Furthermore, a clitic copy of the subject is left behind attached to the initial element which triggered movement of the subject. This rule will be seen in action in the relative clause examples.

Hottentot nouns take endings for grammatical gender (masculine, feminine, neuter/common) and number (singular, dual, plural), which are identical with the clitic forms of third person pronouns (the nonclitic forms consist of a stem *//ei* to which appropriate gender endings (i.e. clitic forms) are added). Modifiers, adjectives, possessives, demonstratives and relative clauses may either precede or follow the head. If they follow, the gender-number endings are copied onto them, if they precede, they are not. There is also an accusative case-marker *a* which is attached to the last member of the NP. The language is post-positional, forming possessive phrases with a post-position *di*. These points of Hottentot grammar are illustrated in the following examples:

(50) a. gei /gõa-n
big child-N(FUT).PL
"big children"

b. //g̃u-b   di   /on-s
father-M(ASC).SG GEN name-F(EM).SG
"the father's name"

c. ao-gu   gei-gu
   man-M.PL big-M.PL
   "the big men"

d. ǂgòa-b   /à-s   di-b
   wall-M.SG city-F.SG GEN-M.SG
   "the wall of the city"

e. mũ ta   go   ao-b   gei-b-a
   see I(clitic) PAST man-M.SG big-M.SG-ACC
   "I saw the big men"

Like other modifiers, relative clauses may precede or follow the head, and when they follow, the agreement marker of the head shows up on the last word of the clause, which in all the examples I have found is a verb. When the clause follows the head, it is introduced by a particle $h\tilde{\imath}a/ia$ (I can find no basis for the variation), and when it precedes, there is no introductory particle. NP_{rel} is deleted. Note especially that when NP_{rel} is the underlying subject of S_{rel}, there is no clitic form left behind.

(51) a. narí ta   gye mũ kho-b   gye ǂgei te
        today I PERF see man-M.SG. PERF call me
        "The man who I saw today called me."

     b. khoi-b, ia go   //ari   ha-b   gye mĩ
        man-M.SG REL PAST yesterday come-M.SG. PERF say
        "the man who came yesterday said ..."

     c. /gõa-b   hĩa-s   tara-s-a   gye si-b   gye
        boy-M.SG. REL-F.SG woman-F.SG.-Acc PERF send-M.SG
        go   //hawu
        PAST get lost
        "The boy whom the woman sent got lost."
        (gye in the main clause of this example is a sort of emphatic particle, not a tense/aspect marker)

     d. tara-s   , hia-ts gye sats-a   ǂgei ha-s   go
        woman-F.SG REL-you PERF you-ACC call be-F.SG PAST
        neti ha
        now   come
        "the woman whom you called has now come"

Note the subject extraposition, which has applied in (c-d). Unfortunately, available examples all involve relative clauses modifying the subjects of sentences, so it is impossible to exhibit the accusative case-marker tacked onto a relative clause following the head. But the workings of the agreement rule can be clearly seen. Note that the form attached to the relative clause is determined by what the head is, and not by what the subject of the clause, is, or any other such thing. These facts show that the Hottentot relative clause is a constituent of an NP containing its head, and has roughly the same external syntax as an adjective.

I shall now turn to some general discussion of the effects of order in the pre- and post- relative clause constructions.

1.1.1.4 *Differences between Pre- and Post- Relatives:* I will here comment on two respects in which the grammar of relative clauses appears to be asymmetrical with respect to linear order. Both observations are quite tentative, and their profferred explanations correspondingly speculative.

First, I believe that pre-relative clauses are more prone than post-relatives to having their subjects put in the genitive case. A functional explanation for this fact is not difficult to think of. In order to avoid center-embedding of S, pre-relative clauses lack COMP or similar introductory particles. The function of a genitive marker on the subject of the relative clause may then be to signal the beginning of a complex constituent: the genitive may serve as a cue that the NP bearing it is not a major constituent of the clause being processed but an initial subconstituent of a major constituent.

Second, we observed that Japanese lacks any formal distinction of restrictive and nonrestrictive clauses. Such a distinction is also lacking in the other pre-relative clause structures I have examined: Korean, Basque and Turkish.

In Korean[5] we can stack nonrestrictive relations. (52) is a Korean parallel to the Japanese example (40):

(52) [$_{NP}$[$_{\bar{S}}$ tehak-e tani-nın][$_{NP}$[$_{\bar{S}}$ ne-ka chowa-ho-n n][$_{NP}$ Mary]]]
     college-to go-REL   I NOM like-do-REL   Mary
"*Mary, who goes to college, who I like"

nın is a particle that follows relative clauses. This structure is distinct from one in which the two relative clauses are coordinated. I illustrate such a structure in (53):

(53)   [$_{NP}$[$_{\bar{\bar{S}}}$[$_{\bar{S}}$[$_{S}$ tehak-e   tani] ko [$_{S}$ ne-ka chowa-ho]] nın]
              college-go go and   I-NOM like-do REL
       [$_{NP}$ Mary]]
       "Mary, who goes to college and who I like"

The fact that *nın* can be attached to a coordination of S suggests that it is a *bona fide* occupant of a clause-final COMP.

Although I know of no language that marks the restrictive/nonrestrictive distinction in pre-relative position, it is not the case that in all languages pre-relatives can be interpreted nonrestrictively. According to (Perkins 1974), Navajo pre-relatives can only be interpreted restrictively, and my own inquiries have confirmed this finding.

We may prevent restrictive and nonrestrictive pre-relatives from having distinct constituent structures by requiring in universal grammar that when CP expands to CASE, NP and $\bar{\bar{S}}$, the $\bar{\bar{S}}$ follow the NP. There are other aspects to the distinction in English, such as the requirement that non-restrictives have a relative pronoun. Their status is unclear.

With these speculations I end my discussion of pre- and post- relative clauses.

1.1.2 *Headless Relative Clauses:* There are many languages in which there are relative clauses which lack a head in surface structure. Instead, the relative clause appears dominated by NP, with NP$_{rel}$ being either a pronoun or a full NP, and perhaps bearing a special mark (such as *wh* in English).

I propose the following structure (or its mirror-image) for such relative clauses:

(54)

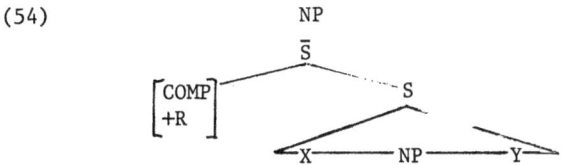

Most languages appear to have headless relative clauses

in which NP_{rel} is a pronoun. These are generally called free relative clauses, and have been discussed in English by Baker (1968) and Kuroda (1969). *Bill ate what was lying on the table* is a typical free relative clause in English. Less widespread are those constructions where NP_{rel} is a full NP. To distinguish these from free relatives I shall follow Gorbet (1974) in calling them internal head relatives. Such a relative clause in English is *what beer we drank was flat*. In English, the internal head relative clause is a very minor construction, but in other languages, such as Diegueño and Navajo, it is the major vehicle of relativization.

Internal head relative clauses may coexist in a language with either pre- or post- relative clauses, and in some languages, such as Diegueño, may be the only kind of relative clause other than free relatives. In this language, internal head relative clauses coexist with a variety of structures whose analysis is dubious.

Below I give a list of languages having internal head relative clauses, indicating whether they coexist with pre- or post- relative clauses:

(55) Languages with Internal Head Relative Clauses:

Hopi	(pre-)	Crow	(pre-)
Navajo	(post-)	Diegueno	(pre- and post- ?)
Dagbani	(pre-)	English	(pre-)

In this section I will discuss Navajo and English. Later in the chapter I will consider Dagbani and Crow. Diegueno receives a major treatment in (Gorbet 1974), and Hopi is discussed in (Jeanne 1974).

1.1.2.1 *Navajo:* Navajo is an SOV language with postpositions and conjunctions that follow the subordinate clauses they are associated with.

I shall identify four relative clause constructions in Navajo: a free relative, indistinguishable in form from a kind of indirect question, a pre-relative, an internal head relative, and an extraposed relative. My information on these constructions is drawn from (Platero 1974), (Kaufman 1974) and (Perkins 1975). The latter types appear to be

related to each other as against the free relatives.
Therefore, after some more general discussion of Navajo
grammar, I will first discuss the pre-, internal head and
extraposed relatives, and then turn to the free relatives.
My discussion on many points will be incomplete, as a much
fuller treatment is given in (Platero 1974) and (Kaufman
1974).

Navajo has agreement processes whereby verbs are marked
for the person and number of their subjects and objects.
Postpositions are also marked for these features of their
objects, and possessed NP for these features of their
possessors. In the examples here we shall see only marking
of verbs. The agreement markers are prefixes, and are
placed in the order *Object-prefix Subject-Prefix*, and are
interspersed with a great variety of other prefixes of
diverse functions. We shall encounter a future tense, and
perfective and imperfective aspects (IMP and PERF). Phonological rules of great complexity obscure the underlying
form and arrangement of the prefixes, rendering futile any
attempt to gloss formatives in the surface phonological
form. The phonology is discussed in (Stanley 1969).

We thus have the simple transitive and intransitive
sentences (56):

(56) a. ashkii ałháá'
boy   IMP:3:snore
"the boy is snoring"

b. ashkii at'ééd yiztał
boy   girl   3:PERF:3:kick
"the boy kicked the girl"

There is an interesting rule of Subject-object inversion, which interchanges the positions of subject and
object, and replaces *yi*, the 3rd person object prefix for
transitive verbs, with *bi*. Applying this rule to (56b) we
get (57):

(57) at'ééd ashkii biztał
girl   boy   3:PERF:kick
"the girl was kicked by the boy"

All relative clauses end in a formative *í(gíí)* or its
alternate *ęę* (sometimes *ąą* due to phonology), which is a

complementizer used in various sorts of nominal subordinate clauses other than relative clauses. These complementizers are discussed extensively in (Kaufman 1974). NP_{rel} in a relative clause can be subject, object, possessor, or the object of a postposition. I will illustrate the first two possibilities. The others may be found in (Platero 1974).

(58) is an intransitive clause. In (59 a, b, c) I embed it as a pre-, internal head and extraposed relative, respectively:

   (58) tl'éédą́ą́' ashkii ałháá'
       last:night boy   IMP:3:snore
       "the boy was snoring last night"

   (59) a. tl'éédą́ą́   ałháá'-ą́ą   ashkii yádoołtih
          last:night IMP:3:snore-REL boy   FUT:3:speak

      b. tl'éédą́ą́ ashkii ałháá'-ą́ą   yádoołtih
         last:night boy   IMP:3:snore-REL FUT:3:speak

      c. ashkii yádoołtih   tl'éédą́ą́ ałháá'-ą́ą
         boy   FUT:3:speak last:night 3:PAST:snore-REL

      "the boy who was snoring last night will speak"

The clause internal position of *ashkii* in (59b) shows that it is NP_{rel} rather than NP_{hd}.

(60) is a transitive clause with first person subject, and in (61) I embed it in the three constructions just as in (59):

   (60) łééchąą'í sétał
       dog   3:PERF:1:kick
       "I kicked the dog"

   (61) a. sétał-éé   łééchąą'í nahał'in
          3:PERF:1:kick-REL dog   IMP:3:bark

      b. łééchąą'í sétał-éé   nahał'in
         dog   3:PERF:1:kick-REL IMP:3:bark

        łééchąą'í nahał'in   sétał-éé
        dog   IMP:3:bark 3:PERF:1:kick-REL

      "the dog that I kicked is barking"

A question that arises immediately, especially in the light of some of the constructions we will be considering in section 1.1.3., is how we know that the purported internal head relative clauses of (59b) and (61c) are actually dominated by NP, taking the place of ordinary nouns in the syntactic structure of their matrices. We can see this by observing examples in which there are internal head relative clauses both in object and in subject position, and in which the subject-object inversion rule applies:

(62) a. adą́ą́dą́ą́' shi-zhé'é łį́į́' nayiisnii'-ę́ę́
yesterday my-father horse 3:PERF:3:buy-REL

ashkii łééchąą'í bishxash-ę́ę́ yiztał
boy dog 3:PERF:3:buy-REL 3:PERF:3:kick

"the horse which my father bought yesterday kicked the dog which bit the boy" or
"the horse which my father bought yesterday kicked the boy whom the dog bit"

b. ashkii łééchąą'í bishxash-ę́ę́ adą́ą́dą́ą́' shi-zhé'é
boy dog 3:PERF:3:bite-REL yesterday my-father

łį́į́' nayiisnii'-ę́ę́ biztał
horse 3:PERF:3:buy-REL 3:PERF:3:kick

(same as (62a) in meaning)

We see that the internal head construction is subject to considerable ambiguity: *ashkii łééchąą'í bishxashę́ę́* in (62) can be interpreted either as "the boy who the dog bit" or "the dog that bit the boy" (note the application of Subject-object inversion in the relative clause).

We would expect the pre-relative construction to likewise be ambiguous. But in that structure, there are principles discussed by Platero that eliminate ambiguity in most cases. (63a) thus gets the reading (63b) but not (63c):

(63) a. ashkii yiyiiłtsá-(n)ę́ę́ at'ééd yáłtih
boy 3:PERF:see-REL girl IMP:3:speak

b. the girl who saw the boy is speaking

c. *the girl who the boy saw is speaking

Platero proposes to derive the three structures we have been considering from a common source: a prerelative structure in which NP_{rel} and NP_{hd} are represented by full NP. The extraposed relatives are derived by a rule of extraposition. Evidence against this discovered by Perkins (1975) will be discussed in section 1.1.3.6. Here I shall discuss and criticize the proposed derivation of pre- and internal head relatives.

By Platero's proposal, the common source for the examples of (61) will be (64):

(64)
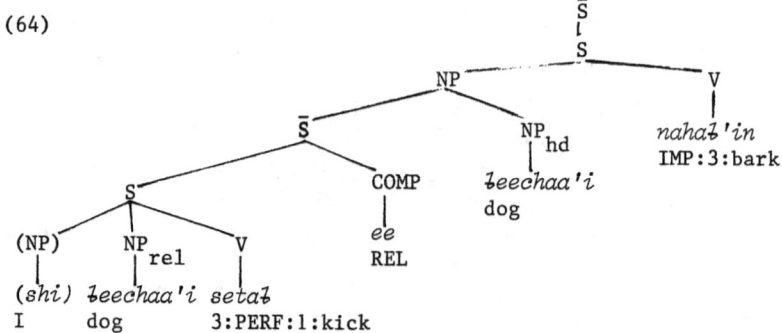

We can apply deletion forwards, deleting NP_{hd} and deriving (61b), or we can apply deletion backwards, deleting NP_{rel} to derive (61a). There are thus no internal head relative clauses in underlying structure.

Platero hypothesizes that the deletion rule applying in relative clauses is the same as ordinary pronominalization, which in Navajo may be effected by deletion. Pronominalization by deletion may go forwards, or backwards into a subordinate clause. These points are illustrated in example (65), in which there is an initial subordinate clause in the adverbial complementizer *go*:

(65) a. ashkii yah-ííyá-(a)go neezdá
       boy   into-PERF:3:go-COMP PERF:3:sit

    b. yah-'ííyá-(a)go   ashkii neezdá
       into-PERF:3:go-COMP boy   PERF:3:sit
       "when the boy$_i$ came in, he$_i$ sat down"

Between coordinated clauses we can delete forwards, but not backwards:

(66) a. ashkii yah-'ííyá   dóó neezdá
       boy   into-PERF:3:go and PERF:3:sit
       "the boy entered and sat down"

    b. yah-'iiya   doo ashkii neezda
       into-PERF:3:go   and boy   PERF:3:sit
       "he$_i$ entered and the boy$_j$ sat down"

This restriction manifests itself in the relative clause system as the fact that in the extraposed construction

NP_{hd} cannot be deleted:

(67) *nahał'in łééchąą'í sétał-ę́ę
    IMP:3:bark dog   3:PERF:1:kick
    "the dog that I kicked was barking"

Platero observes a significant defect of this solution, which is that while the deletion effected by ordinary pronominalization is optional, in the relative clause construction either NP_{rel} or NP_{hd} must go. Hence we have (68) as an alternative to (65), and (69) as an alternative to (66):

(68) ashkii yah-'ííyá-(a)go   ashkii neezdá
    boy   into-PERF:3:go-COMP boy   PERF:3:sit
    "when the boy$_i$ came in, the boy$_i$ sat down"

(69) ashkii yah-'ííyá-(a)go   dóó ashkii neezdá
    boy   into-PERF:3:go-COMP and boy   PERF:3:sit
    "the boy$_i$ entered and the boy$_i$ sat down"

But (70), the sentence derived from (64) by applying no transformations, is ungrammatical:

(70) *łééchąą'í sétał-ę́ę   łééchąą'í nahał'in
    dog   3:PERF:1:kick-REL dog   IMP:3:bark
    "the dog I kicked is barking"

In his article, Platero suggested that perhaps deletion of NP_{rel} was optional in extraposed relative clauses, but he stated that this was not true for all speakers, and has since then decided (personal communication) that deletion of NP_{rel} is obligatory in these structures.

Platero and Hale (1974) propose a reanalysis in which an internal head structure is underlying for the relative clause, and the head is extracted optionally. A further alternative would be to say that there are underlyingly both pre- and internal head relative structures, and that deletion of NP_{rel} is obligatory in the pre-relative. On either of these analyses, the obligatory disappearance of NP_{rel} in the pre-relative construction is easily accounted for.

These analyses are also rendered more attractive by the fact that, as we shall shortly see, internal head relative clauses may co-exist with post-relatives as well as pre-

relatives. A rule deleting the head of a post-relative
clause on identity to NP_{rel} would violate the normal conditions on deletion. Other arguments against head-deletion
will also be adduced.

I finally observe that the relative clause constructions
in Navajo cannot be used nonrestrictively. Hence the following are all ungrammatical:

(71) a. *Kii sétał-ę́ę   neezdá
       Kii 3:PERF:1:kick-REL PERF:3:sit
       "Kii, who I kicked, sat down"

    b. *sétał-ę́ę   Kii neezdá
       3:PERF:1:kick-REL Kii PERF:3:sit
       "Kii, who I kicked, sat down"

    c. *Kii neezdá   sétał-ę́ę
       Kii PERF:3:sit 3:PERF:1:kick-REL
       "Kii sat down, who I kicked"

One might be tempted to associate the absence of a nonrestrictive interpretation with the hypothesis that underlying
internal head structures cannot be interpreted nonrestrictively: this would entail accepting a head-extraction analysis for the pre-relative structures. This suggestion is
obviously highly speculative.

I shall now briefly consider the free relative clauses.
I shall consider them only in connection with another construction, the enclitic phrase. The enclitics are a class
of particles that are suffixed to NP and PP in order to
express various notions of direction and other concepts
associated with motion and location. With the enclitic
di "at," we can thus form (72):

(72) hastiin kin-di   sidá
     man   house-at IMP:3:sit
     "the man is sitting at the house"

Platero (1974) notes two presumably related peculiarities of enclitics: their object NP cannot take demonstratives, and their object NP cannot be relativized:

(73) a. *shí díí tsékooh-di sédá
        I   this canyon-at IMP:1:sit
        "I am sitting in this canyon"

b. *hastiin kin-di sidá-(h)ígíí naa'íízhoozh
   man   house-in IMP:3:sit-REL PERF:3:collapse
   "the house the man was sitting in collapsed"

With free relatives, however, we find the situation quite different.

Kaufman (1974) observes a construction that appears to be used both as an indirect question and as a free relative clause. The target NP of the construction can be an enclitic phrase with no full NP head, and the enclitic migrates to the *í(gíí)/ęę* COMP that terminates both constructions.

(74) illustrates the construction used as an indirect question:

(74) díí bilagáanaa diné bizaad yíhooł'áá'aa-di
     this whiteman Navajo language 3:PERF:3:learn:COMP-at
     doo shił bééhózin-da
     NEG 1:with 3:know-NEG
     "I don't know where this Anglo learned Navajo."

The use as a free relative is illustrated by (75):

(75) gałbáhí a'áán-góne' yah-eelwod-í-gí   hatl'éé'
     rabbit hole-in   into-PERF:3:run-REL-at area is dark
     "It is dark in the area around where the rabbit ran into
        the hole"
     *"It's dark in the hole which the rabbit ran into"

The second, incorrect, translation is what the sentence would mean if it were a relative clause on *a'aangóne'* 'in the hole.' Instead, it appears to be a free relative on a deleted enclitic phrase with the enclitic *gí* 'at,' the free relative giving the location around where the rabbit ran into the hole.

Any number of things might be happening with these constructions. They might be superficially homophonous but underlyingly distinct constructions, as are the free relatives and indirect questions of English. On the other hand, they might all syntactically be free relatives, with the 'indirect question' of (74) a kind of 'concealed question' (see Baker 1968). What seems certain, however, is that free relatives have some significantly different properties from the others.

Here I conclude my discussion of Navajo.

1.1.2.2 *English*: We observed above that in addition to free relatives and *ever*-clauses, English has an internal head relative clause exemplified in such examples as *what beer we found was flat*. I shall first distinguish this latter construction, which for reasons that will become apparent I will call the paucal relative, from the others, and then I will provide an argument that in paucal and in free relatives the *wh*-marked NP is a constituent of the relative clause rather than a head. Finally, I will briefly consider a reason to suspect that the *wh*-marked NP may be generated in initial position rather than preposed.

The paucal relative looks like a free relative with a full head nominal supplied. Perhaps the first thing we notice is that we can only supply such a nominal when the NP is plural or mass:

(76) a. I drank what was provided.
 b. I drank what beer was provided.
 c. *I drank what glass of milk was provided.

(77) a. Fred hit what was on the table
 b. Fred hit what weapons were on the table.
 c. *Fred hit what weapon was on the table.

This requirement that the NP be non-individual (see Fiengo 1974) distinguishes the paucal relative not only from the free relative, but also from the *whatever*-clause, insasmuch as we can say *Fred hid whatever weapon was on the table*.

We may next observe that while we can add the paucal quantifiers *few* and *little* to NP_{rel} in the paucal construction, these are the only quantifiers that may be added:

(78) a. Fred hid what few weapons were on the table.
 b. Bill drank what little wine we had.
 c. *I saw what three people arrived early.
 d. *I know what many people came to the party.

With the *whatever* construction, numerals, but not paucal quantifiers are possible:

(79) a. *I greeted whatever few people came to the door.
 b. I hid the coats of whatever three people he brought.

(79b) is not terribly good, and for many other quantifiers the judgements are too shady for me to wish to make any claims about them.

We may finally observe that the paucal relative clause makes the imputation that the referent of the clause is present in meagre, insufficient amounts. Hence (79b) implies that not much beer was provided, and (77b) that not many weapons were on the table. Nonetheless, this imputation seems to be weaker than it would be were a paucal quantifier present, as may be seen by examining (78a, b); and examples can be found where the imputation of paucity is very weak or perhaps nonexistent: *we will take what steps are necessary*.

Nonetheless as a preliminary explanation I shall propose that there is an underlying element PAUC in the quantifier phrase position of the paucal relatives without overt surface quantifier. PAUC is an abstract member of the class otherwise comprising *few* and *little*, and it is weaker in force. By supposing that it shares with *few* and *little* the requirement that the quantified NP be non-individual, we may explain the impossibility of count singular heads in the paucal construction, as well as the interpretation of the clauses.

While the postulation of abstract elements in syntax is dangerous, it is worth pointing out that the quantifiers are a closed rather than an open class, so that their members may be distinguished from each other by a finite set of features that may be properly said to be a part of the grammar of the language. We can thus treat PAUC as the archi-quantifier embracing *few* and *little*. The effect of our analysis is to connect the requirement that the relative NP be non-individual with the restrictions on the quantifiers possible for this NP.

We now turn to the problem of proving that the *wh*-NP in the free and paucal relative constructions are really constituents of the relative clause. I shall first offer and dispose of a potential argument that does not go through, and then establish the point by a consideration of the behaviour of returning pronouns.

We may observe that the free and paucal relatives do not permit the *wh* NP to be followed by the particle that:

(80) a. *I drank what (little) beer that was on the table.
b. *I drank what (little) beer that we found.
c. *I ate what that we brought.

It strikes me that the *that* is much better with the paucals (80a, b) than with the free relative (80c). I have no explanation for this.

This argument fails to fully convince, because Ø, *that* and relative pronouns are not in free variation as initials for relative clauses in English. Consider the following series of examples:

(81) a. I met a girl I liked.
b. I met a girl that I liked.
c. I met a girl who I liked.

(81a) has the sense that I met one of the girls who I liked, while (81c) means most preferably that I met a girl and liked her. (81b) appears to be ambiguous. (I am indebted to William Cantrall for some discussion of these and related subtleties of meaning). The 'contact' relative construction, the one with neither *that* nor relative pronouns, thus appears to be distinct from the other two, as they are from each other. We could therefore claim that the free and paucal relatives consisted of a *wh* marked NP as head together with a contact relative.

We now consider the argument from the behaviour of returning pronouns. Returning pronouns are pronouns occupying the pre-*wh* movement or relative pronoun deletion position of NP_{rel}. They are fully grammatical in certain geographical regions, such as Texas, and many other speakers, such as myself, are highly tolerant of them. In the following examples we see returning pronouns:

(82) a. The people who Bill says that they stole his car are standing over there.
b. He is a criminal that the FBI will be pleased if they catch him.

Carlson and Martin (1974) note a restriction that resumptive pronouns must be fairly deeply embedded in the relative clause in order to be acceptable, and that they sound best if they are in a position from which island constraints and other such restrictions would prevent one from moving or deleting a pronoun. Hence *the girl who I saw her* is ungrammatical.

I will here note two further restrictions on returning pronouns. First observe that they can occur neither with questions nor with free relatives:

(83) a. the ice-cream that Fred says if you eat it you'll get off has been withdrawn from the market

   b. the automobile that the policeman who impounded it got a citation was a Buick

(84) a. *what does Fred think (that) if you eat it you'll get off?

   b. *what (automobile) did the policeman who impounded it get a citation?

(85) a. *what Fred says (that) if you eat it you'll get off has been withdrawn from the market

   b. *what the policeman who impounded it got a citation is being held at the courthouse

(86) a. *what few drugs Fred says (that) if you take them you'll get off have been withdrawn from the market

   b. *what few weapons the policemen who impounded them got citations are being held at the courthouse.

We may next observe that even in a headed relative clause returning pronouns cannot co-refer with a constituent preposed by pied piping:

(87) a. *There is the boy whose mother Bill says that she's a stripper.

   b. *This is the car the owner of which the patrolman who arrested him got a citation.

We can see from (83-87) the generalisation that a returning pronoun is ungrammatical without a head with which it can corefer without anomaly. In (84-86) there is no head at all, and in (87) the returning pronoun cannot be coreferential with the head without destroying the semantic interpretation of the clause. It is clear that if the *wh*-NP of (85-86) were analysed NP_{hd} rather than as NP_{rel} we could not achieve this unification of restrictions on returning pronouns.

I shall finally observe a reason for suspecting that the NP_{rel} in the headless relative constructions are generated in COMP position. It was observed by Joan Bresnan (in as yet unpublished work) that pied piping is impossible with free relatives. It is also impossible with paucal relatives:

(88) a. I stole what Bill was writing with.

b. *I stole with what Bill was writing.

(89) a. Bill alienated what few girls he danced with.

b. *Bill alienated with what few girls he danced.

We might semantically analyse a relative clause as consisting of a sentence open on a variable x to which an operator R binding x is prefixed. We might further suppose that the operator is restricted by whatever nominal material is in NP_{rel}. Hence *who Bill saw* would translate as (R x:human) (Bill saw x). R would be interpreted in the obvious way as an abstraction operator. Now suppose that a *wh*-NP that is in an ordinary sentence-internal position is preposed in the translation from syntactic to semantic structure, but that one that is in COMP position is merely left in place, with the S translating into a sentence open on some position which in the syntax is 'empty.' Then *what few people I saw* will translate out as (R x:few people) (I saw x), but *with what few people he danced* will come out as (with (R x:with few people)) (he danced?) or some similar piece of garbage, provided that the *wh*-phrases are underlyingly initial. I suggest, then, that it might be the case that (a) semantic interpretation precedes *wh*-movement and works in the manner suggested (b) headed relatives and questions don't (or needn't) have their *wh* NP in COMP position (c) headless relatives require their *wh* NP to be in initial position. This must, of course, all be regarded as the rankest speculation.

I will close with the observation that the free and paucal relative clauses would both correspond to restrictive relative clause with definite heads when rendered in a headed construction. Likewise, the Navajo relative clause, which Hale and Platero (1974) suspect to have an underlyingly headless structure (pre-relatives being derived by extraction), also corresponds only to a restrictive relative on a definite head. Such interpretations may then be a universal property of the headless relative, and there may thereby be a way to distinguish pre- and post-relatives that are derived by extraction from those that are not. This too must be regarded as highly speculative.

1.1.3 *Adjoined Relative Clauses:* Adjoined relative clauses appear not within an NP in their matrix S, but rather at the beginning or the end of that S, possibly separated from their head by an unbounded stretch of material.

I propose that adjoined relative clauses come in three varieties: anticipatory, extraposed and trailing. Anticipatory and trailing relatives I propose to be generated by a rule $\bar{S} \longrightarrow \text{COMP} (\bar{S}) \text{ S } (\bar{S})$, the first $\bar{S}$ on the right being anticipatory, the second being trailing. Extraposed relatives I propose to be introduced by $S \longrightarrow S \bar{S}$. Extraposed relatives are the extraposed relatives familiar from English, while anticipatory and trailing relatives are a type that is present in English only in the form of an assortment of marginal constructions, but is in many languages the major vehicle of relativization. The justifications for distinguishing trailing from extraposed relatives will emerge gradually: essentially the trailing relative is a counterpart to the anticipatory relative, while the extraposed relative is related to the embedded relative. It is obvious that these structural proposals are tremendously oversimplified. There is need for a great deal more work on the ways in which subordinate clauses may be attached to the margins of matrices. Nonetheless the present proposal will suffice as a beginning.

We thus attain the following three constituent structures for relative clauses not forming a constituent with their head:

(90) a. Anticipatory Relative:

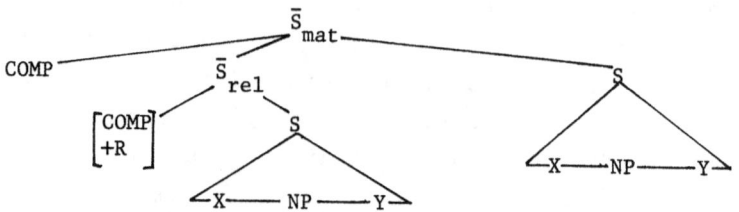

b. Trailing Relative:

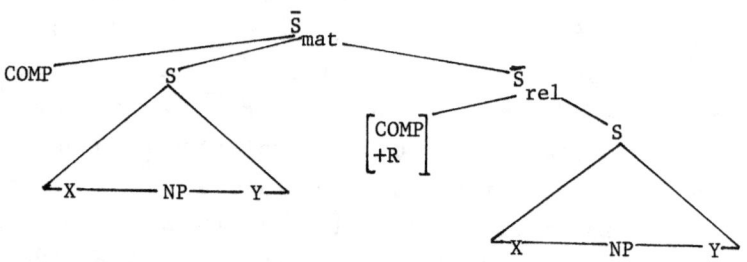

c. Extraposed Relative:

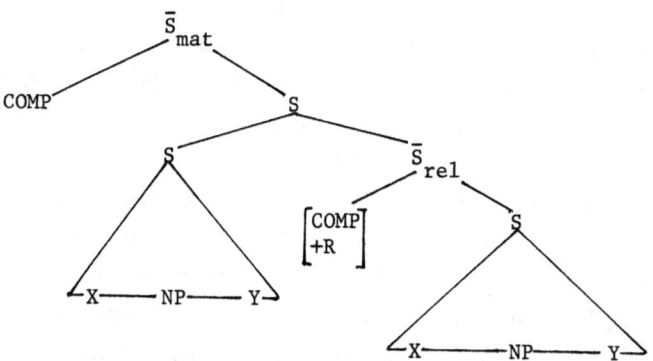

Some languages with anticipatory and trailing relative clauses as major relative clause structures are the following:

(91) Languages with Anticipatory and Trailing Relatives:

Warlpiri		Sanskrit
Mabuiag	Australian	Bengali
Kaititj		Hindi
Papago		Marathi
Hittite		Bambara

English and Navajo have extraposed relatives without anticipatory relatives (excepting marginal constructions in English).

I shall first discuss the Australian languages Warlpiri and Mabuiag, then the Indic languages Hindi, Sanskrit and Marathi, and finally, Navajo and English. Among the highlights will be the exhibition of double headed anticipatory relatives in Sanskrit and Marathi, double headed extraposed relatives in English and Navajo, and finally, cases from Marathi and Navajo where adjoined relatives are separated from their heads by unbounded stretches of material. Such cases have also been given for Hindi by Satyanarayana and Subbarao (1973).

1.1.3.1. *Warlpiri*: This is a somewhat oversimplified account of material presented by Ken Hale in class (1971).[7] I am of course responsible for any errors in the presentation.

Warlpiri is a basically SOV language with very free scrambling and a case system including ergative, absolutive, dative, etc. A constituent with considerable presence in the surface structure is an Aux-node, the contents of which are realized as a single word and which contains tense/aspect and mood markers, as well as agreement morphemes expressing the case and number of various complements of the verb. Curiously, the case-system of the agreement formatives is nominative-accusative while that of the NP is ergative-absolutive. This suggests that the underlying case system is nominative-accusative, and that after the agreement rule applies, an ergative-absolutive rule applies to the full NP and causes the earlier nominative-accusative marking to be obliterated.

Warlpiri speakers do not like constituents of more than one word length to appear in surface structure, preferring to scramble apart even such constituents as NP consisting of head and adjective or demonstrative. Especially, Warlpiri speakers do not like embedded S, and sentences with center-embedded S are definitely ungrammatical in Warlpiri. Thus there are both anticipatory and trailing relative clauses, but no embedded relatives.

In a relative clause, there is a formative *kutja* at the beginning of the AUX, to which various tense-aspect and agreement markers (which may add up to ∅, since many of them are ∅) are added. In the simplest constructions, whichever of NP_{rel} or NP_{hd} comes second may be deleted, or both may be left untouched. It is hence reasonable to believe that in this language, the deletions are accomplished by pronominalization, as is not the case in Navajo.

Below are some examples:

(92) a. timana-lu ∅   kuḍu kutju-nu
     horse-ERG AUX child throw-PAST
     "the horse threw the child."

   b. ŋatju ka-ṇa-la   kuḍu-ku maritjari-mi
     I   PRES-1-3(DAT) child-DAT feel sorry for-NONPAST
     "I feel sorry for the child."

   c. timana-lu kutja kuḍu kutju-ṇu ŋatju ka-ṇa-la
     horse-ERG REL   child throw-PAST I   PRES-1-3(DAT)
     (kuḍu-ku) maritjari-mi
     child-DAT) feel sorry for-NONPAST
     "I feel sorry for the child that the horse threw."

   d. ŋatju ka-ṇa-la   kuḍu-ku   maritjari-mi
     I   PRES-1-3(DAT) child-DAT feel sorry for-NONPAST
     timana-lu kutja kutju-ṇu   (kuḍu)
     horse-ERG REL   throw-PAST (child)
     "I feel sorry for the child that the horse threw."

The surface independence of the relative clause from its head is shown by the fact that there is no necessary constituent structure relationship holding between NP_{hd} and S_{rel}, and by the fact that the case-marking of NP_{hd} and NP_{rel} is entirely determined by the role each NP plays in its clause.

Sometimes, when under great stress, Warlpiri speakers violate the rule against embedding relative clauses, and then a relative gets stuffed into an NP between the head and the case-marker. In this construction, the clauses look like an adjective formating a surface constituent with its head. I believe that such relative clauses are ungrammatical, because Hale reports that a Warlpiri speaker will not admit that he pronounced such a sentence, even if confronted with tape-recorded evidence, much less admit that they are possible in Warlpiri.

From this ungrammatical embedded structure, one can actually get up an argument against deriving relative clauses from an embedded source: for when an ordinary adjective is removed from an NP it takes along with it a copy of the case-marker of the NP. Therefore, if relative clause were to move out of an NP, one would expect it to take with it the case-marker of that NP.

A construction like that of Warlpiri obviously puts strong limitations on the number of relative clauses that can occur modifying NP in a single S. The structure I have given permits two, but it is difficult to tell whether two or one is the permitted number. Only one relative clause can occur at either end of the S, but the occurrence of S with relative clauses at both ends as made possible by my $\bar{S} \rightarrow COMP\ (\bar{S})\ S\ (\bar{S})$ rule is doubtful. Hale reports that when such structures occur, the following relative clause has very much the flavour of an after-thought. A construction that suggests that the trailing relative clause in such cases is an afterthought is an extremely common one in which the trailing relative clause is a copy of the anticipatory one, giving such a sentence as *the man came yesterday, I hit the man, the man came yesterday* as a rendition of *I hit the man who came yesterday*. Perhaps the second relative clause is tacked on because the speaker has forgotten about the first. The 'afterthoughtty' character of many trailing relative clauses is interesting in light of the fact that Thiersch (1974) has observed similar properties of clauses in English that I will in section 1.1.3.7 analyse as trailing clauses.

I have already noted that whichever of NP_{rel} and NP_{hd} comes second is optionally deletable, and since Warlpiri has widespread deletion of anaphoric pronouns, we can safely assume that this optional deletion is accomplished by pronominalization. There are other more complicated configurations involving determiners in which NP_{rel} and NP_{hd} may appear, but since I have not determined their relation to other sorts of anaphoric processes, I shall not discuss them here.

Warlpiri supports the $\bar{S} \to COMP\ (\bar{S})\ S\ (\bar{S})$ rule, inasmuch as (a) there is no evidence that relative clauses are extracted from their heads, and (b) if relative clauses were extracted from their heads, there would be no way to capture the one-to-a-side restriction.

1.1.3.2 *Mabuiag*: I will here briefly sketch some of the results arrived at by T. Klokeid (1970) in his research on Mabuiag, another Australian language. Klokeid identifies three types of relative clauses: participials, which appear to be some sort of reduced relative, and are hence beyond the scope of this paper; full relatives with a *wh* word; and full relatives without such a word. The former type occurs in both anticipatory and trailing position, the latter only in trailing position.

I will first discuss the clauses without a *wh*-word. These clauses are always anticipatory, and NP_{rel} remains a full NP within them, exactly as it would in an unembedded S. NP_{hd}, which always follows the relative clause, may either be deleted or pronominalized. Deletion is a regular alternative to pronominalization. One suspects that NP_{hd} could also be left intact, but Klokeid does not give us information on this point.

Some examples are:

(93) a. moegekaz$_i$ uzarai-dhin Panai-ka, Zon $\{\emptyset_i / \text{nubi-ka}_i\}$
      child   go-PAST   Panai-DAT John him-DAT
      mulai-dhin
      talk-PAST
      "John talked to the child who went to Panai."

   b. moegekazi-n$_i$ gulaig$_j$ gasam-dhin, $\{\emptyset / \text{nui}\}$ or j
      child-ERG   captain   touch-PAST   he$_i$ or j
      uzarai-dhin Panai-ka
      go-PAST   Panai-DAT
      "The child who touched the captain went to Panai."
      "The captain who the child touched went to Panai."

The same essential considerations apply here as do in Warlpiri: there is no compelling reason for deriving these clauses from anywhere but from where they appear in surface structure.

These relative clauses are identical in form to a sort of *because*-clause. In the *because*-clause, there needn't be any NP coreferential with anything in the main clause, but if there is, it gets pronominalized or deleted, just as when a relative clause is present. Hence the examples of (93) also have the *because*-clause readings "John talked to the captain because he went to Panai" and "the captain went to Panai because the child touched him" or "the child went to Panai because he touched the captain". Therefore, if the base rules which generated the *because*-clauses also generated the anticipatory relative clauses, no great syntactic implausibilities would result.

The other form of relative clause uses a *'wh'* word *ngadh* (occurring, of course, in many case-forms) as a relative pronoun or relative determiner of NP. One would of course presume that the uses as pronoun and determiner are in fact the same, the pronominal use being when pronominalization has removed the rest of the NP. *ngadh* is also used as the interrogative pronoun-determiner, as well as as an identity-of-sense pronoun like English *one* in *a red one*. Clauses with *ngadh* can never be interpreted as *because*-clauses, and they may either precede or follow the matrix. They may also occur as post-relatives, but this construction is strained, and is said to have weird intonation.

Some examples of relative clauses with *ngadh* are the following:

(94) a. ngadh mabaig-an os   guudthapam-dhin uzarai-dhin
    Wh-ERG man-ERG horse kiss-PAST   go-PAST
      Bessai-da
      Bessai-DAT
    "The man who kissed a horse went to Bessai".

    b. mabaig uzarai-dhin Bessai-ka, ngadh mabaig-an os
      man   go-PAST   Bessai-DAT wh-ERG man-ERG horse
      guudthapam-dhin
      kiss-PAST
    "The man who kissed a horse went to Bessai".

(c) Zon mabaig, ngadh os   guudthapam-dhin, matham-dhin
    John man   wh-ERG horse kiss-PAST   hit-PAST
    "John hit the man who kissed the horse."

    The greater positional freedom of the clause with *ngadh* is probably a consequence of the fact that it contains a signal that it is a subordinate clause: if the relative clause without *ngadh* were permitted to occur both at the beginning and the end of the main clause, it would be impossible to tell which was which. I am not sure how such a constraint should be built into the grammar.

    Mabauiag is like Warlpiri in having relative clauses introduced by the $\bar{S} \longrightarrow$ COMP ($\bar{S}$) S ($\bar{S}$) rule, and in having pronominalization processes be the ones responsible for reducing whichever of NP_{hd} and NP_{rel} gets reduced; but unlike Warlpiri, it optionally has a special determiner for NP_{rel}, and there is a slight possibility for there to be post-relative clauses of some sort as well. We shall see that on the whole, the relative clauses introduced by $\bar{S} \longrightarrow$ COMP ($\bar{S}$) S ($\bar{S}$) do not have special rules deleting NP_{rel}.

1.1.3.3 *Hindi*: In this subsection, I will briefly summarize the main points of relativization in Hindi as described by Donaldson (1971). Relative clauses may be anticipatory, trailing, or embedded as post-relatives. NP_{rel} has a relative determiner *jo* (occurring in many inflectional forms) which is distinct from the interrogative pronoun. NP_{hd} has the demonstrative determiner *vəh* (also occurring in many inflectional forms) which normally means 'that'. As in the preceding languages, whichever of NP_{rel} and NP_{hd} comes second has everything but the determiner optionally deleted, presumably by pronominalization. Hence Hindi is essentially similar to Mabuiag. Hindi provides the pattern for the other Indic languages: hence, I will discuss in later sections examples from Sanskrit and Marathi without going into great detail with these languages.

    Below are a series of examples from Hindi, first preposed relatives (95), then extraposed (96), and finally post-relatives (97):

(95) a. Jo lərka mere pas rəhta hai, vəh mera chota bhaii hai.
       wh boy me   near lives   that my little brother is
       "The boy who lives near me is my little brother."

   b. Mere pas jo lərka rəhta hai, vəh mera chota bhaii
      me   near wh boy lives   that my little brother
      hai.
      is
      "The boy who lives next door to me is my little brother."

   c. Jo per nadii ke kinare pər tha, pəkshii us pər
      wh tree river of bank on was bird   that on
      baitha tha.
      sitting was
      "The bird was sitting on the tree that was on the bank
      of the river."

(95b) reveals that the *wh*-word needn't front, while (95c) shows S_{rel} and NP_{hd} separated by the subject of the matrix S, so that they cannot be a constituent.

(96) a. Vəh lərka mera chota bhaii hai, jo mere pas rəhta
        that boy my   little brother is wh me   near
        hai.
        lives
        "The boy who lives near me is my little brother."

   b. Gay sərək cəlii ja   rəhii thii, log   jis pər baithe
      cow street on going was   people wh on sitting
      hue the.
      were
      "The cow was walking on the street on which people were
      sitting." (I don't understand why there is no *vəh*
      with *sərək*)

(97) a. Ram ne,   jo əmiir hai, ek məkan khəriida
        Ram INSTR wh rich is a house bought
        "Ram, who is rich, bought a house."

   b. Us   admii ne,   jo əmiir hai, ek məkan khəriida.
      that man   INSTR wh rich is a house bought
      "The man who is rich bought a house."

The instrumental cases on the subject NP in the matrices of (97) are due to the fact that in certain tenses, the subject is put in the instrumental.

There are various special points to be made. First, when the head noun is definite, as we have seen, it usually acquires the determiner *vəh* 'that.' Ordinary definite NP bear no determiner at all. But if the head NP bears the determiner *yəh* 'this', it keeps this determiner, as shown in (98) below:

(98) Yəh kal shant nəhĩĩ hai jisme həm rəhte hai.
　　　this age peaceful not　is　wh-in we live
　　　"This age in which we live is not peaceful."

Secondly, there is a restriction that if the head NP is indefinite, with the determiner *ek* 'a, one,' then the relative clause must follow the head:

(99) a. Us ne ek jhiil dekhi jo bəhut bəṛii thii.
　　　　he INSTR a lake　　 wh very big was
　　　　"He saw a lake which was very big."

　　　b. *jo jhiil bəhut bəṛii thii, us ne ek dekhi

Finally, there is a restriction that nonrestrictive clauses such as those of (97a) can occur only in post-relative position, not as trailing or anticipatory relatives. Hence one has the following:

(100) a. *Ram ne ek məkan khəriida jo əmiir hai.
　　　　 Ram INSTR a house bought wh rich is

　　　 b. Us admii ne ek məkan khəriida jo əmiir hai.
　　　　 that man INSTR a house bought wh rich is

　　　 c. *Jo ram əmiir hai us ne ek məkan khəriida.
　　　　 wh Ram rich is he INSTR a house bought

　　　 d. Jo admii əmiir hai us ne ek məkan khəriida.
　　　　 wh man rich is he INSTR a house bought

I suspect that the constraint that anticipatory relatives require definite heads is universal. It holds in the other Indic languages (making certain allowances), and Hale suspects that it is also true of Warlpiri. Inasmuch as restrictive relatives with definite heads are generally 'old information', this may be related to the tendency for old information to appear first. Also, this construction might be related to the 'left dislocated' structures of such examples as *the guy who did that, I think he should be shot*.

1.1.3.4 *Sanskrit*: Inasmuch as the adjoined relative clause constructions do not have to form constituents with their heads, there is no reason why they should be restricted to having one head, or even one *wh* word.

Examples of multiple headed relative clauses may be found in Classical Sanskrit, such as the following:

(101) a. Yasya$_i$ yat$_j$ paitṛkam   ritkam   sa$_i$
         who:GEN what:NOM paternal:NOM inheritance:NOM he:NOM
         tad$_j$ gṛhnīta,   netaraḥ.
         that:ACC should get not another
         "Of whom what is the paternal inheritance, he should
            get it and not somebody else."

   b. Yena$_i$ yāvān$_j$ yathā$_k$ 'dharma
      who:INSTR to what extent in what manner injustice
         dharma veha samīhitia, sai eva   tatphalam
         justice or is done he exactly the fruits
              būnkte   tathā$_k$ tāvad$_j$ amutra
         thereof will enjoy in that way to that extent in the
                vai.
         other world indeed
         "By whom to what extent [and] in what manner justice or
          injustice is done, he will indeed enjoy the fruits
          thereof to that extent [and] in that manner in the
          other world."

In (101a) we have the *wh* relative words (the simple *ya* series is used only as a relative pronoun, although more complex forms built on *ya* have other uses) *yasya* and *yat*, which are NP$_{rel}$ correlating with demonstratives *sa* and *tad*, which are NP$_{hd}$ in the main clause. In (101b) the *wh* relative words are *yena*, *yāvān* and *yathā*, correlating with *sa*, *tavad* and *tathā*.

If the reader, upon looking at these sentences, feels at a loss as to how to interpret them, then there is a simple algorithm for constructing a paraphrase. Replace the *wh* words with indefinites in *some*, and recast the relative clause as a conditional. Thus one obtains: "if someone has something as a paternal inheritance, then he should get it and not someone else", "if someone does good or evil to some extent in some way, then he shall enjoy the fruits thereof in the next world to that extent and in that way".

I am informed that multiple headed relative clauses in Sanskrit characteristically have this property of being 'generic' statements of laws. One might think, therefore, to derive them from conditionals in some fashion. While this might suffice in Sanskrit, we will find in Marathi examples of multiple headed and multiple *wh*-worded relative clauses which are not generic, but rather referential.

One might also think of assocating the generic anticipatory relative clause with the anticipatory *wh-ever* clause of English, exemplified in (102):

(102) Whoever steals my chickens, I'll set my dogs on him

We may note, however, that the *wh-ever* clause of English (a) allows only one *wh-ever* word (b) does not require a correlative definite in the matrix for every *wh-ever* word in the subordinate clause:

(103) *Whoever gives whatever to Lucy, she'll thank him for it.

(104) Whoever gets the job, I'll be displeased.

Structures like (104) are impossible for Sanskrit relative clauses.

1.1.3.5 *Marathi*:[8] Relativization in Marathi is roughly comparable to relativization in Sanskrit, but is made much more complex by the presence of a bewildering variety of alternative constructions. These are discussed by Junghare (1973). I will make no attempt to review them here, but will rather use the more straightforward constructions to exhibit a number of phenomena that are of theoretical interest.

Marathi is an SOV language with scrambling. It has postpositions and many following conjunctions, although some conjunctions, such as *ki* 'that', precede their clauses (as predicted by Kuno (1974), *ki* clauses are obligatorily extraposed to post-verbal position), and other words that correspond to conjunctions in English, such as *jər* 'if' and *jəri* 'although', may occur within their clauses as if they were adverbs.

There are four cases: nominative, dative-accusative, instrumental and genitive. The marker of the nominative is null. The dative-accusative has a marker *la* which is obligatory with humans, optional with animals, and omitted with inanimates. The marker of the instrumental is *ni*, and the genitive is marked by *c+Agr*, where Agr is a formative expressing the gender and number of the head N which the genitive NP modifies. The genitive marker takes the form *jha* when the possessed NP is masculine singular.

In intransitive sentences, of course, the subject is

nominative. In a transitive sentence in the present tense, the subject is nominative and the object is dative-accusative. In a transitive sentence in the past tense, the subject is instrumental, and the object remains in the dative-accusative. There is, finally, a construction taken by many 'psychological' verbs such as *awəɾ* 'like' in which the experiencer-of-affect takes the nominative. In this construction, the unmarked order is experiencer-object-verb: hence the dative-accusative is occupying the constituent structure position of the subject, and the nominative the position of the object. Verbs agree with their subjects and objects in person, gender and number in complex patterns which I will not describe.

We will be much concerned with the two determiners *j* 'wh' and *t* 'th'. Both may be used as determiners preceding their heads, or independently as pronouns. When used as pronouns, they take the case endings that would otherwise appear on the head N. Hence we have *ǰa muli-la* 'what girl-DA', *ǰa-la* 'who:FEM-DA'. *j* is used on NP_{rel} of relative clauses, but not as an interrogative, and *t* is used as a demonstrative pronoun/definite article, as well as on the NP_{hd} of relative clauses.

As in Hindi, we can find restrictive relative clauses preceding or following the matrix, NP_{rel} marked with *j*, NP_{hd} with *t*, and optional deletion of the head N of whichever NP comes first:

(105) a. Mĩ   ǰa muli-la pahili, mə-la ti (mulgi) awəṛte.
         I:INSTR wh girl-DA saw   I-DA   th (girl) like
         "I like the girl who I saw".

    b. Mə-la ti mulgi awəṛte, mĩ   ǰa (muli)-la pahili
       I-DA th girl like   I:INSTR wh (girl)-DA saw
       "I like the girl who I saw".

The relative clauses in these examples illustrate the instrumental - dative-accusative construction in the past tense, and the matrices illustrate the dative-accusative - nominative construction with psychological verbs. The first, rather than the second instance of the head may be deleted under various circumstances which I do not understand and will not undertake to report.

Jungare (1973) analyses restrictive relative clauses as being extracted from within the NP they modify, a view that we have rejected for Warlpiri and Mabuiag, due to the absence of any convincing evidence to support it. In Sanskrit, we found evidence against the view in the form of double and triple headed relative clauses, but the evidence was weakened in the light of the fact that the clauses receive an interpretation which makes them semantically similar to conditionals. I will exhibit referential multiple headed relative clauses in Marathi, but first I will discuss a relation between the position of a relative clause and its semantic interpretation.

The sentence *Ram thinks that the woman who is in the kitchen is not in the kitchen* is said (see Postal 1974) to have a reading in which a woman is in the kitchen and Ram thinks that she is not in the kitchen, and a reading in which Ram holds the contradiction that the woman who is in the kitchen is not in the kitchen. Following the philosophical tradition, these readings are generally called the transparent and the opaque readings, respectively.

In Marathi, these readings may be distinguished by the positioning of the relative clause: if it is placed initial to the matrix clause, we get the transparent reading; if it is placed initial to the complement clause we get the contradictory opaque reading. (106a) is the matrix with no relative clause, (106b) has the relative clause attached to the matrix to yield the transparent, coherent reading, and in (106c) the relative clause is attached to the complement to yield the contradictory opaque reading:

(106) a. Rama-la waṭṭe ki   ti bai   kičən mədhe nahi.
         Ram-DA thinks that th woman kitchen in   is not
         "Ram thinks that the woman is not in the kitchen."

      b. Ji bai   kičən   mədhe ahe, Rama-la waṭṭe ki   ti
         wh woman kitchen in   is   Ram-DA thinks that th
         (bai)   kičən   mədhe nahi.
         (woman) kitchen in   is not
         "Ram thinks that the woman who is in the kitchen is
          not in the kitchen (Transparent & Ram sane)"

c. Rama-la waṭṭe ki ǰi bai kičən mədhe ahe ti (bai)
   Ram-DA thinks that wh woman kitchen in is th (woman)
   kičən mədhe nahi.
   kitchen in is not
   "Ram thinks that the woman who is in the kitchen is not
    in the kitchen (opaque & Ram crazy)"

Note that the relative clause goes between *ki* and the complement S, justifying the order of elements in the
$\bar{S} \longrightarrow$ COMP $(\bar{S})$ S $(\bar{S})$ rule.

This rule is further justified by the fact that two relative clauses cannot occur initially. Similarly, various sorts of adverbial clauses, such as conditionals in *jər... tər...* cannot cooccur initially with relative clauses, showing that they too occupy this slot:

(107) a. *Jo mulga kičən mədhe ahe, ǰi bai ajari ahe,
         wh boy kitchen in is wh woman sick is
         tya-ni   ti-la   mədət keli.
         th(masc)-INST th(fem)-DA help did
         "The boy who is in the kitchen helped the woman who is
          sick."

     b. *Jər to ghora ǰinkel, jo mulga kičən mədhe ahe, mĩ
         if th horse wins   wh boy kitchen in is   I:NOM
         tər tya-la   marin.
         then th(masc)-DA will hit
         "If that horse wins, then I will kill the boy who is
          in the kitchen."

Inasmuch as I later wish to relate *jər...tər* conditionals and related structures to relative clauses, this result is advantageous. I have not investigated the behaviour of trailing clauses, or of combinations of anticipatory and trailing clauses.

I now turn to multiple headed relatives. Below is a series of double headed relative clauses, the first three anticipatory, the last one trailing:

(108) a. Jo mulga ǰa muli-la pahato, *(tya) mula-la *(ti) mulgi
         wh boy wh girl sees   th boy-DA th girl
         awəṛte.
         likes
         "The boy who sees the girl likes her."

     b. ǰa mula-ni   ǰa muli   dueš kela tya-ni
         wh boy-INST wh girl-GEN hatred did tha(masc)-INST
         ti-la   marli.
         th(fem)-DA killed
         "The boy who hated the girl killed her."

c. J̌a mula-ni   ǰa muli-la mərət keli, to   ti-la
    wh boy-INST wh girl-DA help did th(masc) th(fem)-DA
      marli
      killed
    "The girl who the boy helped liked him."

d. Tya mula-ni tya muli-la marli ǰa-ni   ǰi-ca
    th boy-INST th girl-DA killed wh(masc)-INST wh(fem)-GEN
      dueš   kela.
      hatred did
    "The boy who hated the girl killed her."

The translations given are ambiguous. The meanings of the examples are best given in logicalese. (108a), for example, means that for the unique ordered pair (x, y) where x is a boy and y is a girl and x sees y, x likes y; and similarly for the others. I believe that the translations given have these readings along with others.

Inasmuch as these examples are of considerable importance, it is worth mentioning that I have found them with three different speakers, the first of whom volunteered one in the course of a discussion of the Sanskrit examples in the previous subsection. He said that although referential multiple headed relatives were unnatural in Sanskrit, they were acceptable in his own language. I have tried (not very hard) with no success to elicit them in Bengali, and Keenan has tried with limited success to get them in Hindi (personal communication).

We may observe in (108a) that each j-word in the relative clause must have its corresponding t-word in the matrix. This shows that this relative clause construction really does involve multiple NP_{rel}-NP_{hd} connections. Skepticism on this point may be further abated by observing that a multiple j-word relative clause may be used to answer a multiple k-word (interrogative) question:

(109) Q: Konta mulga kontya muli berober dating kərto?
         which boy   which girl with   dating does

      A: J̌a-la   ǰi   awərte.
         wh(masc)-DA wh(fem)   likes

      Q: "Which boy is dating which girl?"

      A: "who likes who."

The answer is presumably a reduced form of *jăla ǰi awəṛte, to mulga tya muli berober dating kərto*, which is of the same general form as the clauses of (108), except that pronominalization between NP_{rel} and NP_{hd} goes backwards.

These constructions have about them somewhat of the air of Bach-Peters sentences. This is not surprising, inasmuch as one of the more obvious ways to go about providing a semantics for them would be to revise the device of the 'double NP' proposed by Keenan (1972, pp.458-459) to do the semantics for Bach-Peters sentences.

I observed in the discussion of Hindi that a relative clause could modify an indefinite NP if it followed the matrix, but not if it preceded:

(110) a. Mĩ   eka muli-la bheṭlə, mə-la ǰi (mulgi) awəṛte.
          I:INST a girl-DA met   I-DA wh girl   like
          "I met a girl who I like."

   b. *Məla ǰi mulgi awəṛte, mĩ eka mulila bheṭlə.

Relative clauses following indefinite heads can also be multiple headed:

(111) Ek mulaga eka muli-la bheṭlə, ǰa-la   ǰi   awəṛte
       a boy   a   girl-DA met   wh(masc)-DA wh(fem) likes
       "A boy met a girl and he likes her."

This construction has a flavour of 'afterthoughtiness' about it, and we find that it cannot be used with interrogatives and indefinites that are controlled by negatives:

(112) a. Tu kona-la pahila?
          you who-DA saw
          "Who did you see?"

   b. *Tu kona-la pahila jo ghorya-la marət hota?
        you who-DA saw   who horse-DA killing was

(113) a. Mĩ   kunalahi   pahila nahi.
          I:INST anybody(DA) saw   NEG
          "I didn't see anybody."

   b. *Mĩ   kunalahi   pahila nahi jo ghorya-la marət hota.
        I:INST anybody(DA) saw   NEG wh horse-DA killing was

This fact suggests that the clauses are in fact nonrestrictive, and this claim would follow from the general claim made by Junghare that relative clauses without *to* are nonrestrictive.

Before leaving the subject of multiple headed relative clauses, I will mention the fact that Schwartz (1971) claimed that they existed in Telugu in a relative clause construction of the same general form as Indic. The construction was, of course, borrowed from Indic. Our observation of the type of structure was independent.

The anticipatory and trailing relative clause structures are also used to express various adverbial ideas. For example *jevha...tevha...* express *when...then...*, and *jithe...tithe...* express *where...there...* . Hence we have the following:

(114) a. Mĩ   jevha alo, tevha to joplela hota.
         I:INSTR when came then he sleeping was
         "When I arrived he was sleeping."

   b. To tevha dokya wər ubha   hota, jevha mĩ   alo.
      he then head   on standing was   when I:INST came
      "He was standing on his head when I arrived."

(115) a. Jithe sawəli hoti, tithe Ram bəsla
         where shade was   there Ram sat down
         "Where there was shade Ram sat down."

   b. Ram tithe bəsla,   jithe sawəli hoti.
      Ram there sat down where shade was
      "Ram sat down where there was shade."

The anticipatory structure appears to be formally parallel with the English "when I arrived, then I sat down." I personally reject examples with *where...there...*, such as *where we found a four leaf clover, there we built a hut*, but this judgement is not universal.

Geis (1970) argued that adverbial clauses fell into two types: those related to relative clauses on nouns, such as *when* and *where* clauses, and those related to complement clauses on nouns, such as *if* and *although* clauses (consider the expressions *on the condition that...* and *in spite of the fact that...*). The evidence from Marathi undercuts this distinction. For not only do we have the abovementioned pairs, but also *jər...tər...* for *if...then...* and *jəri...təri...* for *although... in spite of that*. Hence corresponding to (114) and (115) we have (116) and (117):

(116) a. Jər to ithə yel, tər mi   tya-la goḷi   marin.
         if he here comes then I:INST he-DA bullet will kill
         "If he comes here, then I'll kill him."

     b. Mi   tər tya-la goḷi   marin,   to jər ithə yel.
         I:INST then he-DA bullet will kill   he if here comes
         "If he comes here, then I'll kill him."

(117) a. Jəri   tya-ni   majha kutrya-la marlə təri
         although he-INST me:GEN dog-DA   killed "thalthough"
         mə-la to awəṛto.
         me-DA he likes
         "Although he killed my dog, in spite of that
         ("thalthough") I still like him."

     b. Mə-la təri   to awəṛto, majha kutrya-la jəri
         I-DA "thalthough" he likes   me:GEN dog   although
         marlə.
         killed
         "Although he killed my dog, in spite of that I still
         like him."

The fact that *jər*, *tər*, *jəri* and *təri* needn't occur clause initially, but rather may occur fairly freely within their clauses, suggests that they are not conjunctions (occupants of COMP), but are rather like adverbs. *jevha*, *tevha*, *jithe* and *tithe* appear to position themselves in roughly the same way as do these other words.

We might still wish to dismiss this situation as a purely adventitious morphological paralellism, but there is deeper evidence of a syntactic relation between *jər...tər...* and *jəri...təri...* and the relative clause. Trailing relative clauses may have the appropriate *t*-word repeated after them. Hence we have (118):

(118) To maṇus ajari ahe jo ithə kam kərto to.
      th man sick is wh here work does th
      "The man who works here is sick."

Correspondingly we have the following examples with the adverbial words:

(119) a. To tevha dokya wər obha   hota, jevha mĩ   alo
         he then head on standing was   when I:INST came
         tevha.
         then
         "When I came, then he was standing on his head."

     b. Ram tithe bəsla,   jithe sawəli hoti tithe.
         Ram there sat down where shade was there
         "Ram sat down where there was shade."

c. Mə-la təri   to awərto, jəri   majha kutrya-la
   me-DA "thalthough" he likes although my   dog-DA
   marlə təri.
   killed "thalthough"

d. Mĩ   tər tya-la sangin   jər mĩ   tya-la bheṭlo
   I:INST then he-DA will tell if I:INST he-DA meet
   tər.
   then

'if' and 'although' in Marathi thus seem closely related to the relative clause construction in this language.

The problem raised by these examples is that it is difficult to think of how a smenatics of the sort that one might envision for relative clauses would extend in any straightforward way to these 'conjunctions'. I will venture the suggestion that perhaps treating the conjunctions with explicit quantification over possible worlds in a fashion suggested, but not explained, by Postal (1974) would provide a satisfactory solution.

In English, also, we can find relative-like conjunctions. Consider first that the *if* in the *if...then...* construction is also used as a wh-word in indirect questions: *I don't know if he will come*. Second, observe that *as...so...* form a clearly correlative pair in *as ye sow, so shall ye reap* and other examples of that ilk. Now in poetry and elevated prose we may find *as...so...* pairs which are not ordinary relative pronouns, but rather relate a clause giving grounds to one giving the consequence, in a construction that is a non-adversative counterpart to the Marathi *jəri...təri* construction. An example of this usage is the following passage from T.S.Eliot's "Little Gidding":

> But, as the passage now presents no hindrance
>   To the spirit unappeased and peregrine
>   Between two worlds become much like each other,
> So I find words I never thought to speak
>   On streets I never thought I should revisit
>   When I left my body on a distant shore.

To conclude the discussion, we have shown that Marathi relative clauses may have multiple *wh* words and multiple heads, thus scotching any hope for a universal derivation of relative clauses from clauses forming a constituent with their head. We have shown some differences between anticipatory and trailing clauses, and we have claimed that lurking among the straightforward relative clauses are a class of clauses that from conventional treatments of semantics one would not expect to betray significant syntactic relations to relative clauses. Marathi is clearly a language worthy of further investigation.

1.1.3.6 *Navajo:* In this section, I will give more thorough consideration to the extraposed relative clause in Navajo, and will contrast it with the extraposed relative in English. The Navajo material here is drawn from Perkins (1975).

The extraposed relative in English obeys the constraint (with various sorts of loopholes, most of which I shall ignore) that the head and the relative clause cannot be separated by another NP. Hence while (120) is acceptable, (121) is not ambiguous:

   (120) A woman came in who was tall.

   (121) A boy kissed a girl who was tall.

In Navajo, on the other hand, there is no such constraint. Hence (122a) is doubly, and (122b) triply ambiguous:

   (122) a. Ashkii at'ééd yoo'į̇   hashtl'izh
            boy   girl   3:PROG:3:see mud
            yiih-yítlizh-ę́ę.
            3:in-PERF:3:fall-REL
            "The boy who fell in the mud sees the girl."
            "The boy sees the girl who fell in the mud."

       b. Ashkii at'ééd łį́į́' ye-inílóóz   ba'níłtsood-ę́ę.
            boy   girl   horse 3:to-3:PERF:3:led 3:PERF:1:feed-REL
            "The boy whom I have fed led the horse to the girl."
            "The boy led the horse to the girl whom I have fed."
            "The boy led the horse which I have fed to the girl."

This Navajo extraposed relative is less restricted than the English in yet another fashion. Extraposition rules in English are subject to an ironclad constraint against extracting elements from subject clauses. Hence we have (123):

   (123) a. That a woman has arrived who knows French is good.

       b. *That a woman has arrived is good who knows French.

In Navajo, we find these data exactly reversed:

(124) a. *łééchąą'í iisxį́-nigíí ba'nił̃tsood-ę́ę yá'át'ééh.
        dog   PERF:3:kill-REL 3:PERF:1:feed-REL it is good
        "It is good that the dog which I have fed has killed
         something."

   b. łééchąą'í iisxį́-nigíí   yá'át'ééh ba'nił̃tsood-ę́ę.
      dog   PERF:3:kill-REL it is good 3:PERF:1:feed-REL

(124a), in which the relative clause *ba'nił̃tsoodę́ę* 'which I have fed' has been extraposed to the end of the subject complement *łééchąą'í iisxį́nigíí* 'that the dog has killed something', is ungrammatical. (124b), where the extraposition has proceeded to the end of the sentence, is acceptable. The ungrammaticality of (124a) I shall deal with later. For the present, let us meditate on the acceptable (124b) in contrast to the English examples (123).

Ross (1967), on the basis of a variety of evidence, including sentences like (123), arrived at the following proposed constraint on transformational application (Ross 1967, ex. 5.58):

(125)   Any rule whose structural index is of the form ...A Y,
        and whose structural change specifies that A is to be
        adjoined to the right of Y, is upward bounded.

However, there is another constraint proposed by Ross that can explain (123), the Sentential Subject Constraint (Ross 1967, ex. 4.254):

(126)   *The Sentential Subject Constraint:*
        No element dominated by an S may be moved out of that
        S if that node S is dominated by a node NP which is
        itself immediately dominated by S.

The reader may observe that the crucial evidence in the discussion that motivates (125) (sections 5.1.1.-5.1.2.) is all explicable by the Sentential Subject Constraint. We have for example the following pairs:

(127) a. That it was obvious that Bob was lying is not true.

      b. *That it was obvious is not true that Bob was lying.
         (5.18)

(128) a. A proof that the claim had been made that John had
         lied was given.

        b. *A proof that the claim had been made was given that
           John had lied. (2.9)

(129) a. That Sam didn't pick those packages up which are to
          be mailed tomorrow is possible. (5.22c)

      b. *That Sam didn't pick those packages up is is
         possible which are to be mailed tomorrow (5.21)

(130) a. That a review came out yesterday of this article
         is catastrophic. (5.55a)

      b. *That a review came out yesterday is catastrophic
         of this article. (5.55b)

These examples illustrate the phenomenon with ordinary Extraposition, Extraposition of Relative Clauses and Complements from NP and Extraposition of PP.

Let us try to construct a series of examples testing for (125) (which I shall henceforth call the Right Roof Constraint) in examples where the Sentential Subject Constraint does not interfere:

(131) a. ?*Bill said that it would be difficult in his
          memorandum to get the project funded.

      b. ?*You promised that a person would come on the
         telephone who would fix the refrigerator.

      c. **He admitted that the hypothesis had been
         disconfirmed in his paper that quarks were
         the major ingredient in baby food.

      d. ?*You said that a man would come today yesterday
         who would fix the faucet.

      e. ?*The professor announced that he had stolen a
         vase in class from the most closely guarded
         temple in India.

These are all rather bad, but they hardly constitute an overwhelming battery of evidence, and to my ear they are not as bad as the (b) examples of (127-130).

If an alternative explanation for (131) can be worked out, which wouldn't surprise me (perhaps on the basis of their ungainly constituent structure), then it might be possible to remove the Right Roof Constraint from the grammar of English. In light of Perkins' and Kaufman's work on Navajo, and Satyanarayana and Subbarao's (1973) work on Hindi and Telugu, this would constitute an advance.

(124b) requires not only that there be no Right Roof Constraint in Navajo, but also that there be no Sentential

Subject Constraint. Happily, this has already been suggested on independent grounds. (Platero 1974, pp.xx) suggests that Navajo relativization does not obey a Sentential Subject Constraint, but instead suffers from an idiolectally varying disability against relativizing into nominal complements. The extraposition process discussed by Perkins would appear to be immune from this disability.

Perkins gives examples that show that a relative clause may be extracted from several clauses deep, but may not be left at the end of any of the intervening clauses. Hence we have the acceptable (133a), and the series of failed variants (133b, c):

(133) a. Łééchąą'í biładideeshdǫǫł nisin dishní
dog 3:FUT:1:shoot 1:want PERF:1:say
shishxash-ę́ę́.
1:PERF:3:bite-REL
"I said that I wanted to shoot the dog that bit me."

b. *Łééchąą'í biładideeshdǫǫł shishxashę́ę́ nisin dishní.

c. *Łééchąą'í biładideeshdǫǫł nisin shishxashę́ę́ dishní.

Perkins further observes that although a relative clause can be extraposed from within a sentential subject, one cannot be extraposed from within a relative clause or a coordinated NP:

(134) a. Łééchąą'í nahał'in-ę́ę́ dóó mási ahigá.
dog IMP:3:bark-REL and cat RECIP:IMP:3:fight
"The dog that was barking and the cat are fighting."

b. *Łééchąą'í dóó mási ahigá nahałinę́ę́.

(135) a. Hastiin dibé ba'niłtsood-ę́ę́ neis'áh-ę́ę́
man sheep 3:PERF:1:feed-REL 3:PERF:3:butcher-REL
adeeshgizh.
REFL:PERF:3:cut
"The man who butchered the sheep which I have fed cut himself."

b. *Hastiin dibé heis'áhę́ę́ adeeshgizh ba'niłtsoodę́ę́.

We are thus confronted with what appears to be an argument that Navajo actually has a rule extraposing relative clauses from their heads: some, although not all, of the island constraints are obeyed, and we could explain the requirement that the extraposed clause wind up at the end of sentence by

having the extraposition rule be a root transformation.
   Nonetheless, mortal counterevidence to this picture exists. Perlmutter and Ross (1970) observed the following sentence pattern in English:

   (136) A man came in and a woman went out who were similar.

I proposed in the introduction to this chapter that this example had the deep structure (3). The fact that the predicate of the relative clause requires a plural subject prevents it from being derived by Extraposition and Right Node Raising from a pair of relative clauses, one in each conjunct.
   We can find examples of this form in Navajo:

   (137) Ashkii yah 'ííyá   dóó at'ééd ch'in-ííyá
         boy   into PERF:3:go and girl out-PERF:3:go
         ałhinoolin'-ęę.
         RECIP:3:look like-REL
         "A girl came in and a boy went out who were similar."

We can also find in Navajo examples of a form impossible in English. In English, the two heads for the relative clause have to be in different conjuncts of a coordinate clause. Hence we cannot say (138):

   (138) *The dog is chasing the cat which were fighting.

But the corresponding structure is perfectly acceptable in Navajo.

   (139) Łééchąą'í mágí yinoołchééł   ahigán-ęę.
         dog   cat 3:PROG:3:chase RECIP:IMP:3:fight-REL
         "The dog is chasing the cat which were fighting."

In light of the Navajo, it is the *(138) of English that is problematical. I would propose that the explanation for *(138) is the same as the explanation for the non-ambiguity of (121). The nonambiguity of (121) shows that there is in English a constraint preventing there from being an NP intervening between a relative clause and its head. This principle would prevent *which were fighting* from taking *dog* as a head in (139) due to the intervention of *cat*. Failure of number agreement then renders the example ungrammatical. Navajo, which lacks this constraint, thus has ambiguity in sentence patterns corresponding to (121) and allows sentence patterns like (139).

Why doesn't the constraint on intervention block (136)? This is presumably a consequence of the general nature of 'Across-the-board' phenomena in coordinate structures. For the present, I shall merely say that when the constraint is presented with a coordination of structures, it applies in each conjunct individually, and not to the coordinate structure as a whole. This proposal predicts that (140) should be unambiguous:

(140) A man saw a woman and a boy saw a girl who were similar.

The relative clause should modify *woman* and *girl*. As best as I can tell, this prediction is borne out.

The proposal that extraposed relatives in Navajo are base-generated in the position they occupy in surface structure appears to contradict the testimony of the evidence that there is a root transformation of Extraposition that obeys island constraints. We can explain why a relative clause can only be extraposed to the end of the main clause by noting that Navajo is absolutely rigid in its requirement that any subordinate clause end with the verb of that clause. Platero (1974) notes processes that may extrapose the subject of a main clause to the end of the clause beyond the verb, but these possibilities of movement are completely absent in subordinate clauses. By imposing the surface requirement that a subordinate clause end with its verb, we may account for the apparent evidence that Extraposition is a root transformation.

Now for the island constraints. Bresnan (1974b) attacks the notion that island constraints constitute diagnostics for movement by showing that they constrain a deletion rule. I propose that these facts from Navajo be taken as evidence that island constraints apply between elements that are related by no transformational rule at all, but rather are connected by the sorts of extra-constituent structure relations that I have been suggesting to hold between heads, relative nouns and complementizers of relative clauses. The ungrammatical (134b) would thus have the structure (141):

(141)

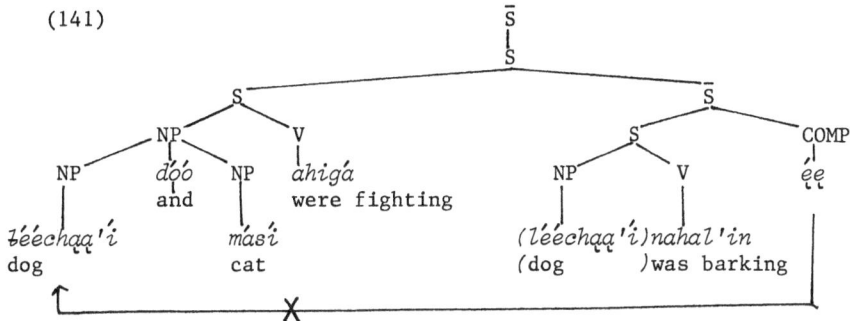

The spot is marked with an X where the Complementizer-Head Connection crosses the coordinate structure boundary.

The reader will note the presence of one assumption that is from the point of view of the Navajo quite gratuitous: I have assumed that the Navajo extraposed relative is introduced by a rule S → S $\bar{S}$. The purpose of this assumption is to create a structural paralellism between the English and the Navajo extraposed relatives.

There are two considerations that motivate introducing extraposed relatives in English with S → S $\bar{S}$ rather than with any of the other alternatives one might imagine. First the construction can stack:

(142) A woman came in who I knew who had taught at Berkeley.

Second, consider what happens when we attach an extraposed relative to a complement sentence:

(143) It is obvious that a man came in and (*that) a woman went out who were similar.

By introducing the relative clause as an expansion of S rather than of $\bar{S}$, we explain why the conjunction *that* cannot be repeated on the second conjunct. I believe that when the sense of the relative clause is such that a derivation by Right Node Raising from multiple relative clauses in a coordinate structure is possible, then the conjunction may be repeated:

(144) It is obvious that a man came in and that a woman went out who were wearing boots.

Why should the English and the Navajo structures be assimilated? They both appear to be in some sense 'variants' of an embedded relative clause structure. In this feature, they are distinguished from the trailing relative clauses of the Australian and Indic languages we have observed above. They have in addition the property of not corresponding to any anticipatory relative clause structure.

Next, we observed in section 1.1.2.1 that extraposed relatives in Navajo obligatorily underwent a rule deleting NP_{rel}. In English, similarly, the NP_{rel} of an extraposed relative clause must be a relative pronoun or it must be deleted (assuming with Bresnan (1970) that English that-relative clauses suffer deletion of NP_{rel}). In contradistinction, we see that in the trailing relative clauses of the previous subsections, NP_{rel} could be repeated. I hypothesize that obligatory deletion or pronominalization of NP_{rel} is a restriction which may be imposed on relative clauses introduced by rules of the form $X \longrightarrow X \bar{S}$ or $X \longrightarrow \bar{S} X$ (where X is any category), but not on relative clauses introduced by other sorts of rules, such as $\bar{S} \longrightarrow COMP (\bar{S}) S (\bar{S})$ or $CP \longrightarrow NP (\bar{S}) CASE$. We are thus led to predict that nonrestrictive relatives in English can have full NP heads, which is indeed the case:

(145) My dog, which faithful animal has guarded me for years, is waiting outside your door.

We might further ask why it seems to be that anticipatory relatives never seem to require pronominalization or deletion of NP_{rel}: under the present approach, we may propose that it is because there is no rule of the form $S \longrightarrow \bar{S} S$ in any language. Of course this fact itself requires explanation.

I finally observe that adjoined, but not extraposed relative clauses may have multiple *wh* words. Hence **a man came in and a woman went out who loved who* is bad in English, and there is no Navajo sentence for "*a dog was chasing the cat which bit which." Perhaps this fact is related to the pronominalization requirement noted above.

I therefore propose that there is a type of relative clause, the extraposed relative, which is essentially a variant of the embedded relative and is quite different from the trailing relative. Extraposed relatives are introduced by the rule S $\longrightarrow$ S $\bar{\text{S}}$. That the Navajo extraposed relative is introduced by this rule is at present more of a prediction than a fact.

1.1.3.7 *Remarks on Multiple Headedness:* We may observe that the multiple headed clauses we have seen fall into two types: those where a single NP_{rel} has multiple antecedents, and cases where a single relative clause has multiple NP_{rel}, each with its own antecedent. This latter case I hypothesize to be impossible with relative clauses introduced by rules of the form X $\longrightarrow$ X $\bar{\text{S}}$ and X $\longrightarrow$ $\bar{\text{S}}$ X.

We are led to suspect that multiple *wh* words may be possible with nonrestrictive relatives in English. The following, suggested by Bill Cantrall, is as good as they come:

(146)　??I scribbled on the cover of a book, which cover of which was orange.

All examples that I can construct are rather dubious, but often less so than one might expect. Note that (146), unlike the relatives of 1.1.3.6, requires a comma pause before the relative clause, making it a sort of nonrestrictive.

Finally, the existence of multiple headed clauses necessitates complications in the abstract relations I have proposed to be involved in relative clauses. In chapter 2, I will cast a proposal in more rigorous terms, but here I will describe a scheme that lets us retain the graphic representation we have been using without too much difficulty. Let us say that COMP of a relative clause expands into an n-tuple R^n. Each R may then be connected by arrows to a single NP_{rel} and to a nonnull set of NP_{hd}. In all English R^n, we have n=1 (with the dubious exception of such examples as (146)), but in Marathi we may have n=2, 3, etc. Sentence (107a) will thus receive the representation (147) on the following page. This expansion of COMP into an n-tuple will offend most readers, and when we move to a more abstract form of representation we shall eliminate it.

Before closing section 1.1, I would like to mention one final fact. It appears that in all cases, the heads of a

(147)

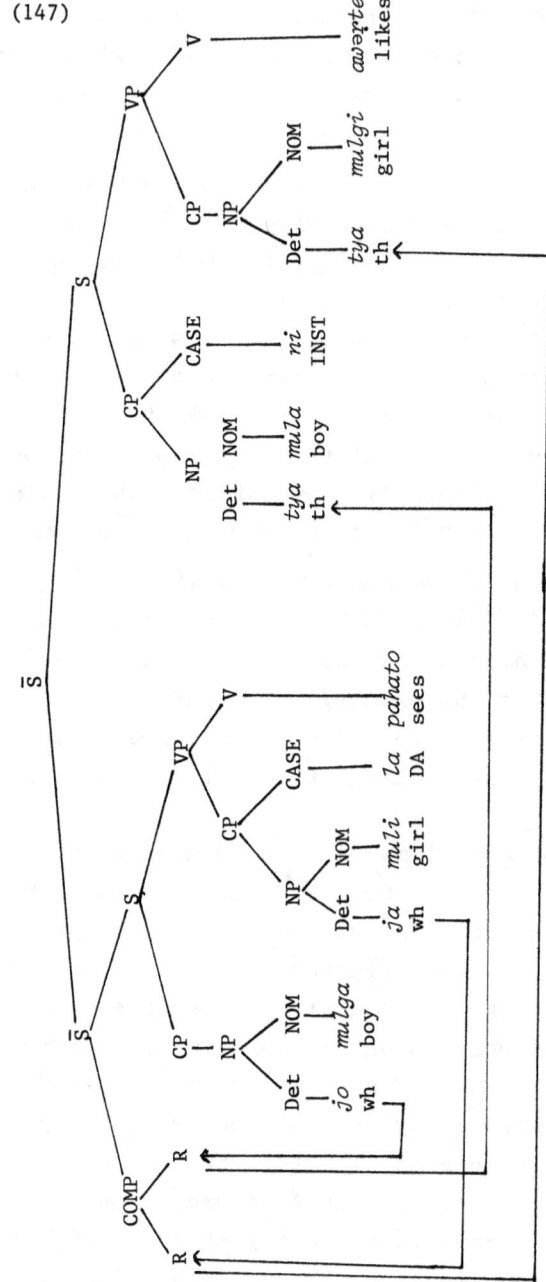

For the unique pair (x, y) where x is a boy, y is a girl and x sees y, x likes y.

relative clause are in construction with that clause, in
the sense of Klima (1964). We may easily accommodate this
with a principle restricting configurations of trees-cum-
abstract relations. Such a principle, along with many
others, will be given in chapter 2.

1.2 *The treatment of NP_{rel}*: In this section, I shall discuss the various things that happen to NP_{rel}. I shall
first in 1.2.1 discuss languages in which NP_{rel} bears a
special morphological mark, but is not deleted by a special
process or moved to the front of the clause. In one of
these languages, NP_{rel} is replaced by a special pronoun,
and in the other, a special agreement marker is placed on
the verb, which may be regarded as a copy of a specially
marked pronoun that subsequently deletes by ordinary pronominalization processes. In 1.2.2 I will discuss some
languages in which NP_{rel} is simply deleted, and in 1.2.3 I
will discuss the preposing of NP_{rel} to the front of the
relative clause. Finally, in 1.2.4 I will give some general
discussion of constraints on the form and position of NP_{rel}.

1.2.1 *Languages marking NP_{rel}*: I will here discuss two
languages with marking but not preposing of NP_{rel}: Crow
and Swahili. Crow is a transparent case of the phenomenon
inasmuch as in the construction we shall discuss there is a
special pronoun that takes the place of NP_{rel}. We require
an analysis to arrive at the conclusion that Swahili has
marking without movement of NP_{rel}.

1.2.1.1 *Crow*: Crow is a Siouan language with about (very
roughly) 4,000 speakers, spoken in southeastern Montana. It
is an SOV language with postpositions and following conjunctions and complementizers, and considerable scrambling.
The person and number of subjects, objects and possessors
are extensively marked on verbs, postpositions and possessed
NP. A particularly interesting feature of the language is a
rich array of determiners on NP which are homophonous with
and semantically similar or identical to "complementizers"
that appear on verbs. The orthography used is that adopted
by the Crow Bilingual Education Project. Dale Oldhorn,

George Reed and Rose Chesarek have been especially helpful in providing me with information about Crow, although many other members of the Crow Tribe have been of assistance.

Crow has at least four relative clause constructions, an internal head relative, an anticipatory relative, a post-relative and a free relative. My knowledge of the language is too small to allow me to say much insightful about most of these. I will therefore make some points which are of general interest with the post-relative structure, then briefly describe the others.

In the postrelative construction, the head NP takes the determiner *-m* and the relative clause takes the termination *e:s*, which serves as an anaphoric definite article on NP, and is attached to clauses representing old, "presupposed" information. NP_{rel} is represented by the word *ak*, which functions only as a subject. We thus attain the NP (148):

(148)　shiká:ka-m ak bi:-lich-é:sh.
　　　　boy-SPEC　who me-hit-DEF
　　　　"The boy who hit me."

I gloss *-m* as SPEC because it generally makes NP specific. So *shiká:ke aw-áka:-ssa:-k* 'boy I-see-NEG-DECL', 'I didn't see any boy', but *shiká:kam awaká:ssa:k* 'I didn't see a (specific) boy.' *k* is a formative that ends declarative clauses.

We may determine that *ak* is a syntactically motile word rather than merely an agentive nominalization prefix by observing that it may occur freely with a relative clause containing several major constituents:

(149)　a.　shiká:ka-m ak hú:le:sh Bill-sh dich-é:sh
　　　　　　boy-SPEC　who yesterday Bill-NM hit-DEF

　　　　b.　shiká:kam hú:le:sh ak Billsh diché:sh

　　　　c.　shiká:kam hú:le:sh Billsh ak diché:sh
　　　　　　"The boy who hit Bill yesterday."

The *sh* formative that I gloss NM is, I believe, a form of the definite article that is attached to proper names.

ak may appear within a subordinate clause in the relative clause. Hence we get (150):

(150)　Shiká:ka-m Bill-sh ak hu:wía-:-k　 hilía:ch-e:sh
　　　 boy-SPEC　Bill-NM who come-will-DECL think-DEF
　　　 "The boy who Bill thinks will come."

There is a constraint in English that if a relative clause has a subject and a complement clause containing NP coreferential to the subject, then the subject can be NP_{rel}, but none of the NP in the complement clause may. This phenomenon along with others is subsumed under the Crossover Principles of Postal (1971, 1972). Hence we have the data of (151):

(151)　a.　the boy who$_i$ thought he$_i$ was smart

　　　 b.　the boy who$_i$ he$_j$ thought was smart

　　　 c.　*the boy who$_i$ he$_i$ thought was smart

Postal (1971) proposed accounting for this with a constraint on movement: the movement of the pronoun *who* in (151c) over the coreferential pronoun *he* was to block the sentence. In the (1972) paper, he suggested retreating from this position. The data from Crow show that this retreat was well-advised, inasmuch as this relative clause construction obeys the constraint even though NP_{rel} is not moved at all, but merely assumes a special form. If we intercalate *ak* between an NP that its appropriate as an object of the complement verb and the complement verb, we prevent it from being analysed as a constituent of the topmost S in the relative clause. Then we get the following:

(152)　a.　shiká:ka-m ak ú:xa-m　 dappeé-k hilía:ch-e:sh
　　　　　 boy-SPEC　who deer-SPEC kill-DECL think-DEF
　　　　　 "The boy who thinks he killed a deer."

　　　 b.　shiká:ka-m ú:xa-m　 ak dappeé-k hilía:ch-e:sh
　　　　　 boy-SPEC　deer-SPEC who kill-DECL think-DEF
　　　　　 "The boy who$_i$ he$_j$ thinks killed a deer."

　　　　　 *"The boy who$_i$ thinks he$_i$ killed a deer."

I shall now briefly run through the other constructions. In the internal head relative clause, NP_{rel} ends in -*m* or nothing, and the complementizer may be at least *e:sh* or nothing, and possibly others, such as *m*, as well. We have for example (153):

(153) a. Mary-sh shiká:ka-m hí:-lich-é:sh
Mary-NM boy-SPEC   meet-sort of-DEF
"The boy who Mary is dating."

b. Mary-sh shiká:ke hí:-lich-é:sh
Mary-NM boy   meet-sort of-DEF
"The boy who Mary is dating."

NP_{rel} may occupy many positions within the relative clause – subject, object, possessor, etc., and it may be in many kinds of subordinate clauses, such as conditionals and indirect questions. This construction thus makes up for the restricted nature of the *ak* postrelative.

There appears to be an anticipatory relative in which a clause ending in *e:sh* precedes the matrix. The NP_{rel} take *m* and the NP_{hd} take the demonstrative *koó*. I consider the analysis of this structure as a real relative clause highly speculative:

(154) Shiká:ka-m bú:bchi-m bía:ka:ta-m kush-shí:ch-e:sh koó
boy-SPEC ball-SPEC girl-SPEC to-throw-DEF   DEM
shiká:ke koo bú:bche koó bía:ka:te ak-dichi-k.
boy   DEM   DEM girl   with-hit-DECL
"Ya know the boy who threw the ball at the girl? Well, he hit her with it."

There are finally the free relatives. These occur in four varieties. When relativising on the subject, one uses *ak*. When relativising on objects, one uses the pronoun *ba:(m)* 'something' to replace NP_{rel}. Adverbial clauses of place, time and manner are formed with *ala* replacing NP_{rel}. These three constructions are illustrated in the following:

(155) a. Bill-sh ak dapp-é:sh sahí:-k.
Bill-NM who kill-DEF Cree-DECL
"The one who killed Bill was a Cree."

b. Ba: aw-áke xawí:-k.
something I-see bad-DECL
"What I saw was bad."

c. Ú:xa-m   an-dá:-ppe, al ú:xam dá:ppe.
deer-SPEC ADV-you-kill
"The time, manner or place in which you killed a deer."

The final construction is that used when NP_{rel} is an instrumental. Crow treats instrumental NP in a very special way: between the instrumental NP and the verb occurs a formative *i:* which may come anywhere between major constituent breaks.

Hence we get the following:

(156) a. Bas-í:la:le i: b-ilápxe chichúche kuss-a:wa:lé:-k.
         my-car   INST my-father Hardin to   I:take-DECL
         "I took my father to Hardin in my car."

   b. Basí:la:le bilápxe i: chichúche kussa:wa:lé:k.

   c. Basí:la:le bilápxe chichúche i:kussa:wa:lé:k

Of these variants, (a) and (c) are the best. To get a relative clause on an instrumental, one merely takes the clause, keeping i: and omitting NP_{rel}, supplying the appropriate complementizer (most often null) to the verb. Hence one gets $i:lia:-we$ 'with do-I', 'what I did it with.' It is worth mentioning that free relative clauses are a very productive source of common nouns: from the relative clause of (157a) comes the noun $amma:ia:schilua:$ 'store', and from that of (157b) comes $i:wa:wara:tua:$ 'pencil':

(157) a. am-ma:-ía:schil-ua:
         ADV-something-buy-Pl
         "Where one buys things."

   b. i:-wa:-wara:t-úa:
      INST-something-write-Pl
      "What one writes with."

The Pl is an agreement marker for a third person plural subject that is deleted, which expresses indefinite agency. Hence we have $dit-ú:-k$ (hit-Pl-DECL) "they killed him (with the indefinite agency use of 'they')." We can spot the nouns because they, unlike relative clauses, can pluralize. Hence we have $amma:ía:schiluo$ 'stores', $i:wa:wara:túo$ 'pencils.'

I am reasonably sure that the construction with $ba:$ cannot be used with a head. The evidence with ala is rather contradictory. Although Crows seem to overwhelmingly reject examples that I concoct with ala in a postrelative structure, they will occasionally let one by. I have found no way to tell whether the instrumental construction appears in a postrelative structure, for the reason that a sequence such as 'pencil letter $i:-$ I wrote' could be analysed either as a postrelative or an internal head relative.

In Crow, we thus find a clear case of replacement of NP_{rel} by a special pronoun, and a variety of further structures which demand more thorough investigation.

1.2.1.2 *Swahili*: The Swahili construction may be regarded as a variation on the Crow. Unlike the Crow *ak* construction, NP_{rel} may occupy almost any grammatical position. Also unlike Crow, NP_{rel} gets deleted, presumably by the ordinary pronoun dropping rules. But the special mark on NP_{rel} leaves a trace in the form of a special agreement marking on the verb.

I shall give much more background information about Swahili than about the other languages in this study, since with this information, we can solve an interesting problem.

1.2.1.2.1 *NP*: Swahili has an intricate noun-class system. For each class, there are two characteristic prefixes (one or both of them sometimes null), a singular and a plural, which are attached to all occurrences of the noun itself. Hence we have *m-tu, wa-tu* 'man, men'; *ki-tabu, vi-tabu*, 'book, books'; *yai, ma-yai* 'egg, eggs.' Furthermore, corresponding to each number/class prefix, there is a 'concord' which is added to words bearing various syntactic relations to the NP, and thus causes them to agree with it. Verbs take a concord which indicates the class/number of their subject: *m-tu a-tatosha, wa-tu wa-tatosha* 'the man will be sufficient, the men will be sufficient'; *ki-tabu ki-tatosha, vi-tabu vi-tatosha* 'the book will be sufficient, the books will be sufficient'; *yai li-tatosha, ma-yai ya-tatosha* 'the egg will be sufficient, the eggs will be sufficient.' Concords are also added to adjectives modifying nouns, both predicate and attributive.

For animate beings, there is a set of personal pronouns, 1st, 2nd and 3rd persons, singular and plural. The first and second persons function like special noun-classes, having their own concord affixes, while the 3rd person uses the concord for animates (the *m-tu - wa-tu* class). One has hence *mimi ni-takufa* 'I will die'; *yeye a-takufa* 'he will die.' Since most pronouns have some concord prefix referencing them, the pronouns are freely deletable when nonemphatic. For inanimates there are no surface pronouns at all: one must make do with concord prefixes, demonstratives and NP such as *kitu* 'thing.'

There are some demonstratives which can be used either as determiners or as independent pronouns. The demonstratives are built from a stem *-le* or *h-* with a concord which is usually similar to that used on verbs to agree with the subject. For the *-le* demonstrative, which means 'that, yonder,' one merely prefixes the appropriate concord: *m-tu yu-le* 'that man,' *ma-yai ya-le* 'those eggs.' The *h-* demonstrative is built by first suffixing to *h-* the vowel of the concord, and then the whole concord itself: *m-tu h-u-yu* 'this man,' *wa-tu h-u-wa* 'these men,' *ki-tabu h-i-ki* 'this book,' *yai h-i-li* 'this egg,' *ma-yai h-a-ya* 'these eggs.' Another demonstrative, supposedly used only to refer to things which have already been mentioned, is formed by suffixing an *o* to the end of the *h-* demonstrative. The *o* causes phonological changes leading to such things as *mtu huyo, watu hao, kitabu hicho*, etc.

One of the most interesting grammatical categories in Swahili is the locative. Swahili locatives are characteristically used to express adverbial thematic relations such as place and time, but they can also be used as surface and even underlying subjects. One locative is the noun *mahali* 'place.' This takes its own special concord *pa*, and one hence gets such sentences as *mahali pa-le pa-meharibika* 'that place has been spoiled.'

More interesting locatives are made from nouns by suffixing *-ni*. One hence has *mji-ni* 'in the town,' *nyumba-ni* 'in the house,' *mlango-ni* 'at the door.' The locatives behave syntactically like NP. Although the locatives themselves lack any class-prefix other than that of the NP they are built from, the concords on the elements agreeing with them show that they fall into three classes, depending on the kind of locative relation they express. The concords are *m(u)* 'within,' *pa* 'at' and *ku* 'around, along' (meanings grossly oversimplified). Demonstratives are built from the locative concords, and one has thus such expressions as *m-le (sanduku-nu)* 'in there (in the box),' *h-a-pa mlango-ni* 'there at the door,' and so forth.

In locative expressions with definite subjects ('the animals are in the forest'), the verb *to be* (usually phonologically null) is used with the subject concord of the subject preceding the verb, and the locative concord of the locative following the verb, followed by the *o* which was mentioned above. One has hence *ki-su k-ko* (<*ku-o nymbani* 'the knife is in the house,' *kisu ki-po* (<*pa-o) mezani* 'the knife is on the table,' and *kisu ki-mo* (<*mu-o) sanduku-ni* 'the knife is in the box.'

There are two prepositions, *kwa* and *na*, which frequently have their objects copied onto them in the form of the concord+*o* combination we have seen several times before. For brevity, I will refer to this combination of concord+*o* as a kihusiano (pl. vihusiano), a term invented by a native grammarian. For each noun-class and number (including the locatives) there is a class-prefix (frequently null), concord affixes and a kihusiano. For one class, the *m-tu* class (singular animate) the kihusiano is irregular, being *ye*, which, interestingly enough, turns out to be the stem from which the third person singular personal pronoun *yeye* is formed. Hence we frequently copy vihusiano onto *kwa* and *na*, getting such forms as *naye* 'with him.' For 1st and 2nd person pronouns, the base from which the pronoun is formed by reduplication is copied onto *na*. Hence one has *mimi*, *nami* 'me, with me.' In the third person plural, the pronoun is *wao*, and the kihusiano is *o*, a contraction of *wao*.

The preposition *na* is primarily comitative and instrumental; hence *nacho* 'with it (say, a book), *nayo* 'with them (eggs).' *kwa* is generally agentive and instrumental; *kwao* 'by them (people).'

There is thus a rule copying underlying pronouns onto these prepositions in the form of a kihusiano. When the object of the preposition is a full NP, the copying generally does not occur: hence *na fimbo* 'with a stick.' The copying rule assures that *na* and *kwa* are never left stranded without any expression of their object, since precisely the things that get deleted freely, nonemphatic pronouns, get copied obligatorily.

1.2.1.2.2 Non-Relative Verbs: The Swahili verb is composed by adding prefixes and suffixes to the stem. The suffixes express for the most part categories of voice which are not my concern in this paper. The prefixes may be regarded as clitics which have become one word with the stem. They fit into the following five slots:

(158) Pre-Verbal Clitic Slots:

I	II	III	IV	V
ha	subject concord	tense/ aspect, si (neg)	relative kihusiano	object concord
(negation)				

In this subsection I will discuss slots I, II, III and V, leaving IV for the discussion of relativization. Slots II and V are well behaved, their contents varying independently of each other (excepting some twitches caused by relativization). I, III and IV have mutual interdependencies. The prefix ha- (in certain forms supplemented with the suffix -i) is used to make negatives. It is used only with certain tense-aspects, and never when there is a relative kihusiano present. ha is never followed by the subject concord ni 'I'. Instead the sequence ha-ni is suppletively replaced by si (distinct from the negative si of slot III).

The occupants of slot III are various. The negative si is used only with relative verbs (those where slot IV is filled): hence si and ha are mutually exclusive. Many of the tense-aspects either do not occur or are expressed by different formatives when I or IV are occupied.

The subject concords we have already seen in operation. They are obligatory, except with the infinitive (taking a ku in slot III) and a 'general' tense with a III-prefix hu. The absence of subject concords with ku is presumably a consequence of the subjects having been deleted, but the absence with hu is unexplained. In Swahili, as in many languages (see Kuno 1971), the locative in a sentence with an indefinite underlying subject becomes the subject, expelling the original subject to a position after the verb.

The advancement of locative to subject manifests itself in Swahili with unusual clarity, because in such sentences the subject slot takes the locative concord appropriate to the locative notion intended, and the locative appears in front of the verb in characteristic subject position. This is true even when the locative is a prepositional phrase in such prepositions as *katika* 'in.'

Thus we have examples such as the following of (159). To keep the interlinear glosses manageable I adopt the following abbreviations: SG, singular class prefix; PL, plural class prefix; SB, subject concord; OB object concord; REL, relative kihusiano.

(159) a. Mwitu-ni   m-me-lala   wa-nyama.
         forest-LOC SB-PERF-sleep PL-animal
         'In the forest sleep animals.'

   b. Wanyama wamelala   mwituni.
      animals SB:PERF:sleep in the forest
      'The animals sleep in the forest.'

   c. Ki-banda-ni m-me-lala   wa-dudu.
      SG-shed-LOC SB-PERF-sleep PL-insect
      'In the shed sleep insects.'

   d. Kule mji-ni   ku-me-kufa wa-tu.
      there town-LOC SB-PERF-die PL-person
      'In the town over there people have died.'

   e. Hapa pa-me-kufa simba.
      here SB-PERF-die lion
      'Here has died a lion.'

   f. Katika sanduku m-me-lala   m-dudu.
      in   box   SB-PERF-sleep SG-insect
      'In the box is sleeping an insect.'

(with stative verbs such as *lala* 'sleep', the perfect aspect marker *me* is used to express the present). This gives us evidence that these locatives are all surface NP. In particular, PP such as those with *katika*, where there is evidence that the whole phrase is an NP, may be contrasted with PP in *kwa* and *na* where there is no such evidence.

Unlike the subject prefix, the object prefix is optional. There appears to be a relation between humanness and copyability; human direct objects are most desirous of being copied, while inanimate objects are least. Nonetheless, they all can be copied. Below are examples:

(160) a. Ni-li-mw-ona   (mtoto).
         I-PAST-him-saw (child)
         'I saw him (the child).'

   b. Ni-li-ki-ona ki-tabu.
      I-PAST-OB-saw SG-book
      'I saw the book.'

Swahili has an almost always obligatory Dative-movement rule which takes indirect objects (which occasionally appear unmoved as prepositional phrases with the preposition *kwa*) and places them directly in front of the direct object and after the main verb. Hence the moved indirect object acquires the syntactic position of a direct object. At the same time, the verb gets its object concord from the moved indirect object rather than from the direct object:

(161) a. Ni-li-m-pe   m-toto   ki-tabu.
         I-PAST-him-give SG-child SG-book
         'I gave the child the book.'

   b. *Nilikipe kitabu mtoto.
      (O.K. with the nonsensical reading 'I gave the child to the book.')

   c. *Nilikipe mtoto kitabu.

This shows that the verb is agreeing with the first NP in the verb.

We have seen that there are rules copying subject and object clitic forms onto the verb. David Perlmutter has observed that when clitics are formed and moved, there are only two places they can go: to the verb, as they do in Swahili, or to second position in the sentence, as they do in Warlpiri (of course, this applies only to clitics formed from major constituents of the sentence: clitics formed within an NP, such as copies of the possessor of that NP, will move the head N, and likewise in PP). This suggests that a grammatical description of clitics in a language will consist of two components: one which says where, when formed, they will go. The other component describes the conditions under which they are formed in the first place. In Swahili, the grammar will contain a statement to the effect that clitics go to the verb, and it will furthermore contain the two statements that subject clitics are generated obligatorily and that object clitics are generated optionally. The movement statement will then cause them to be swept to the verb. Once they get there, they will be ordered by a Surface Structure Constraint in the manner of Perlmutter (1971).

1.2.1.2.3 *Relative Verbs:* Swahili relative clauses fall into two classes: those with a relative kihusiano in slot IV of the verb of S_{rel}, and those with the kihusiano attached to a particle *amba* appearing at the front of the clause. Since the restrictions on the former construction reveal the nature of the latter and the reasons for its existence, I shall discuss the former first.

When a relative kihusiano appears in slot IV, the number of possible tense-aspect distinctions becomes greatly reduced. If the verb is negative, negation must be expressed by a prefix *si* appearing in slot III, the tense-aspect slot, and all tense-aspect distinctions become neutralized. There is also a generic relative, in which slot III is empty and slot IV hops around to the end of the verb, slots II and V remaining in their old positions, and there are in addition progressive *(na)* past *(li)* and future *(taka)* tenses, to the exclusion of all others.

The question now arises: what fills slot IV and how does it get there? Slot IV is filled with the kihusiano of NP_{rel}. However, in order for the kihusiano to get there, and hence for a relative verb to be possible, NP_{rel} must bear an appropriate syntactic relation to S_{rel}.

I will examine what happens when NP_{rel} bears various syntactic relations to S_{rel}. When NP_{rel} is the subject, both the relative kihusiano and the subject concord appear on the verb. We have therefore examples such as the following:

    (162) a. m-tu   a-li-ye-ki-soma   ki-tabu hiki
             SG-man SB-PAST-REL-OB-read SG-book this
             'a man who read this book'

       b. m-tu   a-si-ye-soma
           SG-man SB-NEG-REL-read
           'a man who does not read'

       c. Mimi n-a-sema   ni-taka-ye-kuwa
           I   SB-PRES-sat SB-FUT-REL-be
             Sultani wenu
             Sutan   your
           'I say it, who will be your Sultan.'

From these examples, you can discern various things about the rule generating relative vihusiano. First of all, it is a rule distinct from the one generating subject concords. In these examples, both rules apply. Secondly, all the rule has to do is specify that a relative vihusiano is created. I propose that this creation itself proceeds in two steps. First, there is a specification that NP_{rel} is specially marked, and then there is a specification that it produces a clitic. The creation of the relative clitic is quite independent of the creation of the subject clitic, and subsequent to these processes, pronoun deletion disposes of NP_{rel}. The vihusiano, as well as all the other clitics, actually get to the verb by a rule which merely moves clitics to the verb. This rule appears to apply at various stages of the derivation: for example, after subject clitic formation, and also after kihuisiano formation. Note from (162c) that even when NP_{rel} is first person, one gets the 3rd person kihusiano. I don't know why this is the case.

If NP_{rel} is object, its kihusiano also appears on the verb, and the object concord may or may not appear:

       (163) a. mtu u-na-ye-m-saidia
                 man you-PROG-REL-him-assist
                 'the person you are assisting'

             b. ki-tabu a-ki-taka-cho Hamisi
                 SG-book he-OB-want-REL Hamisi
                 'the book which Hamisi wants'

             c. kitabu atakacho Hamisi
                 'the book which Hamisi wants'

These sentences illustrate another rule which has the effect of moving the relative verb to the front of the relative clause, instead of leaving it behind the subject where it normally would appear in a main clause.

If NP_{rel} is the direct object of a verb that has an indirect object in the construction where the indirect object is a naked NP preceding the direct object, then its kihusiano still appears on the verb, even though an object concord for NP_{rel} is in this case quite impossible:

(164) barua ni-taka-yo-mw-andikia
 letter I-FUT-REL-him-write
 'the letter which I shall write to him'

This last example illustrates quite clearly the independence of relative kihusiano creation from subject and object concord creation.

Relative vihusiano are found attached to the verb with two further types of NP_{rel}; NP_{rel} which are objects of the prepositions *kwa* and *na* (*kwa* rather rarely), and NP_{rel} which are adverbial modifiers of place, time and manner. Examples of these phenomena are given below:

(165) a. ma-embe ni-li-yo-kuwa na-yo
 PL-mango I-PAST-REL-be with-them
 'the mangoes which I was with,' meaning
 'the mangoes which I had'

 b. fimbo u-li-yo-pig-wa na-yo
 stick you-PAST-REL-hit-PASSIVE with-it
 'the stick that you were hit with'

 c. rafiki ni-li-o-sema na-o
 friends I-PAST-REL-talk with-them
 'my friends who I was talking with'

 d. a-ta-weze ku-salimika na ile ibu
 he-FUT-be able INF-escape from the stigma
 wa-li-yo-m-tia chapa kwa-yo wa-zee wake
 they-PAST-REL-him-put brand with-it PL-elder his
 'Will he be able to escape the stigma with which his parents have branded him?'

While NP_{rel} is a locative in S_{rel}, NP_{hd} may function either as a subject or object or an adverbial in the main clause:

(166) a. tu-me-pa-ona a-li-po-pigana
 we-PERF-OB-see there he-PAST-REL-fight
 (loc)
 na simba
 with lion
 'We have seen the spot where he fought with the lion.'

b. hamna   kitanda chumba-ni a-na-mo-lala
   there is not bed   room-LOC he-PROG-REL-sleep
   'There is not a bed in the room in which he is
    sleeping.'

When NP_{rel} is temporal, locative vihusiano, notably *po*, are used. When it is a manner adverbial, the special kihusiano *vyo* is used:

(167) a. a-li-po-sema,   watu   wakakimbia
         he-PAST-REL-say people fled
         (temp)
         'When he spoke, the people all fled.'

   b. i-li-tuka   jinsi u-li-vyo-eleza
      SB-PAST-happen   manner you-PAST-REL-explain
                                   (manner)
      'It happened in the manner that you have
       explained.'

We can observe that all of the usages of the relative verb have it in common that NP_{rel} is dominated by S_{rel} without there being an NP dominating NP_{rel} and dominated by S_{rel}. In fact, if NP_{rel} is the object of the complement of a verb, the possessor of something, or the object of a substantial preposition such as *katika* 'in' (remember that *katika* phrases show agreement evidence of being NP), the relative verb cannot be used. Relative marking in Swahili thus appears to obey the original A-over-A constraint.

In order to express a relative clause in which NP_{rel} is buried inside another NP, it is necessary to use the *amba*-construction, which I discuss in the next section. Note that this account of the constraint depends crucially on *kwa* and *na* phrases not being NP at the time NP_{rel} applies (presumably deep structure).

1.2.1.2.4 *Amba*: Relative clauses in which NP_{rel} is buried under NP can be expressed by the *amba* construction, and relative clauses in which NP_{rel} is not so buried can be too. Hence the *amba* construction can always be used in place of a relative verb. In this construction the kihusiano of NP_{rel} appears attached to the word *amba*, which begins the clause, and the verb is a normal verb with all the tense, mood and negation possibilities of a main clause verb. Some examples of the *amba* construction are as follows:

(168) a. Wi-tu   amba-vyo h-u-ta-vi-taka   kesho
       PL-thing *amba*-REL NEG-you-FUT-them-want tomorrow
       vi-weke   sandukuni.
       them-put into the box
       'Put the things which you will not want tomorrow into
       the box.'

   b. Yale   amba-yo kwa-yo a-li-wa-dangaya
      those PL-word *amba*-REL by-them he-PAST-them-deceived
      wenziwe   ha-ya-sahaulik-i.
      companions-his NEG-they-be forgotten-NEG
      'Those statements by which he deceived his companions
      will not be forgotten.'

   c. Wa-na-weze   ku-chukua ma-sanduku ma-kubwa,
      they-PROG-be able to-carry PL-box   PL-big
      amba-yo sisi watu   wawili au watatu
      amba-REL us people two   or three
      ha-tu-wez-i   ku-ya-inua.
      NEG-we-be able-NEG INF-them-lift
                           (*not* REL)
      'They are able to carry huge boxes which two or even
      three of us could not lift.'

   d. Walifika   katika bustani amba-yo ndani   yake
      they arrived in   garden *amba*-REL interior its
      mna   ma-ua   ya kila rangi.
      were in PL-flower of every color
      'They came to a garden in which were flowers of every
      color.'

   e. Ile nyumba amba-yo paa   lake li-me-ungua.
      the house amba-REL roof its   SB-PERF-scorched
      'The house, the roof of which was scorched'

   f. Yule jumbe   amba-ye tu-li-zugumza   habari zake.
      the messenger *amba*-REL we-PAST-converse news his
      'the messenger about whom we were conversing'

It is clear from the above examples that NP$_{rel}$ in the clause following *amba* is being treated exactly as an ordinary pronoun. The question then is how does *amba* preserve NP$_{rel}$ from marking, and why does it allow NP$_{rel}$ to appear within NP and complement S?

The *amba* construction is rather new: until around the turn of the century, structures that one must use *amba* to relativize were unrelativizable in Swahili. Furthermore, *amba* is the stem of a verb meaning 'to speak.' Although *amba* alone has dropped out of usage, one of its voice-derivatives, *ambia* 'to speak to' is still widely used. D. Permutter tells me that in languages where there are strong restrictions on what may be relativized, a very common way of evading these restrictions is to say such things as 'the book of which I say that Mary believes John wrote it.' Note that in this sentence, NP_{rel} is in the topmost clause, and it has a coreferent embedded inside a *believe*-clause, which in a language like Swahili would be an impossible context to relativize out of directly. I therefore propose that *amba* is in fact a highly defective, semantically empty verb, which takes two arguments: NP_{rel}, and the S which expresses the content of the relative clause. This would allow us to keep a simple restriction on NP_{rel} marking in Swahili, with the *amba* construction being a frozen form of a construction designed to evade the effects of the constraint. I believe that this hypothesis is attractive, and its further verification should prove an interesting task.

There are two further sets of facts which the hypothesis must come to grips with, although I am not sure of their significance. First, there are sentences in which a relative kihusiano appears both on *amba* and on the verb:

(169) a. mimi amba-ye ni-taka-ye watoto si-wa-pata
I *amba*-REL I-want-REL children NEG:I-them-receive
'I who want children do not get them.'

b. mahali amba-po i-li-po-fungiliwa bandera ya
place *amba*-REL SB-PAST-REL-be unfurled flag of
Kiingereza
England
'a place where the British flat had been unfurled'

I suspect that this may have something to do with the 'double relativization' in English that we find in such sentences as 'The man who they tortured by burning holes in with cigarettes was not pleased.' For some reason, both NP_{rel} and its coreferent in the complement of *amba* acquire the NP_{rel} mark, and both are treated as usual by the cliticization rule applying to NP bearing this mark.

Secondly, there are certain dialects in which not only does *amba* get the kihusiano of NP_{rel} suffixed to it, but it also gets the subject concord of NP_{rel} prefixed to it, just as if NP_{rel} were its near-surface subject. Hence in the KiVumba dialect of the southern Kenya coast (East African

Swahili Committee, 1956-1958) we have sentences such as the following:

(170) a. Jambo l-amba-lo   l-a-ni-dhuru   ndi-lo hili.
         thing SB-*amba*-REL SB-PRES-me-hurts is-it this
         'The thing that hurts me is this.'

   b. Wewe w-amba-e   ku-na-n-amba   ni mwivi mbona
      you SB-*amba*-REL you-PERF-me-say   I thief why
      k'-u-vi-ono   vy-amba-vyo si-kw-achii.
      you-NEG-them-see   SB-amba-REL I-you-left
      'You who accuse me of being a thief, why did you not
       notice the things I left for you?'

A final fact is that in this dialect, as well as in the standard language, the *amba* may be followed by *kwamba*, a complementizer frequently used to introduce indirect discourse. Hence we have these examples:

(171) a. Ni-me-sikia   kwamba mwitu u-ki-washwa   moto,
         I-PERF-heard that   forest SB-if-is put to fire
         u-ta-ungua   wote.
         SB-FUT-burn   all
         'I have heard that if fire is put to the forest it
          will burn away completely.'

   b. Watu   amba-o   kwamba wa tayari.
      people amba-REL that   SB ready
      'people who are ready'

These examples suggest that the surface structure of the *amba*-relative is roughly like (172):

(172)
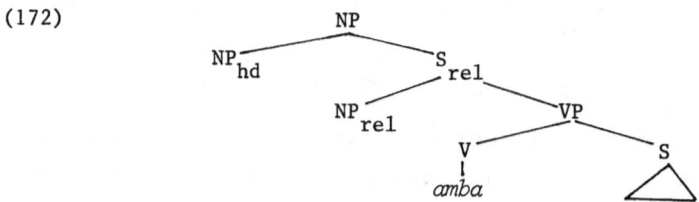

The apparent peculiarities of the *amba*-relative clauses may thus have a reasonable explanation, with the complexities in NP$_{rel}$ marking being consequences of its interaction with other constructions. This concludes my discussion of Swahili.

1.2.1.3 *General Remarks on NP$_{rel}$ Marking:* We may observe that there is also NP$_{rel}$ marking not associated with movement in the Indic languages discussed earlier: Sanskrit, Hindi and Marathi, as well as in Mabuiag. Although relative pronouns often wind up at the front of the sentence in the Indic languages, their propensity for scrambling makes it difficult to tell whether NP_{rel} is scrambled to the front, or gets there by a special optional rule.

What is the mechanism for NP_{rel} marking? We could have the markers be generated in the base, or transformationally. There is little solid ground to determine the choice. In Section 2.3 I will describe a proposal for performing the marking in the base.

One will observe that the vast majority of languages that have marking of NP_{rel} in an embedded relative construction have it in a post-relative structure. I know of only two languages that have it in pre-relatives, the closely related Northwest Caucasian languages Abkhaz and Abaza. In these languages, NP_{rel} is deleted by ordinary pronominalization processes, but regular rules which put agreement markers on constituents to which the NP bears certain grammatical relations (subject, object, possessor, etc.) put the markers in a special form when the NP is NP_{rel}. These phenomena are described in Anderson, (in preparation).

We may finally observe that the paucal relative of English (section 1.1.2.2) provides an example of NP_{rel} marking in an internal head relative clause. We thus see that NP_{rel} may be marked in all the varieties of relative clause structure that we have discerned.

1.2.2 *Deletion of NP_{rel}*: In many languages, NP_{rel} merely disappears. There is a fundamental question of mechanism to which we have no answer: does the disappearance come about by a *bona fide* deletion transformation, or is there instead generation of a phonologically null element in the deep structure position of NP_{rel}? Lacking an answer to this question, I shall speak of NP_{rel} Deletion knowing that the term 'Deletion' is perhaps merely suggestive.

Perlmutter (1972) suggested a test for distinguishing languages with deletion of NP_{rel} from languages in which there was free deletion of anaphoric pronouns, including NP_{rel}. He proposed that the former, but not the latter, languages obeyed island constraints. Recent work by Keenan (1972) calls this into doubt. Keenan observes that many languages in which NP_{rel} is represented by a pronoun rather than being deleted obey island-like constraints on where NP_{rel} may be found.

For these reasons, I will accept as true NP_{rel} Deletion languages only languages in which there are NP_{rel} that disappear that could not be removed by free pronoun deletion. I will consider two such languages: Turkish, where the deletion happens in a pre-relative clause, and Modern Greek, in which it takes place in a post-relative.

1.2.2.1 *Turkish*: In section 1.1.1.2.2, I said that Turkish had deletion of NP_{rel}, but I did not demonstrate it. This I will now proceed to do.

In Turkish, unstressed subject and possessor pronouns are regularly dropped. Hence one gets examples like (173):

(173) a. Gel-di.
         come-PAST
         'He came.'

b. Hasan baba-sı-nı   gördü.
    Hasan father-his-ACC saw
    'Hasan saw his father.' (Hasan's or someone else's)

c. Hasan Orhan-ını baba-sı-nı   gördü.
    Hasan Orhan-GEN father-his-ACC saw
    'Hasan saw Orhan's father.'

In (173a) the subject pronoun has disappeared. In (173b) the genitive pronoun with which the agreement suffix $-sı$ is agreeing has vanished. In (173c) we see a sentence with full NP in the place of these missing ingredients.

Though subject and genitive pronouns vanish, object pronouns do not. Hence we have these sentences:

(174) Hasan, Fatma-nın *(o-nu)   öl-dür-eceğ-i-ni   düşünüyor.
       Hasan Fatma-GEN (he-ACC) die-CAUSE-FUT-her-ACC thinks
       'Hasan$_i$ thinks that Fatma will kill him$_{i,j}$.'

We see that the object pronoun of (174) is not freely deletable. But when NP_{rel} is a direct object, it always disappears:

(175) Orhan-ın (*o-nu) gör-düg-ü adam çıktı.
Orhan-GEN (he-ACC) see-NOM-his man left
'The man who Orhan saw left.'

This deletion of the pronoun shows that there is in fact a rule of NP_{rel} deletion at work.

We can see an interesting contrast between Turkish and English. Both English and Turkish have free relatives. The Turkish free relative looks exactly like a pre-relative, but has no head. Hence we have (176):

(176) Hasan-ın al-dığ-ı-nı gördüm.
Hasan-GEN buy-NOM-his-ACC I saw
'I saw what Hasan bought.'

In English, however, we must form the free relative with a relative pronoun: we cannot use the *that*-relative or the *that*-less relative construction. It would appear then that we would need two kinds of NP_{rel} deletion: one kind sensitive to the presence of a head, and the other kind not. There is, however, a possible escape from this conclusion.

We can paraphrase (176) with (177), which is identical in structure, except that the relative clause is a pre-relative on the head *şey* 'thing.':

(177) Hasanın aldığı şeyi gördüm.

We could claim that (176) was derived from (177) by a rule of *şey*-deletion. An immediate objection to this proposal is that one should not delete lexical items. This may be countered by proposing that *şey* is a 'pronominal N': a noun head that is really a pronoun, like 'place,' 'time,' and 'thing' in English. Since pronouns are members of a closed category, their deletion is not in principle as objectionable as deletion of real lexical items. See Andrews (1974) for discussion. I add as a cautionary note, however, that Navajo, which offers a free relative construction that cannot be analysed as a headed relative clause, does not need to have a rule of NP_{rel} deletion. This potential source of testimony as to whether there is NP_{rel} deletion in underlying headless relative clauses is not in fact available.

1.2.2.2 *Modern Greek:* Modern Greek has two relative clause constructions. One, characteristic of the literary (Katharevousa) language, has a relative pronoun *o opíos* (taking various inflectional forms) that is preposed to the front of the relative clause. *o opíos* is distinct from the interrogative pronouns *piós* 'who?' *ti* 'what?'. The other construction, characteristic of the colloquial (Demotic) language, has a relative complementizer *pu*. NP_{rel} is deleted or retained as a pronoun. I shall here investigate the properties of the *pu*-relative.

Modern Greek is an SVO language with scrambling, prepositions, preceding complementizers and conjunctions, and post-relative clauses. There are three cases on NP: nominative, genitive and accusative. Pronouns come in both clitic and nonclitic forms. Verbs are inflected for the person and number of their subjects, and there are no subject clitics, nonemphatic subjects being simply deleted. Nonemphatic direct and indirect objects appear as clitic pronouns on the verb, the direct object clitics being accusative, the indirect objects genitive. Full NP indirect objects do not appear in the genitive, but rather as objects of the preposition *se*, of which we will have more to say in the sequel. In addition to case, nouns and their dependents are inflected for number (sg/pl) and gender (masc/fem/neut). These markings will not be noted in the glosses.

We can see from the following examples that ordinary anaphoric object pronoun clitics are not deleted freely:

(178) a. O   leonídhas   vríke ton   kósta   ke
         The:NOM Leonidas:NOM found the:ACC Costa:ACC and
         i   marika   *(ton) skótose.
         the:NOM Maria:NOM him:ACC killed
         'Leonidas found Costa and Maria killed him.'

   b. O   leonídhas   nomízi oti i   marika
      the:NOM Leonidas:NOM thinks that the:NOM Maria:NOM
         tha *(ton)   skotosi.
         FUT him:ACC kill
         'Leonidhas thinks that Maria will kill him.'

However an NP_{rel} object of a verb must be deleted:

(179) O   ándras pu (*ton)   ídha íne o   leonídhas.
      the:NOM man:NOM REL him:ACC I is the:NOM Leonidas:NOM
      'The man who I saw is Leonidas."

Indirect object and possessive clitics, on the other hand, must be left behind in clitic form as 'returning pronouns':

(180) a. i yinéka pu *(tis) édhosa to vivlío
         the woman REL she:GEN I gave the book
         'the woman who I gave the book to'

      b. i yinéka pu éklepsa to vivlío *(tis)
         the woman REL I stole the book   she:GEN
         'the woman whose book I stole'

It is worth noting that in poetry, accusative NP_{rel} may be left behind, as, for example, in the following two lines of Seferis:

(181) páno s-to dzámi afto pu to xtipá i vroxí apo ton
      upon at-the window this REL it strikes the rain from the
         ékso   kósmo
         outside world
      'upon this window struck by the rain/from the outside world' (Mythistorema 6, Keeley and Sherrard (1969)).

We may observe that it is the genitive clitics that are left behind, and the accusatives (and presumably the nominatives) that are deleted.

There is a constraint on relativization that NP_{rel} must either be deleted or appear as a clitic pronoun. Full NP or nonclitic pronominal NP are ungrammatical. This fact, together with some features of the system of prepositions, leads to there being an entertainingly unsayable class of sentences in Modern Greek. To exhibit them, we must investigate the syntax of prepositional phrases.

There are two kinds of prepositions in Modern Greek. There are first the simple prepositions, which take accusative NP objects. Some of these are *se* 'to, at, on'; *me* 'with'; *apo* 'from'; *ya* 'for'; *xorís, dhíxos* 'without'. The simple prepositions take their objects in the accusative case. Hence we have *s-to trapézi* 'on the table', *me tin kopéla* 'with the girl', *apo to xorió* 'from the village'. Nonclitic pronouns are treated exactly like ordinary NP: *s' aftón* 'to him'. But there is a constraint that the object cannot be a clitic: **ston, *stou, *me ton, *me tu,* etc. Since *se*, *me*, and *apo* are clearly proclitics, we might explain the phenomenon by proposing a restriction that a clitic cannot take a clitic as head. But since the status of the other simple prepositions is not clear to me, I cannot rely on this explanation for the constraint.

Then there are the adverbial prepositions, which are much more numerous than are the simple ones. These include *mazí* 'with', *kondá* 'near', and *káto* 'under'. They take as objects not NP, but prepositional phrases in the three simple prepositions *se*, *me* and *apo* ('at/to', 'with' and 'from'). We hence find *mazí me to korítsi* 'with the girl', *kondá sto spíti* 'near the house', and *káto apo to trapézi* 'under the table', *mazí me aftín* 'with her'. There is also a construction in which the adverbial prepositions take a clitic pronominal object. In place of the simple prepositional phrase, one merely puts a genitive clitic: *mazí tis* 'with her', *kondá tu* 'near him', *káto tu* 'under it, him'. It is thus the case that clitic objects can only appear with the adverbial prepositions. It is also worth noting that the adverbial prepositions, but not the simple ones, can take 'predeterminer modification' as described by Bresnan (1973) and extended to English prepositional phrases by Jackendoff (1973): *pio pera apo ta vuná* 'further beyond the mountains'. This fact, as well as the cliticization phenomena, suggests that the adverbial prepositions have a significant featural relationship to the major categories. There is no such evidence for the simple prepositions.

Now let us consider relativization. If NP_{rel} is the object of an adverbial preposition, NP_{rel} is represented by a genitive clitic on the preposition, and there is no problem:

(182) i   kopéla pu   káthisa kondá tis
       the girl   REL I sat   near   her:GEN
       "the girl I sat near"

If, however, NP_{rel} is the object of a simple preposition, the *pu* construction simply can't be used:

(183) *i   kopéla pu   mílisa   me   tin
       the girl   REL I spoke with   aftín
                                         her

We are forced to use the relative pronoun *o opíos*:

(184) i kopéla me tin opían mílisa
the girl with whom I spoke
"the girl with whom I spoke"

The morphologically sensitive reader will perhaps have noted that *o opíos* is of the form *Definite Article + opíos*, a form parallel in its make-up to Fr. *lequel*, It. *il quale* and the archaic English *the which*. It is surely not accidental or a consequence of borrowing that so many relative pronouns are of this form.

On the basis of Modern Greek, we make an observation that is of interest in the formalization of relativization rules. There are two morphological entities that may serve as NP_{rel}: a clitic pronoun, and the relative pronoun *o opíos*. The latter, but not the former, preposes. This shows that the rule is being conditioned not merely by the fact that a certain NP is NP_{rel}, but by the presence of an actual formative.

1.2.3 *Movement of NP_{rel}*: Movement of NP_{rel} is sufficiently familiar to need little discussion here. I wish, however, to make certain observations.

It is generally held that the head of a relative clause is part of the environment for fronting in a relative clause. If English headless relatives are derived from underlyingly headless structures, then this position is untenable. Rather, the conditioning factor would presumably be the 'R' that I propose appears as the complementizer of relative clauses.

Recent work by Chomsky (1973) is compatible with this claim. Chomsky writes *wh* Movement as follows (Chomsky 1973 ex. 199b):

(185) *wh* Movement: in the structure
$[_S[_{COMP} X_1, X_2, X_3, \pm WH], X_5, wh, X_7]$
the sixth term fills the position of X_2 and is replaced by PRO.

+WH is Q; -WH is R and also the *that* in ordinary complements. Hence (185) is *wh* Movement in both questions and relative clauses. The '*wh*' in term 6 is not the formative *wh*, but a feature attached to the constituent that actually moves. Hence, in *to whom did you talk?*, the *wh* is attached to the prepositional phrase *to whom*.

This treatment avoids a difficulty which would otherwise appear in Chomsky's theory of *wh* Movement. Chomsky proposes that *wh* Movement removes a *wh* word from an embedded S by moving it on each cycle to the COMP of the $\bar{S}$ being cycled on. Hence one gets *who does Bill think Mary likes* by way of the intermediate stage *Bill thinks who Mary likes*. Since *wh* Movement may either extract an NP from within a PP or else move the whole PP, we have a problem in explaining the ungrammaticality of *who does Bill think to Mary gave a record*. By saying that in the underlying structure of *to whom does Bill think Mary gave a record*, the feature *wh* is attached to the PP, we explain why the entire PP must again move when we reapply (185) to the intermediate structure *Bill thinks to whom Mary gave a book*.

This formalization also accomplishes the desirable effect of eliminating the 'Pied Piping Convention' of Ross (1967). In Pied Piping, the *wh* movement transformation mentions a *wh*-marked term, and the rule actually moves another. An attempt to build this into a theory of rule application would involve substantial complications. Under Chomsky's treatment, the terms mentioned in the structural description are those used in the structural change.

Recent work by Bresnan, some of which is presented in Bresnan (1974b), promises to provide an alternative to Chomsky's account in which both the Pied Piping Convention and the abstract *wh* are eliminated.

I will close by pointing out that preposing of NP_{rel} is a minority strategy: it is quite common in Indo-European, but rather rare otherwise. I might also add that I have found no counterexamples to the claim of Bresnan (1970) that *wh* words in relative clauses and questions move across variables to the left, but not to the right.

1.3 *The Extraction Analysis:* I will here discuss a variety of languages in which there exist phenomena that suggest the correctness of the proposal that the heads of embedded relative clauses with heads are extracted from within them. I do not believe that these descriptions contain knockdown arguments for the proposals, but the situations described are such that both friends and foes of this analysis should investigate carefully.

1.3.1 *Japanese:* In many languages, we observe a restriction that when the embedded relative clause has a head, NP_{rel} must be pronominal. This is compatible with and somewhat supportive of the extraction analysis. On the other hand, it would appear that if NP_{rel} and NP_{hd} could be full NP with different head NP, the extraction analysis would be completely disconfirmed.

At first blush this is the situation obtaining in Japanese. In section 1.1.1.2.2 I observed the grammaticality of the following:

(186) watakusi ga   sono hito   no namae   wasurete simatta
      I   SUBJ that person GEN name OBJ have forgotten
      okyaku-san
      guest
      "a guest whose name I have forgotten"

Martin (1972) describes a similar construction which appears in certain dialects of English: "They are the guys who Bill says the bastards stole your car!" This construction is highly marginal, many speakers rejecting it out of hand. The position of NP_{rel} is occupied by an epithet, and the entire construction has a distinctly pejorative tone. (186), on the other hand, is a perfectly ordinary noun phrase of Japanese. I suspect, then, that Martin's examples are derived by some sort of non-transformational deformation of syntactic structures: amalgamatory insertion of an epithet into an empty position created by the preposing of *who*. The process is perhaps a syntactic counterpart to the phonetic and morphological deformations described in Nootka by Sapir (1963).

(186), on the other hand, appears to be a *bona fide* product of Japanese syntax, and to destroy any hope for an extraction analysis of Japanese relative clauses. There are, however, considerations which potentially reverse the import of (186).

Kuno (1973) has proposed that NP_{rel} in Japanese is always the theme of NP_{rel}: the theme being the preposed NP followed by *wa* that was mentioned in 1.1.1.2.2. The theme needn't have a co-referent in the clause. If there is a coreferent, however, it is most usual for it to be deleted. But under certain circumstances it needn't be, and may surface as a full NP with head N distinct from that of the theme. I refer the reader to Kuno (1973) and McCawley (1972) for discussion. We have thus (187), in which the theme has no coreferent, and (188), in which the coreferent of the theme is a full NP distinct from the theme:

(187) Sakana wa   tai   ga   ii
      fish   THEME red-snapper SUBJ good-is
      "Speaking of fish, red snapper is the best."

(188) Ano okyaku-san wa   watakusi ga   sono hito   no
      that guest   THEME I   SUBJ that person GEN
         namae o wasurete simatta.
         name OBJ have forgotten
      "Speaking of that guest, I have forgotten his name."

There is, however, the requirement, common to all anaphora, that the coreferent be a more general noun phrase than the initial theme. Hence (189) is ungrammatical:

(189) *Ano hito   wa   watakusi ga   sono okyaku-san no namae
       that person THEME I   SUBJ that guest   GEN name
          o wasurete simatta.
          OBJ have forgotten.

With this in mind, we may reconsider (186).

It is required that there be no theme on the surface in relative clauses. Hence (190) are ungrammatical noun phrases:

(190) a. *Sono okyakusan wa watakusi ga sono hito no
            namae o wasurete simatta okyakusan

      b. *Sono hito wa watakusi ga sono hito no
            namae o wasurete simatta okyakus-san.

This theme must then obligatorily disappear.

Fiengo (1974) has pointed out the suspicious nature of positing elements which are 'positive absolute exceptions' to deletion: elements that are obligatorily identical to some other element and obligatorily delete under identity with it. We have two alternatives to postulating that the vanishing theme of the relative clause is obligatorily identical to the head and obligatorily deleted due to identity with it. We can suppose that the theme is moved into head position, or we can suppose that it is underlying a pronoun or a null element. If we pick this latter alternative, we will be violating the generalization noted with respect to *(189), that a theme must be less general than its coreferent. The former analysis avoids this problem, as well as the problem of positing such obligatorily identical obligatorily deleting elements.

As the extraction hypothesis would predict, and as we would expect anyway, the head of the relative clause must be less general than any surviving coreferents within it. Hence (191) is bad, just as is (189):

(191) *Watakusi ga   sono okyakusan no   namae o
      I   SUBJ that guest   GEN name OBJ
      wasurete simatta hito.
      have forgotten person
      "the guest/person whose name I have forgotten"

Kuno's hypothesis removes (186) from the class of clear counterexamples to the extraction anlysis, and may well convert it into a strong argument for the proposal. It also eliminates a counterexample to the general claim that when there is a head to an embedded relative clause, NP_{rel} must delete or be pronominal.

1.3.2 *Micmac:* This example was presented by Hale (1970). It involves the category of obviation. When there are two third person NP in an S, the second becomes obviative. This is illustrated in the following:

(192) a. Tjĩmn elogoet.
         man   work
         "The man is working."

      b. Ēpit nemiat-l   tjĩmno-l
         woman see-OBV.OB man-OBV
         "The woman sees the man."

But if the subject of a sentence (the first NP in it) is NP_{hd} of a relative clause in which NP_{rel} is the object (second NP in S_{rel}), then NP_{hd} becomes obviative in accordance with the structure of the main clause:

(193) Tjĭmno-1 tān ēpit nemiat-1 na
 man-OBV REL woman see-OBV.OB prt work-OBV.SUBJ
 "The man who the woman sees is working."

NP_{hd} is thus here being assigned to a grammatical category on the basis of the status of NP_{rel}.

1.3.3 *Persian:* Persian is an SOV language, but it has prepositions preceding conjunctions, and following modifiers in NP. Relativization is reminiscent of that in Demotic Greek. The relative clause is a post-relative, with NP_{rel} deleted if it is a subject or an object, otherwise left behind as a pronoun. There is, however, no clitic/nonclitic distinction.

There is a formative *e* (which I gloss MD for 'modifier'), which is attached to the head of any post-head modifier if that modifier is itself followed by a modifier. There is also a Specific Accusative marker *ra*, which I shall gloss as ACC. This marks direct objects that are specific. See Browne (1972) for discussion of the function of *ra*. *ra* follows the NP, and *e* is not inserted before it. Hence we have the following:

(194) a. ketab-e bozorg (ra)
 book-MD big ACC
 "(the) big book"

 b. ketab-e bozorg-e mæn (ra)
 book-MD big-MD I ACC
 "my big book"

Note that possession is rendered as in (194b) by placing the possessor NP after the head as if it were an adjective.

In the relative clause construction, the *e* does not appear. Instead, NP_{hd} is followed by a formative *i* which may also be placed after an NP to render it indefinite. Hence:

(195) a. ketab-i (ra) ke didæm
 book-IND ACC REL I saw
 "the book I saw"

 b. mærd-i ke be u ketab didæm
 man-IND REL to him book I gave
 "the man I gave a book to"

But there is a strange twist in the use of *ra*. Normally, *ra* is obligatory in a specific object. But if one has an NP_{hd} that is a direct object in the main clause, and NP_{rel} is a subject in the relative, then *ra* is optional on NP_{hd}, and likewise, if NP_{rel} is subject in the main clause and NP_{rel} is object in the relative clause, then *ra* is also optional. Hence it appears that when an NP is modified by a relative clause one may look either at the role of NP_{hd} in the matrix or of NP_{rel} in the relative clause to determine the case-marking of NP_{hd}.

Some examples of this from Lambton (1953) are:

(194) a. An   zæni   (ra) ke diruz   amæd didæm.
         that woman:IND (ACC) REL yesterday came I saw
         "I saw the woman who came yesterday."

   b. Zæni   (ra) ke didid injast.
      woman:IND (ACC) REL you saw is here
      "The woman you saw is here."

   c. Ketab-i (ra) ke be mæn dadid   gom šode æst.
      book-IND (ACC) REL to me you gave is lost

From these facts of case-marking, and from the appearance of the *i* (recall that NP_{rel} in Crow internal head relative clauses have indefinite morphology), one might well be able to work up an argument that the heads of Persian relative clauses are extracted from within them.

Jeanne (1974) has proposed an analysis of Hopi relativization which makes crucial use of the inheritance by NP_{hd} of the case of NP_{rel} in a manner somewhat reminiscent of, although significantly different from, Persian.

Before leaving the subject, I will observe that the available evidence for the extraction analysis all involves cases where NP_{rel} is not a relative pronoun, but is an ordinary pronoun or is deleted. Consider in English the contrast *the headway (that) we made* and **the headway which we made*. This is comforting in light of the fact that one of the major problems with the analysis is insuring that the *wh* formative on relative pronouns gets universally left behind during extraction.

FOOTNOTES TO CHAPTER 1

1. Much of the research in this chapter was supported by grant OEC-0-70-4986(8234) from the Office of Education to Stephen Anderson at the Language Research Foundation. The contents of this chapter differ substantially both from the report to OEC co-authored with Anderson and also from various preliminary drafts of mine that have been informally circulated. Motu, Tagalog, French and Breton were omitted because Anderson wrote or revised the sketch, and Hopi, Welch and Dagbani were omitted for reasons of space and time. Japanese was added, and Navajo and Marathi were substantially expanded.

   I am indebted to Ken Hale, Dave Perlmutter, Hu Matthews, Paul Kiparsky, Haj Ross, Mary Lou Walch and Roy Wright for commenting on earlier drafts of this chapter. I am also indebted to many people for helping me with particular languages. They are indicated in footnotes, in the text, and in the index of languages and sources that appears as an appendix to this chapter. I finally thank Stephen Anderson for getting me interested in the subject and supporting much of my work in it.

2. But note:

      *Nobody got a pen, and he wrote a letter with it.

   Nonrestrictive relatives seem to presuppose existence (example by Ross (personal communication)).

3. Sandy Chung has informed me that Churchward (1934), upon which this is based, is accurate for the modern language.

4. Robert Underhill taught me most of what I know about Eskimo.

5. I have been greatly assisted with Japanese by Susumu Kuno and Shosuke Haraguchi.

6. Wha-Chun Kim provided the information about Korean.

7. This analysis has now been published by Hale (1976).

8. Sharad Gupti was extremely generous of his time in teaching me enough about Marathi to write this section. S.D. Joshi volunteered the first referential multiple-headed relative clause I encountered. Kashi Wali has also

been quite helpful.
9. Wayles Brown has given me advice on Persian.

APPENDIX TO CHAPTER 1 - INDEX OF LANGUAGES AND SOURCES

I give first the language, then the pages on which I discuss it, then references works on it, and finally those who have provided me with information about it. Only languages receiving substantial discussions are mentioned.

Crow:	pp. 83-88; Lowie 1944; Dale Oldhorn, George Reed, Rose Chesarek.
English:	pp. 11-17, 48-53, 73-81.
Eskimo:	pp. 21-25; Kleinschmidt 1851, Schultz-Lorentzen 1945, Bergsland 1955; Robert Underhill.
Faroese:	pp. 20-21; Lockwood 1964.
Greek (Md.):	pp. 104-107; Dimitri Konstantinidi.
Hindi:	pp. 60-62; Donaldson 1971.
Hottentot:	pp. 36-38; Meinhof 1909.
Japanese:	pp. 26-30, 108-111; Kuno 1973, McCawley 1972; Susumu Kuno, Shosuke Haraguchi.
Mabuiag:	pp. 58-60; Klokeid 1970.
Marathi:	pp. 64-73; Southworth and Kavadi 1965; Sharad Gupte, Kashi Wali, S.D. Joshi.
Micmac:	pg. 111; Hale 1970;
Navajo:	pp. 40-47, 110-121; Platero 1974, Perkins 1974, Kaufman 1974, Platero and Hale 1974; Ken Ḥale, Paul Platero.
Persian:	pp. 112-113; Lambton 1953, Brown 1970; Wayles Brown.
Samoan:	pp. 18-20; Churchward 1934; Sandy Chung.
Sanskrit:	pp. 62-64; Wackernagel 1930.
Swahili:	pp. 88-100; Ashton 1944, Loogman 1965, East African Swahili Committee 1956-58.
Tibetan:	pp. 34-35; Lalou 1950.
Turkish:	pp. 30-34; Lewis 1953, 1967, Underhill 1972.
Warlpiri:	pp. 55-58; Hale 1970, 1971, 1974 class lectures, 1976.

2. *Comparative Clauses:* In this chapter, I will devote my attention to the comparative clause construction of English. I will follow the arrangement, and, to a large degree, the content, of the classic article on the subject by Bresnan (1973).[1] I will first consider the head to which comparative clauses are attached, and then the relation between the head and the clause.

In the treatment of the head, I will adopt (with minor revisions) the analysis proposed by Bresnan, and will extend it to a construction not considered by her, the indefinite comparative construction of such examples as *the more you study, the less you know*. My primary concern will be, however, with the metatheory in which the analysis is formulated. I shall formulate certain processes which Bresnan leaves vague, such as the rule of QP Raising, and, more significantly, will propose a system of conventions on rule application and constraints on structure which, given some rather strong assumptions, allow one to make a case that the analysis given is in fact the most highly valued one for the data considered, and that in several cases, the most highly valued analysis for subsets of the data predicts the remainder. This amounts to making the claim that Bresnan's analysis is internally justified within a linguistic theory with a significant degree of explanatory adequacy.

Bresnan supposed that comparative clauses were generated within the determiners of the quantifier phrases that they modify. Using multiple headed comparatives that are similar to the multiple headed relative clauses of the preceding chapter, I will show that such a source is untenable. I shall propose that comparative clauses are generated in underlying structure in the position that they occupy on the surface, and will explain the phenomena previously taken to support determiner generation of comparatives in terms of a theory of extra-constituent structure relations of the sort extensively used in the previous chapter. This time, however, I will take a far more formal approach to the material, providing a formalization of the

representation of the relations, and proposing a system of
language-universal conditions governing permissable assignments of systems of relations to constituent structures.
These principles will also cover relative clauses as presented in the previous chapter, and will therefore constitute a unified theory of determiner complementation.

2.1 *The Head, Revisited:* I will here review the analysis
provided by Bresnan of the head constituent to which the
comparative clause is attached. I shall assume Bresnan's
base rules, and recast the transformational part of her
analysis within a particular metatheory. I shall make a
case that if the basic data from which language learning
proceeds is assumed to consist of a set of surface string-
deep structure pairs, then the transformational part of
the analysis is the most highly valued analysis provided by
the metatheory that is consistent with the data. I will
furthermore attempt to support certain articles of the metatheory on the grounds that they lead to analyses being
selected by subsets of the total range of data which those
analyses explain. The analysis will thus be argued to be
internally justified, and the metatheory to be explanatorily potent.

The assumption that the basic data from which language
learning takes place consists of surface string-deep structure pairings is unrealistically strong. Nonetheless, I
believe that results attained by means of it may be valid
and interesting. For it is likely that given a sufficiently restrictive theory of the semantic interpretation of
deep structure, there may be relatively few ways of construing a string of words and phrases of known meaning
into a sentence with a coherent reading.

Consider, for example, the phrase *many too many marbles*.
Suppose we are ignorant of the syntax of the language, but
we know that *many* and *too many* are quantity expressions,
the latter signifying excessive amount, and that *marbles* is
a count noun. Then one of the few ways of taking the phrase
semantically will be to take the first *many* as qualifying
too many, and *many too many* as qualifying *marbles*. About

the only alternative I can think of is to take it as the
predication *many is too many marbles*, or something like
that. The context might well serve to eliminate many formally possible ways of semantically combining the elements
of the string.

Given a sufficiently restrictive theory of semantic
interpretation, this string could lead to a uniquely determined addition to the base component of the language being
learned: namely, the addition of the rules that generate
a deep structure that can be interpreted as having the formally possible and pragmatically plausible reading, and
which can be related to the string by a minimal, in this
case by a null, set of transformations.

These results, if valid, have an interesting implication for research directed at constraining linguistic
theory. The greatest part of such work has been devoted to
constraining the transformational component, the base being
comparatively neglected. In the following pages, I will
assume a transformational component that is quite uncon-
strained by current standards of work in the Extended Standard Theory. It seems to me likely that if a sufficiently
restrictive theory of the base were found, one could show
that the theory determined the analysis for the data without making the assumption that the data included the deep
structures for the strings considered. Rather, one would
suppose the data to include information on the semantic
type of words and phrases in the strings. The implication
is that work on constraining linguistic theory should be
focussed not on the transformational component, but on the
base.

2.1.1 *Basic Structures:* I shall begin by reviewing Bresnan's basic analysis of QP, AP and predicative NP. I shall
be concerned with the material in her sections 1.1 - 1.4,
omitting partitives.

Bresnan has no analysis for nodes of type V (V, VP, and
perhaps S, etc.), and her analysis of N nodes was essentially limited to the predicative or adjectival NP found in
predicate nominal and certain nonreferential positions (e.g.

I have never seen as magnificent a coelacanth as this specimen), although she ventures an occasional diagram for ordinary NP. I shall remain within these limitations. Although she did not formally adopt an X-bar analysis, her analysis was so given as to be easily translated into one.

In Chomsky's (1970) exposition of the X-bar notation, he proposed that there was a small set of language-universal primitive categories including at least N, V, A and S, which might themselves be composed of features. There are then four diacritic features: 0, 1, 2 and Spec.

The following rule skeletons are then specified:

(1) a. $S \rightarrow N^2 V^2$
 b. $X^2 \rightarrow [\text{Spec}, X^1] X^1$
 c. $X^1 \rightarrow X \ldots$

'...' is to be the material in the complement of the various categories. $[\text{Spec}, X^1]$ is taken to comprise the system of articles, possessives and demonstratives; $[\text{Spec}, V^1]$ the auxiliary system; and $[\text{Spec}, A^1]$ is hypothesized to comprise the system of degree modification.

Chomsky's schema (1a) is irrelevant to her discussion; the other two, however, she accepts, but makes certain changes in the framework. She adopts a new category Q, which contains the quantifiers, such as *few, more, enough,* etc. Note that the Q are the linguistic quantity expressions, rather than the logical operators $\exists$ and $\forall$. I shall thus take the category variables in the rules as ranging over N, V and A, with A comprising both adjectives and adverbs. It would be wrong to attribute to Bresnan the positions that the basic category features are N, Q and A. Rather, she should be taken as suggesting that the basic feature system should be so constructed to deliver these categories, presumably along with others.

Furthermore, she alters the interpretation of the Spec nodes. For $[\text{Spec}, N^1]$, she preserves Chomsky's interpretation, especially in putting the indefinite article there, and also a null article that she postulates to be present in anarthrous mass and plural NP such as *beer* and *linguists* (see Fiengo (1974) for more discussion of this hypothetical null article). [Spec, Q^1] is taken to comprise the degree particles, *er*, *too*, *as*, *so*, etc; *more* being derived from *er much* and *less* and *fewer* from *er little* and *er few*, respectively.

On the subject of [Spec, A^1], however, she departs from Chomsky's speculations and from the work of previous lexicalist writers. Whereas Bowers (1970) and Selkirk (1970) analyze such expressions as *as tall* as having the degree particle *as* as the contents of [Spec, A^1], Bresnan provides a different analysis, to which we shall turn shortly, of degree particles that precede adjectives and adverbs. What she identifies as [Spec, A^1] is rather the class of adverbial intensifiers including *merely*, *utterly*, *perfectly*, *rather*, *quite*, etc.

She also suggests a change in the interpretation of the [Spec, X^m] notation. Instead of taking it as designating a category, that is, a node, she suggests taking it as being an abbreviation for the categories expanded in its position. She omits [Spec, X^1] nodes from her trees, and has the material expanded in these positions dominated by Det in NP and QP nodes, and by Adv in AP nodes. I shall follow these conventions.

Hence we attain the following series of analogously constructed phrases:

(2) a. *a man*:

```
        N²
       /  \
     Det   N¹
      |    |
      a   man
```

b. *beer*

```
        N²
       /  \
     Det   N¹
      |    |
      ∅   beer
```

c. *too much*

```
        Q²
       /  \
     Det   Q¹
      |    |
     too  much
```

d. *utterly crazy*: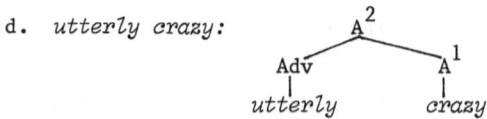

In these structures I have omitted the X^0 nodes, and will consistently do so when they play no role in the discussion.

Bresnan's proposal for degree modification of AP and quantity modification of NP is based on her observation of how degree modification of QP works. She observes that in such examples as (3):

(3) a. (much less) tall
    b. (many (too many)) marbles

the phrasing is as indicated by the parentheses.

Bresnan explains the phrasing by reanalysing QP, AP and NP as Q^3, A^3 and N^3, respectively. The examples of (3) are thus given the structures (4):

(4) a.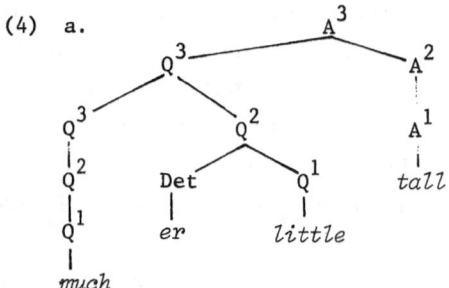

b.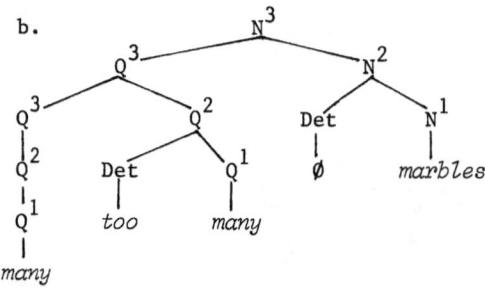

Justification for the constituent structure (4b) is given in the form of a rule of QP Shift (pg. 290) which derives (5) from (3b) by shifting Q^2 around N^2:

(5) many marbles too many.

This rule may be formulated as (6):

(6) *QP Shift:*

$$Q^3 - Q^2 - N^2 \quad \text{OPT}$$
$$1 \quad\ \ 2 \quad\ \ 3 \quad \Longrightarrow$$
$$1 \quad\ \ \emptyset \quad\ \ 3\#2$$

Note that this rule as formulated can misapply rather spectacularly. It can, for example, derive *she gave [many] [many]$_{NP}$[too many marbles]$_{NP}$* from *she gave [many]$_{NP}$ [too many marbles]$_{NP}$*. I will propose conventions to block this and other misapplications. Given the generally well-founded prohibition against moving nonconstituents, the argument for the phrasing indicated in (40b) is immediate.

We thus arrive at the following phrase structure rule:

(7) $X^3 \longrightarrow (Q^3)\ X^2$

An example of a Q^3 preceding a [Spec, A^1] is *he is less crazy than she is*.

We can see that when applied in AP, (7) will yield in addition to the grammatical outputs like (3a) the ungrammatical output of (8):

(8) a. *as much intelligent

     b. *too much intelligent

     c. *that much intelligent.

A rule deleting *much* before A^2 would derive from (8) the grammatical (9), thereby providing a source for degree modification of AP:

(9) a. as intelligent

     b. too intelligent

     c. that intelligent.

There is a difficulty, however, alluded to in Bresnan's footnote 4, in that while most adjectives, such as *tall*, reject overt *much*: *much tall*; some, like *different*, accept it: *much different*. Similar to *different* are a large class of what one might call intrinsically comparative adjectives are not in this class: *much similar; and some that are not comparative, such as *aware* and *amused*. I am indebted to Wayles Brown for pointing out to me that an inordinate number of these adjectives begin with the prefix *a-*.

We find the following sample paradigms:

(10) a. *much intelligent

  b. *little intelligent

  c. as (*much) intelligent

  d. *as little intelligent

  e. more intelligent

  f. less intelligent

(11) a. much alike

  b. little alike

  c. as (much) alike

  d. as little alike

  e. more alike

  f. less alike

From (10), we glean that *intelligent* disdains to be preceded by Q^0: both *much intelligent* and *little intelligent* are bad, but whenever *much* Deletion applies, or the rule applies that permutes *er* around a following Q^0, then the examples are good. *alike* in (11), on the other hand, appears to be devoid of this restriction. Both *much alike* and *little alike* are grammatical.

Bresnan proposes to deal with ordinary adjectives by having *much* Deletion be obligatory, suggesting in footnote 4 that the rule is optional with such adjectives as *alike* and *different*. But this runs afoul of the fact that ordinary adjectives reject *little* as firmly as they reject *much*, without rejecting *less* and *more*. The facts concerning *little* would seem to call for a surface(y) filter ruling out *little* A sequences. But then it is strange that for all adjectives that are exceptions to the filter, *much* Deletion is optional.

These considerations plainly show that in fact *much* Deletion is always optional, and that it is the surface filter that is governed. For it presumably costs less in features to specify the category Q^0 than to specify its member *little*, and therefore the filter motivated by the nonappearance of the *little A* sequences will be a $*Q^0A$ filter rather than a **little A* filter.

We can find further support for this position by noting that ordinary adjective phrases such as *tall* and *intelligent* are not ambiguous between their ordinary senses and a sense in which they mean 'very tall' or 'very intelligent' (under normal intonation and stress). Therefore, a derivation from *much tall* to *tall* or from *much intelligent* to *intelligent* by *much* Deletion is not possible. *much* Deletion can only apply when *much* is preceded by its degree particle. Nonetheless, we find **much tall*, **much intelligent*. Since these forms cannot be blocked by turning them into something else with an obligatory transformation, we need a filter to rule out *much A* sequences as well as *little A* sequences. Both of these effects, as well as the apparent obligatoriness of *much* Deletion with ordinary adjectives, can be accomplished with a lexically governed filter on Q^0A sequences.

Further support for this analysis may be found by considering the behaviour of *enough*: **enough tall, tall enough, enough alike, alike enough*. *Enough* permutes obligatorily around ordinary adjectives, but optionally around those which can be preceded by *much* and *little*. Given Bresnan's conclusion that *enough* is a Q, this is what we predict.

I will now formulate some rules. *much* Deletion I formulate as follows:

(12) *much* Deletion:
Det - *much* - A^1 OPT
 1   2   3 $\implies$
 1   ∅   3

The reader will first note that the rule as formulated can

misapply in a way analogous to that pointed out for (6), misderiving *too stale bread* from *too much stale bread*. This problem will be solved by a constraint on rule application.

Another problem is term 3. Its category features pose no difficulties: they are needed to block **too more bread* and **as soup*, etc. The superscript presents serious problems. Consider the pair *very much so*, **very so*, pointed out to me by Ross. I shall want to analyse *so* in such phrases as having the form (13):

(13)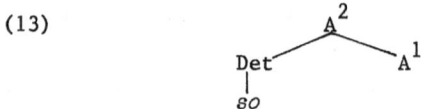

We cannot, therefore, let (12) specify merely category features without bars. Given that bars must be specified, 3 is plainly wrong and 2 is against the evidence just cited. My choice of 1 rather than 0 is arbitrary and descriptively inconsequential.

This solves the descriptive problem, but the explanatory problem remains. If we could find a principle determining a rule with superscript 1 in the last term on the basis of data like *too tall*, **too more corn*, we would explain *very much so*, **very so* rather than merely describe it. At present I have no such principle. The reader will also note that *too utterly crazy*, **too much utterly crazy* presents a descriptive problem for (12), suggesting, contrary to *very much so*, **very so*, that the superscript on term 3 should be 2 rather than 1. I shall meet this problem eventually, but for the present shall defer treatment of it.

The other problem is term 1. Its effect is to block the derivation of *tall* from *much tall*. The problem is how it is learned. In order to require it to be in the rule, one must specify in the data that the string *tall* lacks *much tall* as an underlying structure. It is very unclear where this information might come from. Perhaps having *tall* ambiguous between *tall* and *much tall* is a universally unacceptable form of ambiguity, and grammars producing such ambiguity for sentences in the basic data are automatically discarded. Such a constraint on ambiguity might also explain while the rule deletes only *much* instead of both *much* and *little* (since the category Q^0 is closed, we cannot invoke recoverability of deletions, lest pronoun drop be made an impossible rule).

Finally, the optionality of the rule is no problem, given *too much alike*, etc. in the data.

The innocuous seeming rule of *much* Deletion has proved upon close examination to be rife with explanatory problems. This suggests that efforts should be directed towards eliminating it. I shall nonetheless retain the rule in the present work.

I now consider the rule permuting *er* around Q^0. The problem is to get this rule to keep the filter from throwing out *more intelligent* and *less intelligent*. If we suppose that the only kind of adjunction available is Chomsky adjunction, then the only way to do this is to adjoin *er* to Q^1:

(14)   *er* Shift
     er - Q^1
              OBL
              ⟹
    1   2
    ∅   2#1

(14) will derive (15b) from (15a):

(15) a.

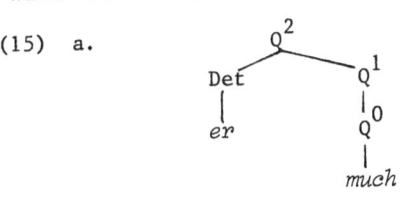

      b.

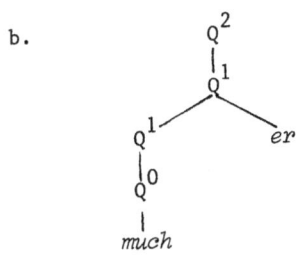

One will note from (15) that I intend a derived constituent

structure convention whereby it is the node mentioned that is moved, with nodes exhaustively dominating it vanishing, as does the Det node in (15a). This kind of application is not possible within the formalization of Peters and Ritchie (1973), although it is possible in Ginsburg and Partee (1969). Note that although these latter authors do not provide for Chomsky adjunction, this could be amended. The rule can be gotten to be obligatory by the presumption that OBL is a cheaper marking than OPT (or is the unmarked instance).

Now for the filter. Since the filter is lexically governed, I shall assume that it must involve the category A^0. We may thus notate it as (16):

(16) Q^0 A^0 Filter:
$*Q^0$ A^0

We may observe the usual form of misapplication: the filter as it stands will star *many old people* and *we gave many stale bread*. This problem will shortly be remedied.

Suppose then that the rules (including the filter) are cyclic, and that rules cycle on X^3 nodes. Then *er* Shift will automatically apply before *much* Deletion and the filter. If we suppose in addition (as will turn out to be necessary) that filters are extrinsically ordered with respect to the rules, then the grammaticality of *too tall* will force us to order the filter after *much* Deletion. The rules with these orderings will then suffice to deliver the facts of (10-11). I think that it is furthermore reasonable to believe that given a metatheory with transformations and filters of the form indicated, the data of (10-11), taken to be a pairing of each string with the set of its deep structures, determines the analysis consisting of (12, 14, 16), excepting the problem of the superscript on term 3 of (12).

None of these rules are formulated with end-variables, since there is nothing in (10-11) that motivates end-variables. Nonetheless, we want the rules to apply as if they had end-variables: we want *er* Shift to derive *much more intelligent* from *much er much intelligent*, we want *much* Deletion to derive *much too intelligent*, and we want the filter to block *much too much intelligent*. We may achieve this effect by supposing that there is a convention that automatically supplies end-variables to rules. Alternatively, we might suppose that there is a requirement on the form of rules that they have end variables: then (12, 14, 16) would have to be replaced by their variants with end-variables. In either case, the rules motivated by (10-11) would then apply in the desired manner in the more complex examples given above.

I will now formulate the rule deriving *taller* from *more tall*. At the beginning of the A^3 cycle, the structure of taller will be (17):

(17)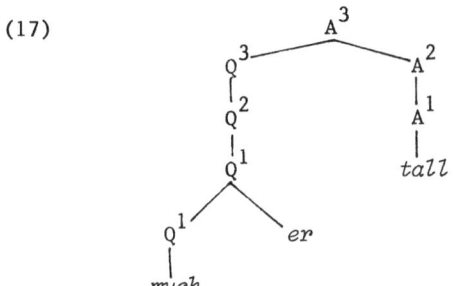

The simplest rule in our theory that could effect the required change is (18):

(18) *more* Shift:

$$\begin{array}{ccc} much & - & er & - & A^0 \\ & & & & \text{OBL} \\ & & & & \Longrightarrow \\ 1 & & 2 & & 3 \\ \emptyset & & \emptyset & & 3\#2 \end{array}$$

Note that we would have to assume it to be in the basic data that *taller* is not underlain by *less tall*. I presume that because the rule is governed by the adjective, term 3 must have the superscript 0.

We may now show the assumption that the rules are strictly ordered does some work. Consider the underlying structure of *too much taller*:

(19)

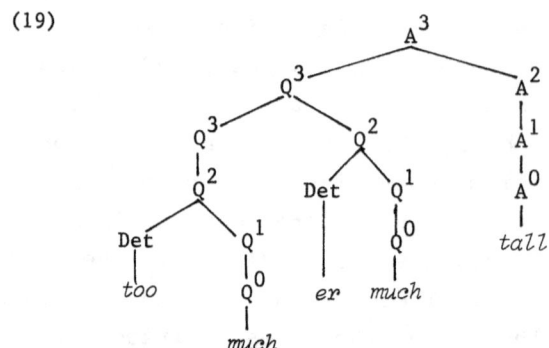

On the second Q^3 cycle in (19) we apply *er* Shift, and subsequently on the A^3 cycle we apply *more* Shift, yielding the derived constituent structure (20):

(20)

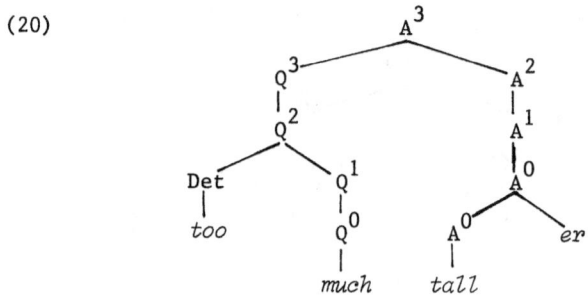

Since *too much taller* is acceptable, and *tall* is not an exception to the filter, we see that the application of the filter must precede that of *more* Shift. We have already noted, on the other hand, that *much* Deletion must precede the filter. We therefore deduce by transitivity of ordering that *much* Deletion precedes *more* Shift. This is independently evidenced by the fact that **too taller*, is ungrammatical. The assumption of strict ordering in conjunction with the preceding data thus predicts **too taller*.

On the other hand, no evidence can be found for ordering *er* Shift. Hence we arrive at an analysis consisting of the following rules:

(21) a. *er* Shift   OBL   (14)
     b. *much* Deletion   OPT   (12)
     c. *Q^0 A^0 Filter   (16)
     d. *more* Shift   OBL   (18)

The rules are assumed to apply cyclically. The reader will be able to discern that this assumption is not necessary for the present data, and that the analyses of this section, 2.1, can be cast into a noncyclic framework. I shall nonetheless assume cyclicity because of its greater elegance. Assuming cyclicity, we shall soon see that a principle of strict cyclicity is necessary. But first it will be necessary to give another constituent structure rule.

Bresnan finds that not only QP, but also AP appear as predeterminer modifiers of QP, AP and predicative NP:

(22) a. far more people
     b. as good an answer
     c. as obviously good an answer
     d. far too tall a man

We may thus replace (7) with (23):

(23) $X^3 \rightarrow \begin{Bmatrix} Q \\ A \end{Bmatrix}^3 X^2$

(21) and (23) will assign to example (22d) the structure (24):

(24)

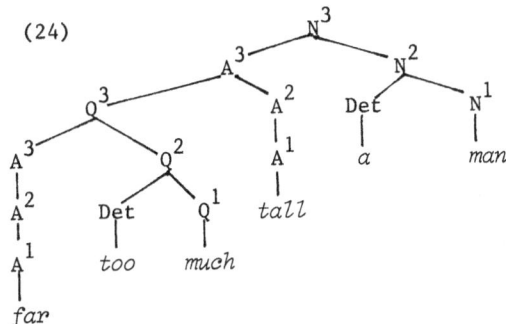

Note that N^3 with initial A^3 have a substantially different distribution from those with initial Q^3 or Det: hence the designation predicative NP. Their properties are discussed by Bresnan (pg. 283, 299) and by Berman (1974), who offers a rather different analysis. Furthermore, observe that the contents of Det determine what can precede it under X^3: in the QP system, for example, only *er* and *too* allow predeterminer QP; in the NP system, only the indefinite and null articles permit any sort of predeterminer modification:

(25) a. *as good the answer
     b. *more the men

We may now consider the question of strict cyclicity. Consider (26):

(26) a. as much better an answer
     b. *as better an answer

(26a) will be underlain by (27a), which at the end of the A^3 cycle will have the derived structure (27b):

(27) a.

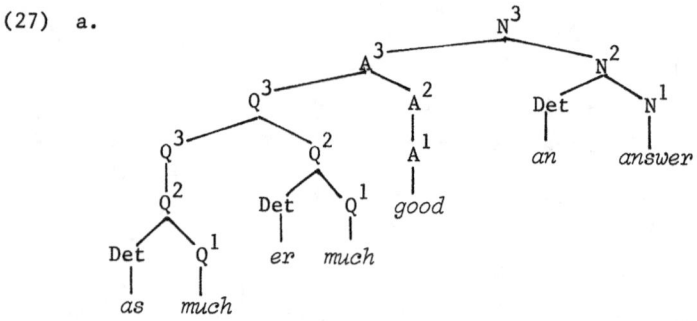

b.

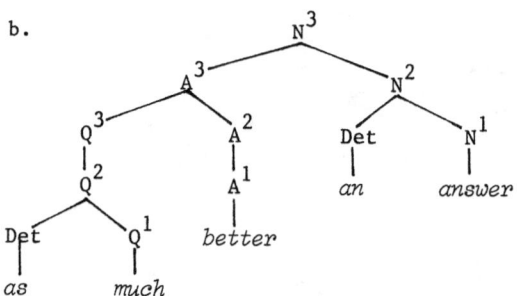

We must keep the filter from ruling out (26a), and *much* Deletion from generating (26b) from (27b). A principle of strict cyclicity would accomplish this, since the first crack that the rules get at applying is on the A^3 cycle, where the extrinsic ordering keeps them in line. Then when we get to the N^3 cycle, strict cyclicity will keep them from working, since they would have to operate entirely within the A^3 domain that has already been cycled on.

A conventional formulation of a principle of strict cyclicity would stipulate that a rule not apply entirely within a domain that has already been cycled on. I will put forth a different formulation, combining strict cyclicity with a principle that blocks a class of misapplications that we have been noting in the preceding pages.

I list these misapplications below:

(28) a. QP Shift (6):

she gave $[many]_{NP}$ $[too\ many\ marbles]_{NP}$ $\longrightarrow$ she gave $[many]_{NP}$ $[marbles\ too\ many]_{NP}$

b. *much* Deletion (12):

too much stale bread $\longrightarrow$ too stale bread

c. Q^0 A^0 Filter (16):

blocks *many old people, we gave many stale bread*

We may also note that *more* Shift will derive *I am angrier than sad* from *I am more angry than sad* (see Bresnan pg. 327, and, for a different account, Ross (1974). Hankamer (1973) discusses similar sentences in Greek and Latin).

In all of these misapplications, we find that the rule applies so that all of its constant terms (terms specified as constituents) lie within domains that have already been cycled on. For example in (28b) we have the structure $[_N 3[_Q 3\ too\ much][_N 2[_A 3\ stale][_N 1\ bread]]]$ (I am not sure of the internal constituent structure of the NP). When *much* Deletion applies, the disappearing *much* and its Det lie within the Q^3, and the A^1 *stale* lies within the A^3. Both of these domains have already been cycled on.

I thus suggest the following principle which subsumes both Strict Cyclicity and what is needed to block these misapplications:

(29) Cyclical Novelty Principle:

The structural description of a cyclical rule is not met unless at least one of its constant terms lies in a domain that has not yet been cycled on.

Observe that this principle would keep from applying a Dative rule that mentioned only the two NP terms. An additional term, such as the verb, would have to be mentioned in order for the rule to ever get to apply. Likewise, rules of Raising into subject and object positions would have to mention some term in the matrix, such as the verb. These results seem reasonable.

Further note that the behaviour of QP Shift and *more* Shift could be accommodated by a constraint against insertion into cyclical domains. It is *much* Deletion and the filter that necessitate a principle like (29).

The necessity for (29) is explanatory rather than descriptive. We could build the effects of (29) into our rules by appropriately deploying brackets within them. For example, she formulates *much* Deletion as follows (Bresnan's example (10)):

(30) Bresnan's *much* Deletion:

much $\longrightarrow \emptyset$ / [... --A]$_{AP}$

(But c.f. Bresnan's fn. 5)

Given the present metatheory and the discussion of the preceding pages, I would recast (30) as (31):

(31) [$_A{}^3$ W$_1$ - Det - *much* - A^1]   OPT $\Longrightarrow$

$\quad\quad\quad$ 1 $\quad$ 2 $\quad\quad$ 3 $\quad$ 4

$\quad\quad\quad$ 1 $\quad$ 2 $\quad\quad$ $\emptyset$ $\quad$ 4

But there is nothing in the basic data of (10-11) that requires the outer A^3 brackets to be there. The simplest rule for that data will lack them. Hence a theory with (29) will explain why *too stale bread* is not derived from *too much stale bread*, while in a theory without (29) one can only describe the fact.

In this subsection, I have revised Bresnan's analysis of the basic structures of QP, AP and adjectival NP, and provided some reason to believe that the analysis is determined for the data by the metatheory, given some assumptions about the form of the latter. I have also shown the explanatory significance of the assumption of strict ordering of transformations and filters, the convention supplying end variables, and an extension of Strict Cyclicity, the Cyclical Novelty Principle. The discussion has finally revealed that the rule of *much* Deletion is from an explanatory point of view the weakest part of the analysis, inasmuch as the least plausible assumptions about the basic data are required to make it take its descriptively correct form. It would be a vindication of the methods of this chapter should it prove desirable on independent grounds to dispense with this rule.

2.1.2 *AP Shift*: I here examine the process of AP Shift discussed in Bresnan (1.5-1.6). My goal will be to collapse Bresnan's AP Shift rule with the rule of QP Raising that Bresnan postulates to crucially feed it, but does not formulate. I shall here ignore much of the original data considered by Bresnan, especially taking no notice of any facts connected with *such*. *such* will be treated in the next subsection.

The attentive reader may have noticed a difficulty with the analysis of 2.1.1, in the form of paradigms like (32):

(32) a. as good a reply
     b. *an as good reply
     c. *better a reply
     d. a better reply

Bresnan proposes to accommodate (32) by a rule of AP Shift to which I shall give the preliminary formulation (33):

(33) AP Shift (preliminary):

$$[_N 3 \ A^2 \ - \ Det \ - \ N^1] \quad OBL \implies$$

$$\begin{array}{ccc} 1 & 2 & 3 \\ \emptyset & 2 & 1\#3 \end{array}$$

(33) will derive (32d) from (32c), but not (32b) from (32a). To see this, consider (34a), the structure of (32a) at the

beginning of the N^3 cycle, and (34b), the structure of (32c) at the beginning of the N^3 cycle:

(34) a.

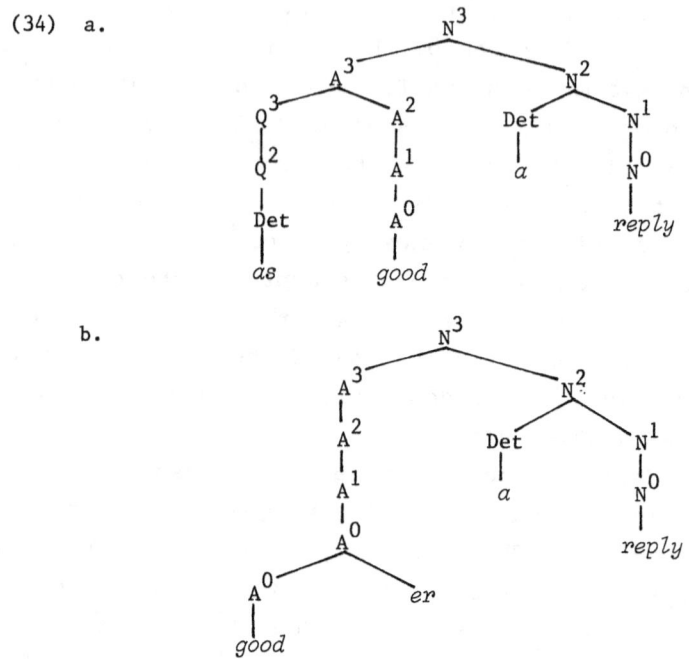

b.

The QP remnant *as* in (34a) prevents there from being an A^2 initial in N^3, as required by the outer brackets of (33). On the other hand, in (34b), the QP that was initial in underlying structure has been destroyed by transformations, the *coup de grâce* having been administered by *more* Shift. Therefore (33) applies, deriving (32d).

(33) was picked arbitrarily from many other formulations that would have sufficed. Our next example will lead us to a reformulation that is almost uniquely determined. Consider (35):

(35) a. as much better a reply
b. *an as much better reply
c. ?? much better a reply
d. a much better reply

Blocking (35b) is no problem: as (33) is currently formulated, it will not derive (35b) from (35a). The problem is to generate (35d) and block (35c). By the end of the A^3 cycle on (36a), the deep structure of (35d), the rules of (21) will have produced (36b):

(36) a.

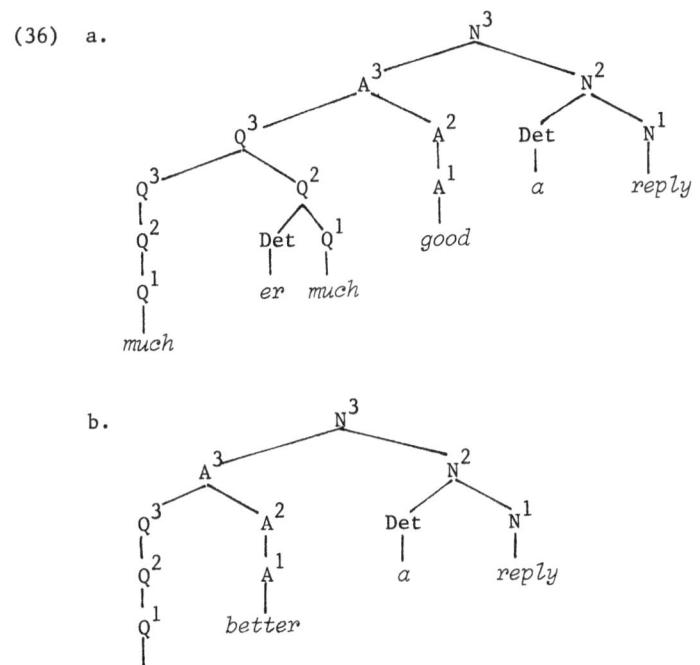

b.

(36b) does not meet the structural description of (33).

But suppose we had a rule that would attach the initial QP *much* to the A^2 *better*: then (33) would be able to apply, deriving (35d). This attachment rule is the QP Raising process. The process will cost less if we can collapse it with AP Shift. We therefore examine the latter more closely.

In the (33) formulation of AP Shift, it is assumed that the A^2 has to move around a Det. We find, however, that what can appear in the Det position after an AP is completely determined: if the NP is count singular, *a* must appear, otherwise the construction is impossible: **as good beer*, **too good the beer*, etc. This suggests that the Det position in this construction is syntactically empty, bearing the features [± sing, ± count], determined by the head N. *a* is substituted by a transformation for a Det that is [+sing +count]. Later in the section I will deal with what happens when the combination of features in Det is otherwise. There are two things we need with regard to the hypothesis that the indefinite article here is underlying null. First, we want some independent evidence that it is true, and second we want some principle to make it true. These will be provided later in the discussion. For the present, I shall show what can be done with the assumption that the Det is underlying null.

Given the underlying nullity of the Det of N in examples like (32) and (35), we may simplify (33) by eliminating from it term 2 and ordering it before the α-Insertion rule (Note that since by assumption the rules have to be put in some order, the particular order one puts them in is free). Next, we will obviously want to have more general category specifications than A and N for the two surviving terms.

Our rule will thus have the general form of (37):

(37) $[_X3 \ Y^m - X^n]$ OBL $\Longrightarrow$

         1   2

         ∅   1#2

It remains to identify m and n. $n = 3$ and $n = 2$ are clearly out of the question, because then the rule could not effect permutation over the empty Det. $n = 0$ is also wrong because then the shifted material would form a compound word with the N (being Chomsky-adjoined to N^0), and the stress shows that this is not what is happening. We see thus that $n = 1$.

To determine m is a little trickier. Consider (38), the structure of (35a) at the beginning of the N^3 cycle:

(38)

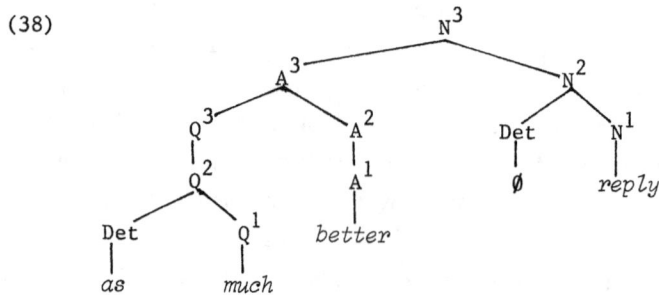

$m = 3$ we already know is wrong. $m = 2$ is also wrong, for on the A^3 cycle we would have been able to attach the Q^2 *as much* to the A^1 *better*, and then on the N^3 cycle we could attach the resulting A^1 *as much better* to the N^1, thereby generating (35b), *an as much better reply*, by subsequent article insertion. We are left with two possibilities: $m = 1$, and $m = 0$. Either would suffice. I shall assume $m = 1$, perhaps on the basis of a principle that high superscripts are cheaper than low.

The rule determined for (32, 35) is thus (39):

(39) X^1 Attachment:

$$[_{Y^3} X^1 - Y^1] \quad \text{OBL} \Rightarrow$$

$$\begin{array}{cc} 1 & 2 \\ \emptyset & 1\#2 \end{array}$$

The only feature of (39) that is not determined by the data is the superscript on term 1. This is not really essential, and I have proposed a principle that would cause it to be determined also.

If we order X^1 Attachment after er Shift and before Indefinite Article Insertion, it will derive (35d) from its deep structure (36a). Below I give the derivation, circling that node in each derived tree that was being cycled on to produce the tree from its predecessor, and boxing the node that will be cycled on to produce the next. Indefinite Article Insertion is abbreviated on the final tree.

(40) a.

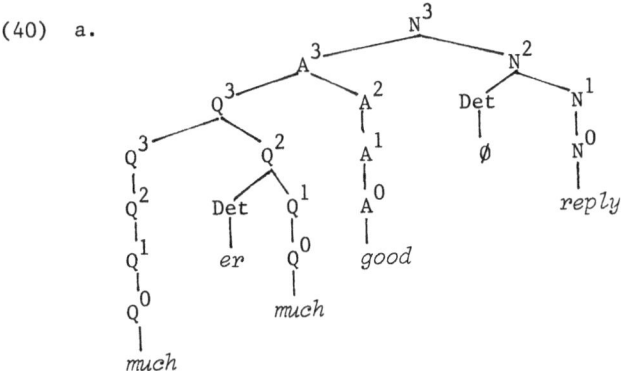

er Shift

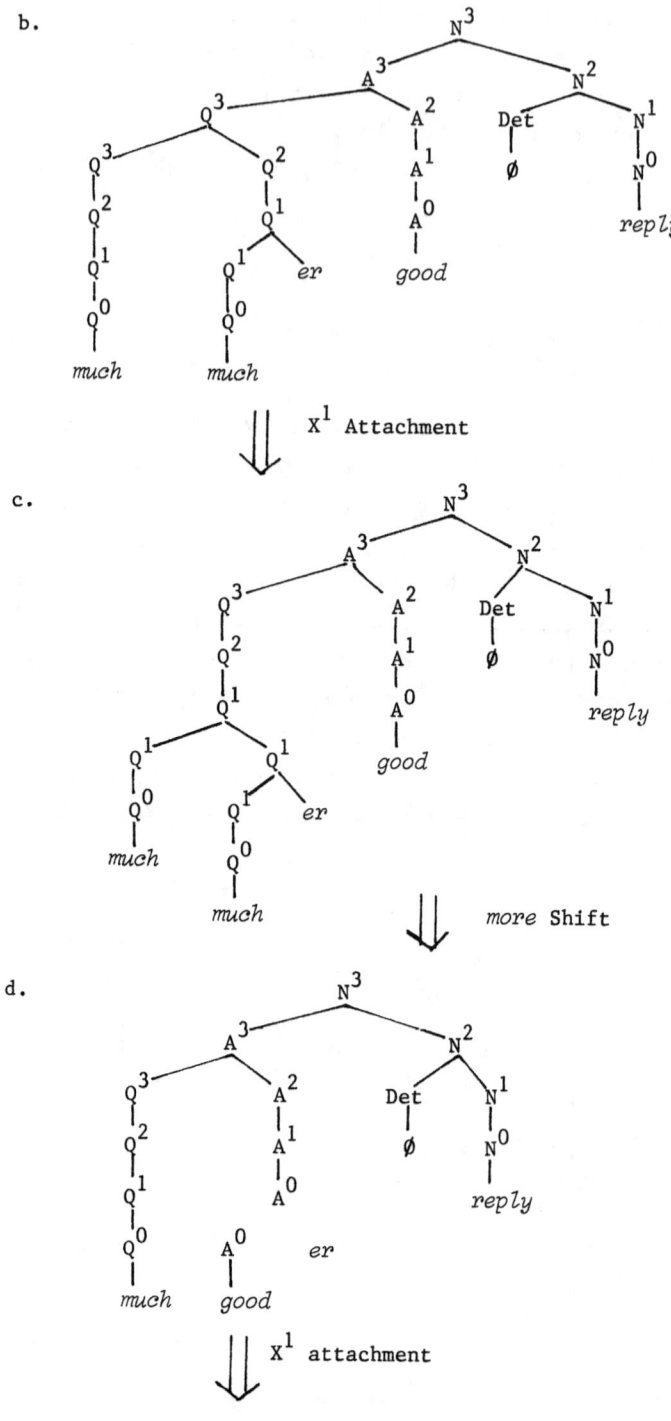

e.
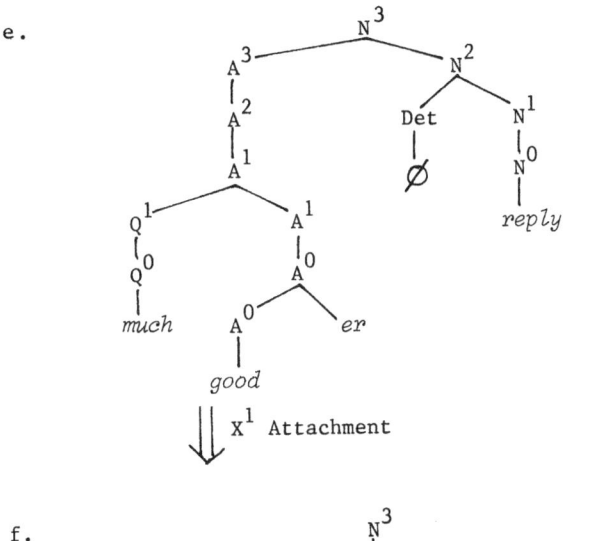

X^1 Attachment

f.
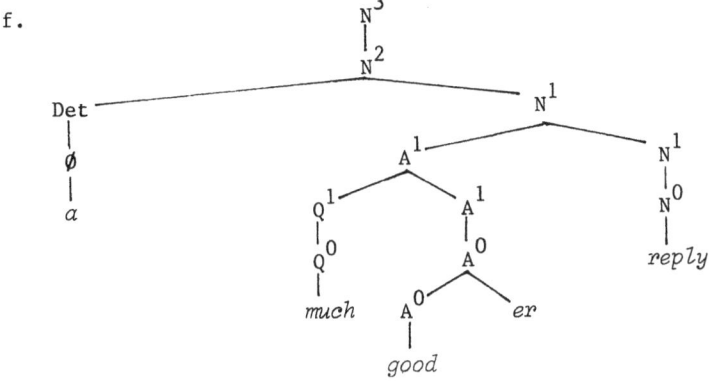

Note that with regard to the A^3 cycle (stages c and d) the rules of *more* Shift and X^1 Attachment could be applied in the reverse order without aborting the derivation. Likewise, the ordering with the Q^0 A^0 Filter and with *much* Deletion is immaterial.

The reader can easily verify that the rules will not derive (35b) from (38), but rather (38) will surface as (35a). Likewise, the rules can be seen to produce the correct results for paradigm (32). One aspect of the derivation (40) that may cause readers to balk is the $[_{Q^1} Q^1 Q^1]$ derived constituent structure in (40c). This is the structure which *much more* in *a much more intelligent answer* would have. This rather unnatural result will be eliminated in 2.1.3. For the present, we may merely observe that it is produced by the metatheory.

The present system of rules may be summarized as follows:

(41) a. *er* Shift   OBL (14)

       b. X^1 Attachment   OBL (39)

       c. Indefinite Article Insertion   OBL (unformulated)

       d. *much* Deletion   OPT (12)

       e. $Q^0 A^0$ Filter   (16)

       f. *more* Shift   OBL (18)

These rules are hopefully a minimum set for data like (10, 11, 32, 35), although some of the superscripts are doubtful.

X^1 Attachment automatically incorporates the special feature of QP Raising noted by Bresnan that it will not incorporate a QP into a QP whose Det is nonnull:

(42) a. much too hard a job

       b. *a much too hard job.

(42a) will be underlain by (43):

(43)

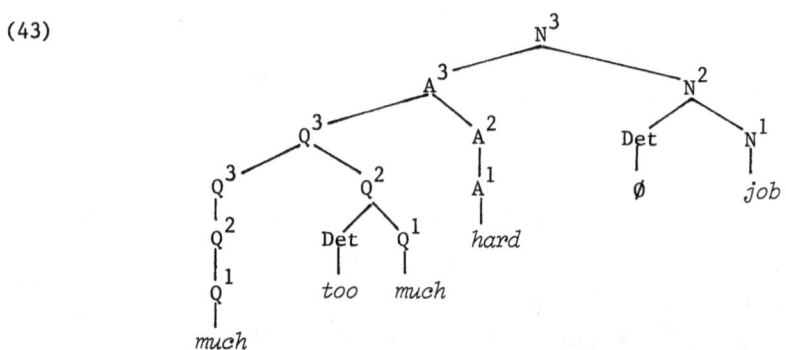

On the two Q^3 cycles, nothing will happen: in particular, X^1 Attachment will not apply on the second Q^3 cycle because of the degree particle *too* intervening between the two Q^1 nodes. Then on the A^3 cycle, *much* Deletion will apply, but again X^1 Attachment will be blocked. Finally, X^1 Attachment will yet again be blocked on the N^3 cycle. Hence the formulation of X^1 Attachment determined by the simpler cases automatically extends to the case of (42).

I will now motivate an additional filter in the analysis.

Consider (44-46):

(44) a. as good a linguist

b. *as good linguists

(45) a. *as good linguists

b. better linguists

(46) a. *as good beer

b. better beer

In precisely those examples where X^1 attachment will succeed in attaching A^1 to N^1, thereby destroying A^3 and A^2, the example is good. Otherwise it is bad. We may suppose then that there is a filter following article insertion that prohibits $A^2\ N^1$ (or equivalently, $A^3\ N^1$) sequences. The formulations of the $*A^2\ N^1$ filter and the article insertion rules are trivial.

We may now consider an apparent counterexample:

(47) a more utterly crazy lunatic

By our rules, the underlying structure for (47) would have to be (48):

(48)
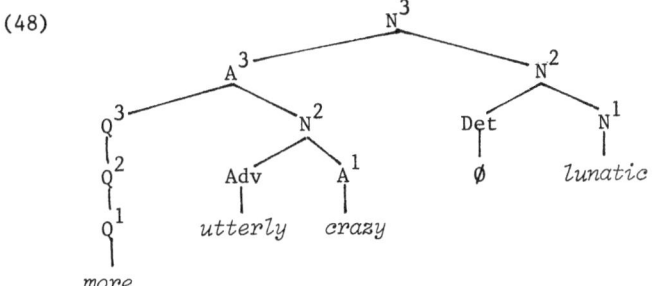

The Adv *utterly* will block X^1 Attachment on its attempt to apply to the circled A^3, so that **more utterly crazy a lunatic* will be derived, and the grammatical form will not be. This is precisely consonant with the problem we noted in the preceding subsection of the grammaticality of *too utterly crazy*, in which *much* Deletion is applying before *utterly* (recall *too *(much) so*, etc.).

I propose that in these examples *utterly* is an ordinary A rather than an Adv. (47) will not then have (48) as its structure, but will rather have a structure parallel to *a more obviously crazy lunatic*.

I now return to the cyclicity principle (29). Strict Cyclicity principles are characteristically thought of as prohibiting operations entirely within a domain dominated by a cyclic node. This leaves open the question of what happens if the cyclic node dominating a domain is removed. We can see that in the case of (29), the newly exposed material should not be resubmitted to rule application. Consider *a much better linguist*. This is derived from X^1 Attachment from *much better a linguist*. X^1 attachment removes the A^3 node from over *much better*, yet the Q^0 A^0 Filter does not get a chance to rule the sentence out on the N^3 cycle.

We can formalize (29) appropriately by introducing into a theory a division between red and green brackets. The base produces structures in which all the brackets are green. When the cycle on a domain is finished, all the brackets (including the outermost) on that domain are painted red. (29) then becomes a constraint that one of the factors covered by a constant term in a rule must contain green brackets in order for the structural description of the rule to be met. I believe that this formalism could be extended to the treatment of idioms given by Kiparsky (1975).

We are finally left with the problem of the indefinite article. The following data can be taken to support either a rule of *one(s)* Deletion or a rule of *one(s)* Insertion (I am indebted to Hankamer for pointing this out to me):

(49) a. I wrecked Bill's old car, and you wrecked Harry's new *(one).

b. I wrecked Bill's car, and you wrecked Harry's (*one).

(50) a. I bought three old records, and you bought three new *(ones).

b. I bought three records, and you bought four (*ones).

We could say that *one(s)* is deleted after quantifiers and possessives, or inserted after adjectives (but note *this one* and *that one*: I suspect that this is a different *one*)

Observe the following contrast:

(51) a. Bill is a piano player and Lucinda is one too.

b. Bill is as good a piano player as Dinu Lapitti, and Lucinda is as good a one as Horowitz.

Perlmutter (1970) suggests that the indefinite article is a stressless form of the numeral *one*, and that there is deletion of the identity-of-sense pronoun *one* after numerals, including the indefinite article. Hence the predicate nominal *one* in (51a) is analysed as underlyingly *one one*, with the second *one* disappearing by *one(s)* Deletion.

But this approach cannot explain the appearance of *a one* in (51b). Even if the *a* were underlying empty, so that we had a structure like (52)

(52)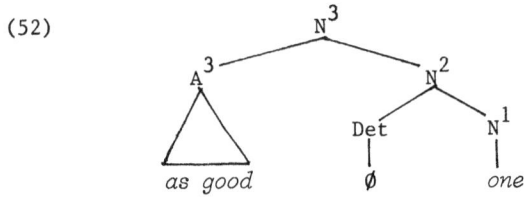

a *one(s)* Deletion rule would still apply, providing that the null Det were of the same grammatical category as a numeral, since terms of transformations can take null factors.

But suppose instead that *one(s)* is inserted, presumably for an empty N^0. We might formulate the rule as follows:

(53) *one(s)* Insertion

$$A^3 - N^0 \quad \text{OBL}$$

1   2   ⟹

1   PRO

Then the appearance of *ones* in (51b) is explained, as long as *one(s)* Insertion follows Indefinite Article Insertion.

I have formulated the rule as insertion of PRO rather than as insertion of *one(s)* because I wish to preserve the solution proposed in Andrews (1974) to the problem presented in (54):

(54) a. I ate Bill's meat and you ate Mary's.

b. *I ate Bill's expensive meat and you ate Mary's cheap.

When the N^0 for which one would substitute *one(s)* is mass, nothing can be done. I proposed that *one(s)* was inserted by surface structure lexicalization for a feature complex, and that there simply wasn't a lexical item that could be inserted for the mass counterpart to *one(s)*. Derivations surfacing with unlexicalizable positions would then block. Thus if (53) inserts PRO into an N^0 that is [-count], there is no lexical item that can fill this position, and the derivation blocks, explaining the ungrammaticality of (54b).

We finally want a principle to force the indefinite article to be underlyingly null. I propose the principle that if an N^3 is analysable as $A^3 N^2$, it is also analysable as $A^3 N^1$. One would hope to derive this principle from more general considerations, presumably of semantic interpretation.

2.1.3 *So and Such*: Bresnan (section 1.4) observes a mass of facts which support the notion that the AP Shift process is capable of moving an AP while stranding an associated *so*, which subsequently becomes *such*:

(55) a. so tall a man

b. *so a tall man

c. *such tall a man

d. such a tall man

Observing in addition the following data:

(56) a. so much better a linguist

b. *such a (much) better linguist

we are led to propose the following reformulation of X^1

Attachment that will accommodate the above data:

(57) $[_Y3 \langle so \rangle_1 - \begin{smallmatrix} X^1 \\ \langle +A \rangle_1 \end{smallmatrix} - Y^1]$ $\langle OPT \rangle_1 \Longrightarrow$

   1   2   3

   1   ∅   2#3

In interpreting this rule, we can take OPT as a feature or as a non-feature with regard to the angle bracket notation If we take it as a non-feature, we want rules with no specification to be obligatory; if we take it as a featur we want [-OPT] = OBL. The rule has an equally highly valued equivalent in which the role of '+A' is filled by '-Q.'

(57) is, I believe, the minimal rule for the data we have seen so far, but it is in fact incorrect, going badly haywire in some rather intricate derivations. Consider (58b), the underlying structure of (58a):

(58) a. such an obviously more plausible suggestion

   b.

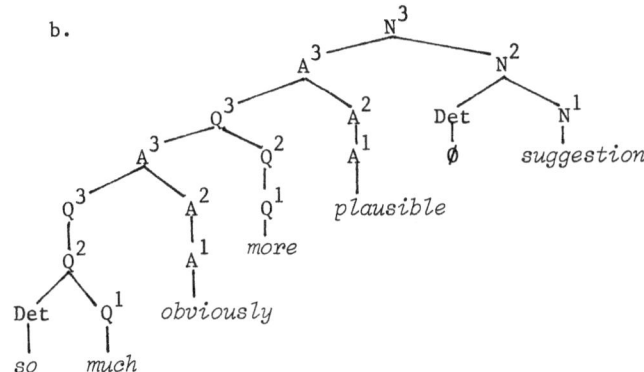

On the A^3 cycle, *much* Deletion will happen. On the Q^3 cycle, *obviously* and *more* will glom together under Q^1, resulting in the derived constituent structure (58c):

(58) c.

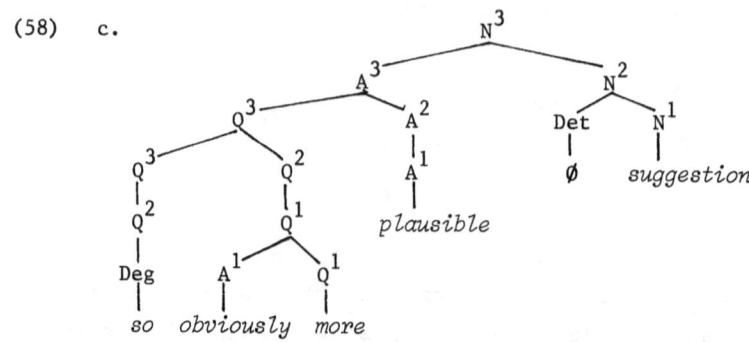

But now we are stuck. To get to a stage where we can shift *obviously more plausible* into the N^2, we have to attach the Q^1 *obviously more* to the A^1 *plausible*, and this operation is prohibited by the formulation of (57).

This formulation is necessary in order to avoid generating *(56b) from (56a). To avoid the generation of *(56b), we must block incorporation of a Q^1 that is preceded by *so* into an A^1, and that is precisely what we must do in order to progress from (58b) to the grammatical (58a).

It is not sufficient to merely change (57): rather, we must alter the metatheory so that it is not in fact compatible with the data of the preceding section and that of (55-56).

The rule of X^1 Attachment produces derived constituent structures such as (59), which have doubtless upset many readers when they have occurred in our derivations:

(59) a.

b.

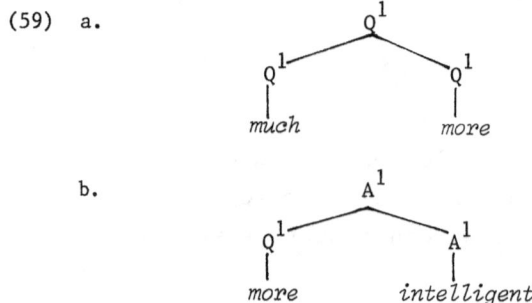

These structures have the property that the basic modifier-head relationships have been obscured. Let us then add to the metatheory a stipulation that structures of the form (60) cannot be produced by a transformation:

(60)

(where, of course, any of X, Y and Z may be equal to one another). We might accomplish this with a restriction that structures of the form (60) are obligatorily interpreted as coordinate structures.

The rule of X^1 Attachment (39) is no longer compatible with the data (32, 32), since it assigns to these sentences impossible derived constituent structures. I believe that instead of the minimal rule is (61):

(61) X^2 Attachment (first try):

$$[_Y3 \ [_{X}2 \ X^1] - Y^1] \quad \text{OBL}$$

$$\qquad \quad 1 \qquad \quad 2 \quad \Longrightarrow$$

$$\qquad \quad \emptyset \qquad 1\#2$$

X^2 Attachment, like X^1 Attachment, produces the additional facts of (42), as desired. We have thus not lost explanatory potency in this direction. We also, however, have attained intuitively far more comfortable derived constituent structures.

The derivation of *a much better reply* goes through as follows:

(62) a.

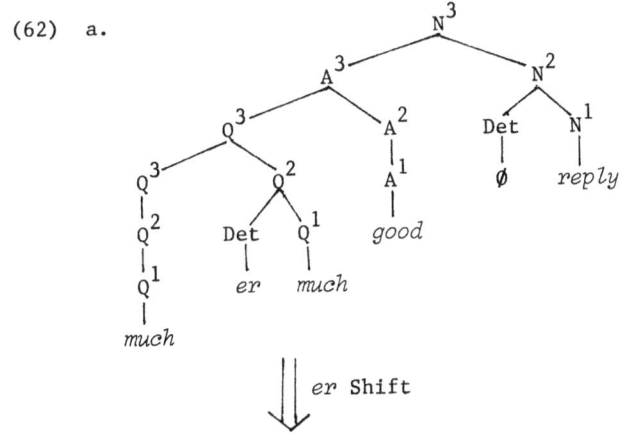

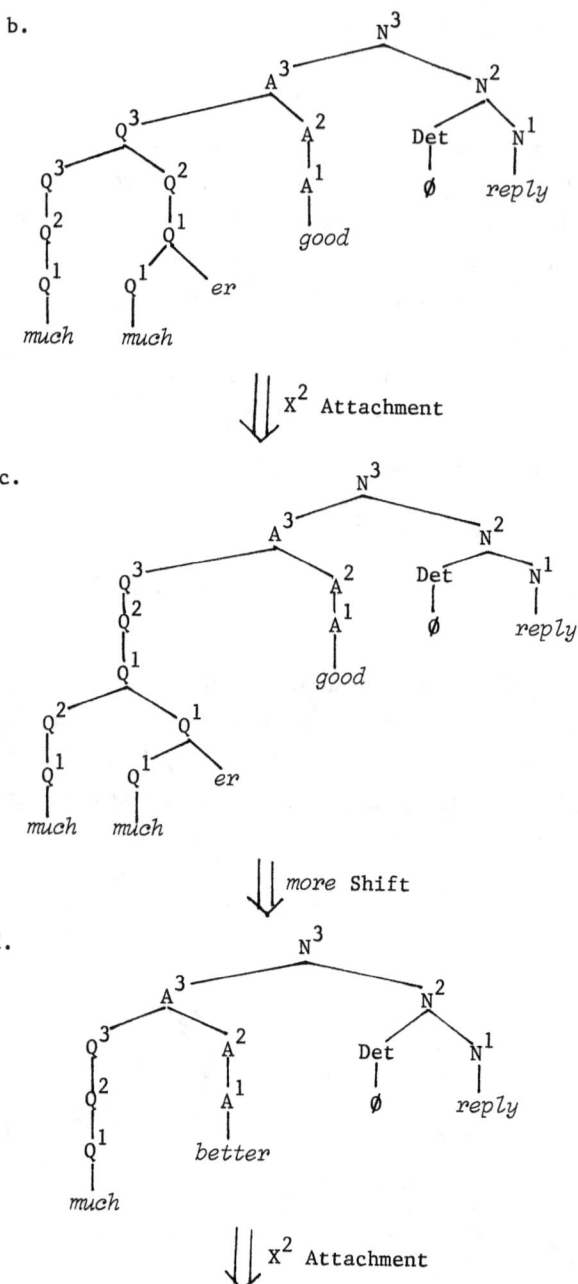

e.

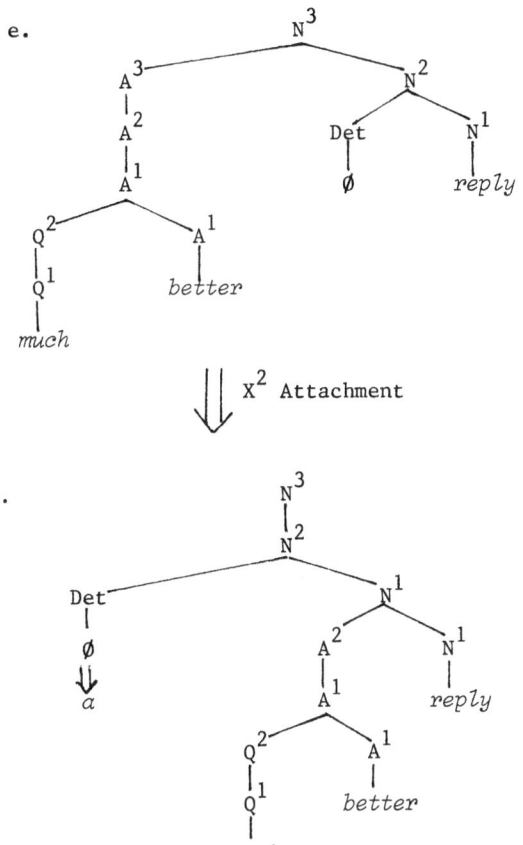

Now let us return to the data of (55). Given the revised metatheory and the data of the preceding sections, the minimal way to accommodate (55) is to reformulate X^2 Attachment as follows:

(63) X^2 Attachment (second try):

$$[_Y3 \langle so \rangle_1 - [_X2\ X^1] - Y^1] \quad \langle OPT \rangle_1$$
$$1 2 3 \quad \Longrightarrow$$

$$1 \emptyset 2\#3$$

Now (63), unlike (57), automatically predicts the facts of (56b). The underlying structure of (56a) will be (64):

(64)

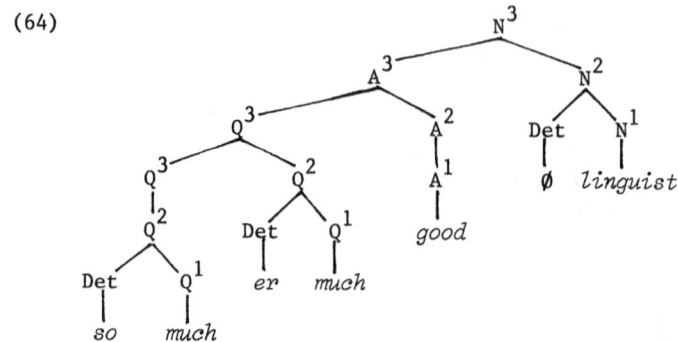

But (64) will never meet the structural description of the new X^2 Attachment, so that the derivation to *(56b) will be blocked. The reason the rule does not get to apply to (64) is that the initial *so* is under the Q^2 of the Q^1 that immediately follows it; while in (65), the underlying structure of (55a), that Q^1 gets deleted on the A^3 cycle, leaving *so* preceding A^2 on the N^3 cycle, so that (63) can apply:

(65)

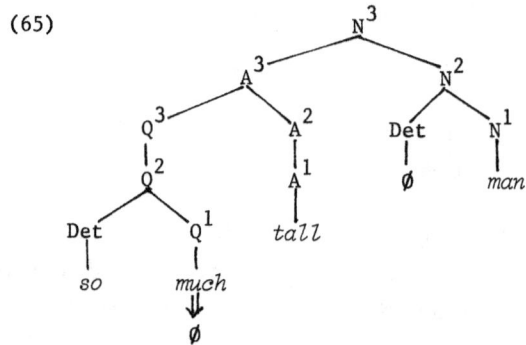

Going back to the example (58) (*so obviously plausible a suggestion*), which defeated the original X^1 Attachment rule, we find that the derivation by X^2 Attachment does not get hung up. On the A^3 cycle *much* disappears, and then X^2 Attachment works smoothly on each following cycle.

The metatheoretical principle ruling out structures of the form (60) thus results in very substantial explanatory improvements: from the data of (55) are predicted both the data of (56) and (58). The principle has the added appeal of ruling out a constituent structure that is counter-intuitive, to say the least.

We may note a pleasant by-product of the reformulation of the attachment rule: the filter to exclude *as good beer receives unique characterization as an $*A^3 \ N^1$ filter. This is, of course, free beer rather than an argument.

We must finally extend the analysis in order to accommodate a few more facts brought forth by Bresnan. Consider such examples as the following:

(66) a. Bill is less a linguist than you are.

b. Ferdinand is too much a scholar to publish junk like that.

c. He has become more a poet than a linguist.

Bresnan assigns to less a linguist the structure (67) (after er Shift):

(67)

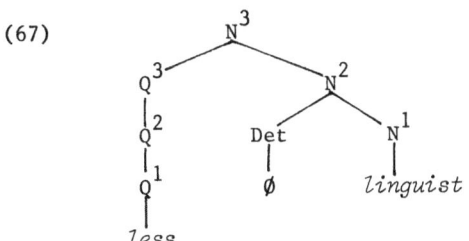

I would be inclined to have the Q^3 immediately dominated by A^3. This would capture the intuitive resemblance of these structures to the predeterminer adjective constructions, and explain less a one by one(s) Insertion, and *this is less beer than that by the $*A^3 \ N^1$ filter.

Regardless of whether we make these emendations, rule (63) will misapply to (67), deriving *a less linguist. Hence (63) must be again reformulated. (68) appears to do the job:

(68) X^2 Attachment (final version):

$$[_{Y^3} \langle so \rangle_1 - [_{X^2} [_{\langle Q \rangle_2}^X]^1] - \langle -N \rangle_2^{Y^1} \quad \langle OPT \rangle$$

$$1 \qquad\qquad 2 \qquad\qquad 3 \qquad \Longrightarrow : \to 1$$

$$1 \qquad\qquad \emptyset \qquad\qquad 2\#3$$

Note how crucially this formulation relies on the differing interpretation of angle brackets around features (as in term 2) and around nonfeatures (terms 1 and 3), as specified in Sound Patterns of English (p.394-395). Also note that (68) merely describes, rather than explains, (66).

I list the salient rules in the analysis we have arrived at as follows:

(69) a. *er* Shift   OBL   (14)
     b. X^2 Attachment   OBL   (68)
     c. Ind. Art. Insertion OBL   (unformulated)
     d. *$A^2 N^1$ Filter   (unformulated)
     e. *much* Deletion   OPT   (12)
     f. *$Q^0 A^0$ Filter   (16)
     g. *more* Shift   OBL   (18)

There are various further data and constructions considered in Bresnan (1.5 - 1.6). The reader can verify that under Bresnan's account of the underlying structures, the rules of (69) work correctly. They also apply appropriately to the indefinite superlative construction of Bresnan (1.7).

2.1.4 *The Indefinite Comparative:* The indefinite comparative is the structure exemplified in the following examples:

(70) a. The more you work, the less you get
     b. The taller you are, the heavier.
     c. The more pizzas Mary eats, the fatter she gets.

My own work on these constructions is a reanalysis of material covered in Thiersch (1974). I will here consider the internal constituent structure of the preposed constituents in *the*: *the more pizza* and *the fatter* in (70c), for example. The clausal relations will be discussed in 2.2.1, though it should be obvious that I am going to say that the initial clause is an anticipatory clause like the anticipatory relatives of the preceding chapter.

The problem is to determine the underlying constituent of the *the*. Thiersch analyses it as a COMP, occurring initially in each clause, which attracts the constituent with *more* to it. The following examples, however, suggest that it is instead an occupant of the Det of QP:

(71) a. The more you practice, the better a pianist you will be.

b. The better a linguist you are, the fewer questions
you have to ask your informants.

Consider the phrases *the better a pianist, the better a linguist*. If the *the* is in COMP, nothing can explain the ungrammaticality of **the a better linguist, *the a better pianist, *the a more obviously competent insurance salesman*, etc. But suppose *the* is in the Det of QP. Then *the better a pianist* will have the underlying structure (72a), reaching the surface as (72b):

(72) a.

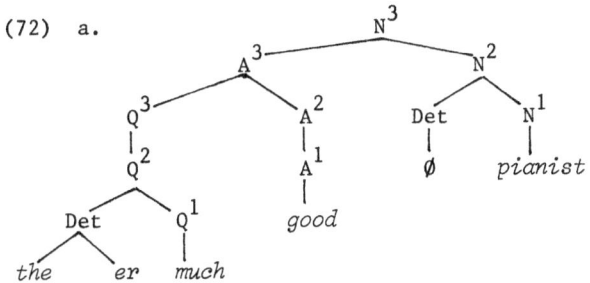

b.

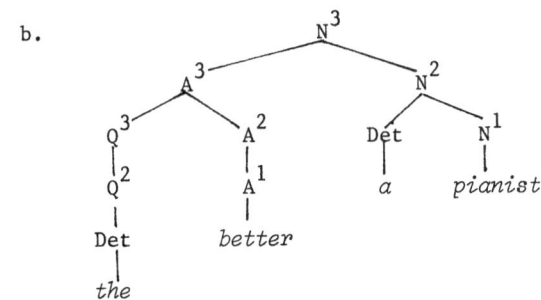

The Q^3 remnant *the* prevents X^2 Attachment from applying on the N^3 cycle.

This analysis further is confirmed when we see such examples as *he tried all the harder, so much the worse for him, he became all the better a psychologist for it*. In these cases the *the* is preceded by predeterminer material, though it is not in the indefinite comparative construction.

This little studied construction thus fits easily into Bresnan's analysis.

2.2 *Comparative Clauses in the Base*: I will here determine the underlying position of comparative clauses. In 2.2.1 I examine and reject the traditional view that comparative clauses are generated in the Det of the QP they modify. In section 2.2.2 I propose that comparative clauses (including the indefinite comparatives of (2.1.4) are generated in the base in the positions that they occupy on the surface, and indicate what the responsible rules are.

2.2.1 *The Determiner Analysis*: Bresnan (pp. 338-343) proposes the traditional analysis of the underlying structure of comparative clauses, in which they are generated within the Det of the QP they modify, and are then moved to their surface position by rules of Comparative Formation and Extraposition. Hence (73) is underlain by (74), which undergoes the movement indicated by the arrow, as well as deletion of a constituent identical to the head except for its special Determiner x in the QP (x is the symbol for the Det of the 'target QP' of the comparative clause, rather than a logical variable):

(74)
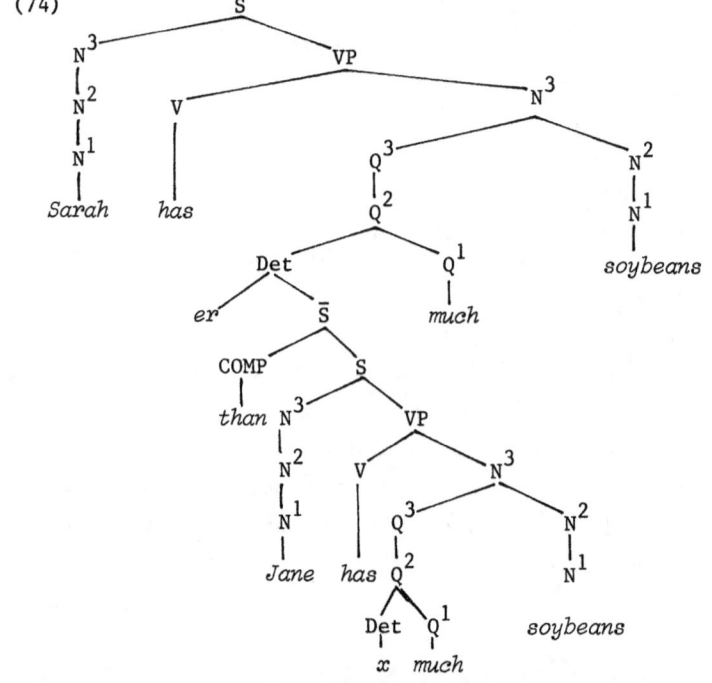

Bresnan cites two motivations supporting this structure. The first is that the cooccurrence restrictions between the COMP of the comparative clause and the Det of the modified QP may easily be stated over these structures. Bresnan observes that these restrictions hold over unbounded distances in surface structure (Bresnan p. 339):

(75) a. Mary doesn't have as many too many too many
... marbles as Jane.
b. Cindy has more nearly as many too many
marbles as Julie than Linda

The second reason is that this structure allows a systematic explanation for the exclusion from the comparative clause of certain modifiers in the head, namely, those that precede the determiner with which the clause is associated. Consider, for example, (76):

(76) Melvin sliced twice as many bagels as Seymour

We wish (76) to be derived from (77) rather than from (78):

(77) Melvin sliced twice as [Seymour sliced x many bagels] many bagels

(78) Melvin sliced twice as [Seymour sliced twice x many bagels] many bagels

Given determiner generation of the comparative clause, the modifiers that are excluded are given a straightforward characterization as those that are to the right of the clause itself in its underlying position.

To these considerations may be added a third, the support of semantic interpretation. The semantics of comparatives will obviously go more smoothly if there is some systematic representation of the relations between a comparative clause and the QP it modifies. Davis and Hellan (in preparation), for example, give a model theoretic semantics for comparatives that is based essentially on Bresnan's analysis, and assume that the comparative clause is generated in the determiner.

There are nonetheless many severe problems with determiner generation of comparative clauses. First, there are difficulties connected with formulating the rule.

The presumed derived constituent structure from the application of Comparative Formation to (74) is (79):

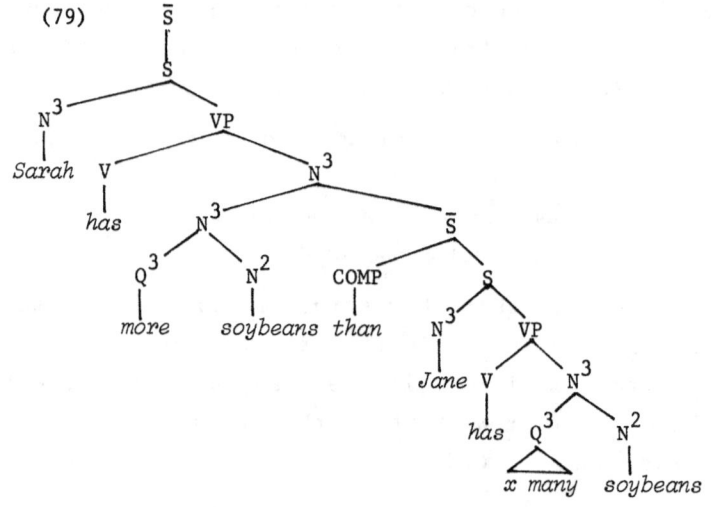

Bresnan suggests that Comparative Formation also effects deletion of the constituent *x many soybeans* in the comparative clause that is identical to the head (when the clause has been removed). I have omitted this feature in (79).

If (79) is the derived constituent structure produced by Comparative Formation, then the rule has to have the effect of Chomsky adjoining the comparative clause to its head, which is an operation of Chomsky adjoining a constituent to a containing constituent (and deleting the original occurrence within that constituent). Because the rule requires operations (deletion and adjunction) on overlapping domains, it is not formulable as a single transformation within the framework of Peters and Ritchie (1973) (cf. Peters and Ritchie p.54, p. 60 def. 210). I do not think one could easily introduce the capacity to perform such operations either into the Peters and Ritchie framework or the Partee and Ginsburg (1969) framework. One could probably find a way by factoring Comparative Formation into two successive operations, an adjunction and an erasure, but my best efforts in this direction are hardly attractive. The rule is thus unformulable as a single transformation in available formalisms, and the necessity for factoring it into two transformations considerably increases its cost and lowers its appeal.

Additional problems arise when we attempt to specify where Comparative Formation is to put the clause it moves. Bresnan (pp. 328-329) notes paradigms such as the following:

(80) a. Bill is more than five feet tall.
b. Bill is taller than five feet.
c. *Bill is more than Max (is) tall.
d. Bill is taller than Max (is).

She shows that the correct phrasing for the AP of (4a) is *(more (than five feet)) tall*, and proposes that the comparative clause originates from an underlying equational sentence 'five feet is x much.' She claims that the verb of this sentence cannot be the copula, but must be a special abstract equational predicate, but the basis for this is not clear to me. The copula would appear to suffice in the light of such examples as *five feet is more than six inches*, etc.

We can thus propose (81) to underly (80):

(81) a. Bill is er [than five feet is x much] much tall.
b. Bill is er [than five feet is x much tall] much tall.
c. Bill is er [than Max is x much] much tall.
d. Bill is er [than Max is x much tall] much tall.

The comparative clause may in these examples be seen to be attaching to that constituent in the head which is identical to the disappearing constituent in the comparative clause. (80c) is ungrammatical because putting the comparative clause after *er much* forces the deleted constituent in the comparative clause to be x *much*, which cannot be equated with *Bill*.

This sort of approach too breaks down because of examples like the following:

(82) a. Bill sliced more salami than Harry did bologna.
b. The table is longer than the door is wide.
c. More men than women (did) made reservations.
d. He gave more cash than he did attention to his mistress.

The sources of these would be (83):

(83) a. Bill sliced er [than Harry sliced x much bologna] much salami.
b. the table is er [than the door is x much wide] much long
c. er [than x many men made reservations] many women made reservations
d. he gave er [than he gave x much attention to his mistress] much cash to his mistress

No condition on Comparative Formation stated in terms of identity can generate (82) but block (84):

(84) a. *Bill sliced more than Harry did bologna salami.
b. *The table is more than the door is wide long.
c. *More than women did men made reservations.
d. *He gave more than he did attention (to his mistress cash to his mistress.

Bresnan notes these problems, but does not give a clear solution.

The situation gets worse if we observe some restrictions found by Pinkham (1974). Pinkham noted that when a comparative clause was attached to its head, rather than extraposed, and neither contained a structure identical to the head nor was identical outside the head to the matrix, then the sentence was ungrammatical. Corresponding to the grammatical (82c, d) are the grammatical (85a, b) and the ungrammatical (86a, b):

(85) a. More men than I expected to made reservations.
b. Bill gave more cash than Maurice did to Brycelinde.

(86) a. *More men than I expected women to made reservations.
b. *Bill gave more cash than Maurice did affection to Brycelinde.

Conditions on a movement rule would appear to be an unlikely way to explain what comparative clauses go where.

Attempts to maintain a determiner source for comparative clauses are finally defeated by multiple headed comparatives like these:

(87) As fair a woman and as foul a man as I have ever seen together are coming toward us.

(88) a.[2] People do crazier things at higher speeds on the McGrath Highway than they do other places.

b. Marcille gave a longer talk at a better attended session than did her husband.

c. Alfred bestowed a heartier kiss on a prettier girl than Maxwell did.

Liberman (1974) also cites multiple headed result clauses: *John hit his car so hard so many times with such a big hammer than it finally started.*

(87) would presumably be underlain by (89), and (88) by (90):

(89) as much fair a woman and as much foul a man [as I have ever seen x much fair a woman and x much foul a man together] are coming toward us.

(90) Alfred bestowed er much hearty a kiss on er much pretty a girl [than Maxwell bestowed x much hearty a kiss on x much pretty a girl]

The other examples of (88) have structures parallel to (90). Note that the 'x' in these examples is not a logical variable, but a symbol for the abstract formative (*so?*) that is the Det of the QP in the comparative clause.

One might think to generate (87) by generating a comparative clause in each conjunct of the coordinate NP, and applying Right Node Raising, but the presence of *together* renders this impossible: *I have ever seen x much fair a woman together* is ungrammatical. This result is preserved under current theories in which many aspects of semantic interpretation are determined from surface structure, because in these theories Right Node Raising would have the comparative clause binding traces in each conjunct, and interpretation would use these to determine the meaning as if the movement had not occurred (see Vergnaud 1974, pp.82-83 for discussion). We get the same result in (88) where there aren't any processes that could yield the comparative clause by combining well-formed clauses on the individual matrix comparative determiners.

(87-88) might be dismissed as marginal phenomena. If they were the sole evidence against Comparative Formation, one might still maintain the rule with a relatively clear conscience. But in the light of the preceding discussion, which shows that the formulation of the rule is highly problematic, if possible at all, they become telling counterevidence.

There is a final consideration that we must discuss before accepting (87-88) as counterevidence to Comparative Formation. There are sentences in natural language which 'sound all right' and suggest a meaning, but certainly don't get their meaning by means of regular rules of grammar. For example, "the more you eat the more you want the more you eat" suggests the presence of a vicious circle, but it certainly doesn't do this by means of regular rules of semantic interpretation. Rather, the meaning is delivered iconically, by an operation of free intelligence. One might correspondingly claim that (87, 88) were not sentences of English, but rather surface patterns resembling sentences, and receiving meanings not by regular rules but by some vague sort of suggestiveness.

The only way to refute such a proposal is to give rules for interpreting multiple headed comparatives, and show that they fit in reasonably well with the rest of the rules of semantic interpretation of the language. The semantics of comparatives is quite complicated, and that of multiple headed comparatives much more so. I wish to spare the reader most of my presently rather ill thought out ideas on the subject. I will, however, bring forth some reasons to believe that multiple headed comparatives are interpreted in a reasonably disciplined fashion.

Postal (1974) suggested a semantics for comparatives in which they were interpreted as two definite descriptions connected by a relational predicate. Hence "Bill has more money than Tom" comes out "the amount of money Bill has exceeds the amount of money Tom has." Now consider an experiment on the effects of marijuana smoking. We may say "50 people smoked 100 joints" and mean either 50 people smoked 100 joints apiece, or 50 people smoked 100 joints between them (there are other readings, but they are not very sensible in the given context). Now suppose we say "more people smoked more joints in this experiment than in the last." We might mean that the total number of participants in this experiment exceeded that in the last and the total number of joints smoked in this experiment exceeded that in the last, or we might mean that more people participated and they each smoked more joints.

We can get this effect by introducing a definite description operator that denotes not an amount, but rather an ordered pair of amounts, and likewise extending the 'exceeds' relation and the others to be relations over ordered n-tuples rather than merely individuals. Our example would thus have a logical structure like (91):

(91) (A X, Y) (X people smoked Y joints in this experiment) exceeds (A X, Y) (X people smoked Y joints in the last experiment).

'A' is the operator forming definite descriptions of amounts or n-tuples of amounts. I would interpret 'exceeds' in '$(x_1,\ldots, x_n)$ exceeds $(y_1, \ldots, y_n)$' as meaning that for $i = 1, \ldots, n$, x_i exceeds y_i, but one might dissent from this. The ambiguity in the example thus derives from the ambiguity of 'X people smoked Y joints', which ambiguity would presumably be eliminated in a reasonable semantic representation. There is much more to be said on the subject of multiple headed comparative semantics, but I shall not try to say it here.

The above discussion, though incomplete, suffices to show that structures like (87-88) are really sentences. Their status as evidence is thereby confirmed.

2.2.2 *The Base Position of Comparative Clauses*: The comparative clauses that we have seen, including the double headed ones, come in two surface positions: attached to a head, and extraposed. I shall propose underlying structures for both in which the deep position is also the surface position. After examining the regular comparatives, I will turn to the indefinite comparatives.

The crucial fact about headed comparatives is that they can stack, and there is a constraint, which I call the mirror-image constraint, that the clauses must appear in the reverse order from that of the determiners of the QP that they are associated with:

(92) a. As many more people than I invited as you predicted came to the party.
b. *As many more people as you predicted than I invited came to the party.

Since they stack, I shall presume that they are introduced by the rule $X^3 \longrightarrow X^3 \bar{S}$. When $X = N$, we get examples like (92). When $X = A$ we get sentences like *the chair is twice as much wider than the door as I expected*. And when $X = Q$, we get those like *the plants grow as much as six feet high*.

Extraposed comparatives also appear to stack, and to obey the mirror-image constraint, even in conjunction with embedded comparatives:

(93) a. As many more people than I invited came to the party as you predicted.
b. *As many more people as you predicted came to the party than I invited.
c. As many more people came to the party than I invited as you predicted.
d. *As many more people came to the party as I invited than you predicted.

By analogy with relative clauses, it would be reasonable to propose that extraposed comparatives be introduced by the $S \longrightarrow S \bar{S}$ rule that introduces extraposed relatives.

This rule leads us to expect to find comparative clauses with a head in each conjunct of a coordinate S, but not of a coordinate $\bar{S}$:

(94) a. More men were singing and more women were dancing than I had ever seen on a stage at once.

b. Bill reported that more men were singing and (*that) more women were dancing than he had ever seen on a stage at once.
   c. than I/he had ever seen x many men and x many women on a stage at once

(94a) illustrates the construction, (94b) shows that a comparative clause cannot be attached to conjoined $\bar{S}$, and (94c) shows the presumed underlying structure for the comparative clauses in these examples.

We see that an extraposed comparative can precede or follow an extraposed relative, and that the mirror-image constraint appears to hold:

(95) a. More men came to the party who were drunk than I expected would.
   b. *More men came to the party than I expected would who were drunk.
   c. More men picked a girl up who was willing than we expected
   d. *More men picked a girl up than we expected who was willing.

These facts strengthen the hypothesis.

Williams (1974) proposed that comparative and result clauses extraposed to the end of the S that was their scope. Consider such examples as these:

(96) a. Bill's teachers said he was so smart he could solve any problem.
   b. Bill's teachers said he was smarter than anybody else was.
   c. Bill's teachers said he was so smart that people doubted their recommendations.
   d. Bill's teachers said he was smarter than anybody else did.

In (96a, b), the scope of the comparative or result clause is the complement sentence. In (96a), Bill's problem solving ability is said to be a consequence of how smart he is, not how smart people say he is; and in (96b) Bill is said to be smarter than anybody else. In (96c, d), however, the scope of the comparative and result clauses is the matrix. In (96c), it is the extent to which Bill's teachers say he is smart that causes disbelief, and in (96d), the extent to which Bill's teachers say he is smart is compared with the extent to which anybody else does.

Williams claims that these scope differences correspond to differences in surface constituent structure as follows:

(97) a. Bill's teachers said [he was so smart he could solve any problem]
b. Bill's teachers said [he was smarter than anybody else was]
c. [Bill's teachers said that he was so smart] that people doubted their recommendations
d. [Bill's teachers said he was smarter] than anybody else did.

This claim is supported by the following contrasts involving the placement of matrix agent phrases:

(98) a. *Bill is said to be so smart by his teachers that he can solve any problem.
b. *Bill is said to know more by his teachers than anybody else does.
c. Bill was said to be so smart by his teachers that people doubted their recommendations.
d. Bill was said to be smarter by his teachers than he was by anybody else.

When the clause has scope within the complement, the matrix agent phrase cannot be interpolated between it and its head. Assuming that nodes cannot be moved into S by the rules that position adverbs or prepositional phrases, the result follows immediately from the bracketing of (97).

We can see that the clause may be indefinitely far removed from its head by contemplating examples such as *Bill is said by his friends.....to be believed by his teachers to be smarter than anybody else is*, etc.

We can produce multiple headed examples precisely parallel to (98):

(99) a. *People are said to do crazier things at higher
         speeds there by Dorothy than they do other places.
     b. *People are said to do such crazy things at such high
         speeds there by Dorothy that they get killed off
         in droves.
     c. People are said to do crazier things at higher speeds
         there by Dorothy than they are by other people.
     d. People are said to do such crazy things at such high
         speeds there by Dorothy that I am getting skeptical.

It cannot be maintained, then, that comparative and result clauses are extraposed to the end of the S that is their scope. Rather, they are base-generated in approximately that area. I propose that they are base-generated as sisters to the S that is their scope.

Notice that we have here rather massive Right-Roof Constraint violations (assuming that the connections between the clauses and their heads obey island constraints), but that the sentential subject constraint is respected: *that Seymour sliced so many bagels is obvious that his arm fell off*. These results strengthen the suspicion voiced in section 1.1.3.6 that the Right Roof Constraint should be retired.

The question arises naturally as to whether certain clauses just happen to be generated in a clause-final position, or whether there is a general prohibition on rules of extraposition. We have only seen two purported varieties of clausal extraposition: extraposition of comparative and result clauses, and extraposition of relative clauses. There have also been purported to be extraposition of noun-complement clauses (*Bill figured a proof out that the circle could not be squared*) and extraposition leaving *it* (*it is obvious that Jack is a commie*). I cannot replicate any of the arguments that relative and comparative clauses are generated in place for these other types.

Furthermore, there is a paradigm discovered by Ross that provides evidence that there is extraposition of relative and complement clauses from NP that have been *wh* Moved to initial position (adapted from Ross (1967:5.1.1.3)).

(100) a. Sam picked somebody up who would sleep with him before nine.
b. Sam picked somebody up before nine who would sleep with him.
c. *Who did Sam pick up who would sleep with him before nine?
d. Who did Sam pick up before nine who would sleep with him?

(101) a. Jane figured six proofs out that the circle could not be squared before dawn.
b. Jane figured six proofs out before dawn that the circle could not be squared.
c. *How many proofs did Jane figure out that the circle could not be squared before dawn?
d. How many proofs did Jane figure out before dawn that the circle could not be squared?

Given the assumptions that *wh* Movement puts the preposed element in COMP, that 'extraposed' relatives and noun complements are generated by a S ⟶ S S̄ rule, and that their heads must be in construction with them at all levels of the derivation, *(100c) and *(101c) are ruled out as desired. But (100d) and (101d) should be out as well, and they are grammatical. It appears that there actually is a rule of Extraposition from NP that applies after *wh* Movement, just as proposed by Ross. Whether this rule applies to clauses in NP outside of COMP I do not know.

This analysis requires that it be impossible for split antecedents of a relative pronoun to be *wh*-Moved, and this indeed we find to be the case:

(102) a. *Who is on the A team and who is on the B team who are related?
b. *What did you buy and what did you sell that were of approximately equal value?
c. *What actor married and what actress divorced yesterday who once were engaged?
d. *Who did you hug and who did you kiss who are sisters?

These are the best examples I can find, and, fortunately, they do not quite make the grade.

It is reasonable to ask whether noun phrase complements always extrapose, or whether they can be generated at a distance from their heads. The following example, of a form pointed out to me by Michael Szamosi, shows that complement-like clauses can hang in space next to an idiomatic S:

(103) The cat is out of the bag that Freebie's on parole.

It thus seems that complement clauses can fill the position created by the S $\longrightarrow$ S $\bar{\text{S}}$ rule. But (103) is clearly not a noun complement. Should noun complements be generable at a distance from their heads, as are relatives and comparatives, the distinction between the predicate complement system and the determiner complement system would begin to fade, which would be unfortunate (but recall Baltin's example: *the proof which we discussed yesterday that Pi was irrational*).

I now turn to the indefinite comparative. Thiersch (1974) proposed that the subordinate clause originated in the Det of the matrix QP. Taking the *the* in the subordinate clause as its complementizer, he arrives at (104b) as the structure for (104a):

(104) a. The more pizza Mary eats, the fatter she gets.

(104) b.

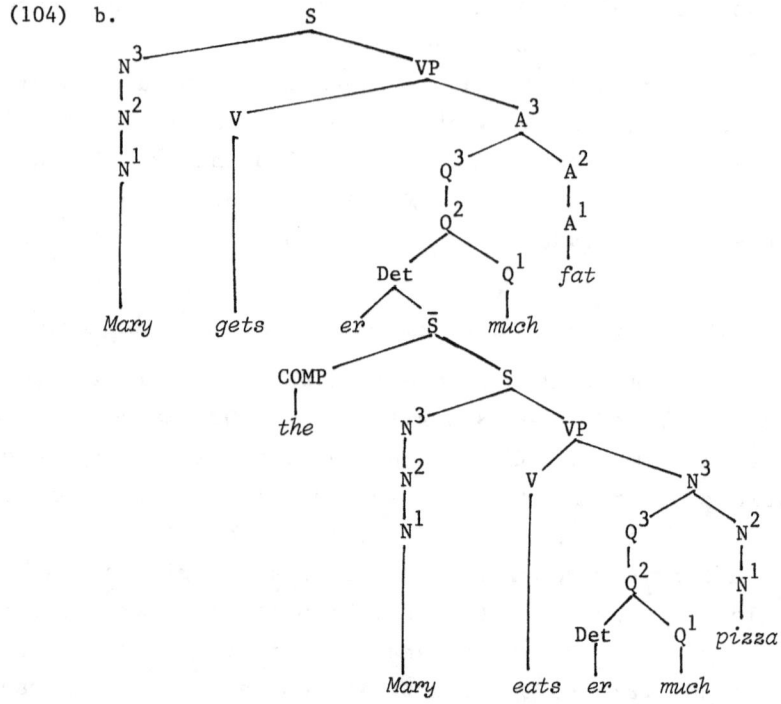

The subordinate clause is then preposed by a rule that replicates the *the*, producing the *the* in the second, matrix, clause of (104).

We have already seen that these *the*'s do not occupy COMP position, but rather Det position in their associated QP. Now the fall of the Det source for comparatives makes this proposal for these constructions considerably less attractive. Enthusiasm for this wanes still further when we observe that the *the*-clause preposing would have to be so constrained as to move the clause to the front of the clause it had 'scope' over:

(105) a. Bill says that the more you study, the less you know.
b. The more you study, the less Bill says you know.

By introducing these clauses with the $\bar{\bar{S}} \longrightarrow$ COMP ($\bar{S}$) S ($\bar{S}$) rule we may subsume them under the generalization noted for Marathi (section 1.1.3.5) that anticipatory clauses go semantically on the $\bar{S}$ they're in. In fact one may say generally that relative and comparative clauses go semantically on the S, if any, that they are sisters with.

Given this proposal, (106) is the deep structure for (104a):

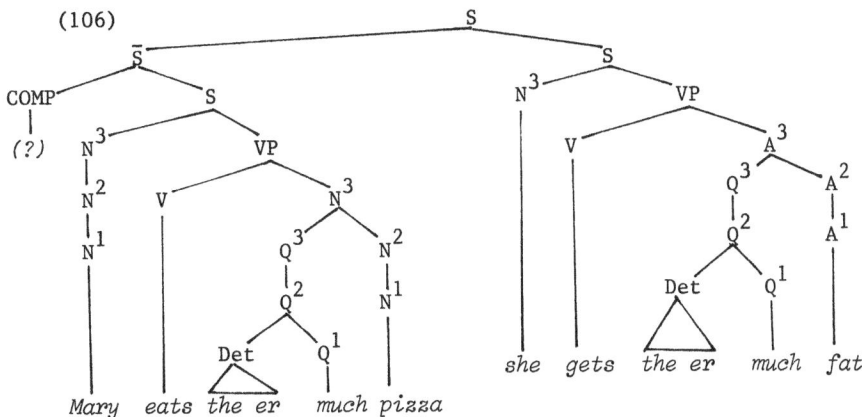

Observe that preposing of the *the-er* determined constituent happens in both the main and the subordinate clause. This suggests that the lexicalists' multi-barrelled COMP is really more like the old notion of 'Pre-Sentence': a place where all manner of things can be put, among them complementizers in Bresnan's original sense.

Taking the indefinite comparative as analogous to the anticipatory relative, we expect to find it in trailing position as well, and indeed we do:

(107) a. You know the less, you more you study.
 b. Mary gets the fatter, the more pizza she eats.

Observe that in the trailing construction the *the-er* determined constituent does not front. This structure reinforces our decision to analyse *the* as part of the Det of QP.

Thiersch observes a construction allied to the trailing indefinite comparative, in which the matrix does not have a *the-er* determiner, but an iterated comparative adjective: *Mary gets fatter and fatter, the more pizzas she eats.* This construction cannot be anticipatory: **the more pizzas she eats, the fatter and fatter she gets.* Thiersch notes that in this construction the matrix may be uttered by one speaker and the following clause by another: A: "*Mary gets fatter and fatter*". B: "*The more of those pizzas she eats!*" The genuine indefinite comparative distinguishes itself from this construction in not being divisible between two speakers in either its trailing or its anticipatory variants: *A: "Mary gets the fatter." B: "The more pizzas she eats!"; *A: "The more pizzas she eats" B: "The fatter Mary gets."

I would tentatively conclude that there is in addition to extraposed and trailing position at the end of the sentence something which I shall call 'afterthought position.' A clause is essentially independent of its afterthoughts, which may be uttered by a different speaker or not at all. Nonrestrictive relatives on sentences in *which*, but not in *as*, have the properties of afterthoughts: *as you know, our funds are being cut*, **which you know, our funds are being cut*; *A:"Ivan, our funds are being cut!" I: "as I told you they would be!"*, *A: "Ivan, our funds are being cut!" I: "which I already knew!"*. *as* thus appears to take the anticipatory/trailing construction, while *which* takes the afterthought construction.

We may finally note for the comparative system a lack paralleling that pointed out earlier for the relative system: extraposed position is a clause-final position that for both comparative and relative clauses has a great deal in common with embedded-headed position. There is no clause initial position that is related to embedded position.

2.3 *Global Relations:* I shall now develop the theory of extra-constituent structure relations that I have frequently invoked in the preceding pages. The theory is a development of interpretive theories of anaphora as explored in such works as Jackendoff (1972), Wasow (1972), Chomsky (1973) and Fiengo (1974), and of the 'global grammar' proposed by Lakoff (1971).

There are a number of objections commonly raised against interpretive theories that I wish to meet in the present one. The first is "How do you put it together?" Interpretive theories characteristically determine such relations as coreference or quantifier scope by examination of various levels of derived structure. How is the information thus determined integrated with that determined by examination of other levels of structure so as to form a coherent level of semantic representation? It is commonplace to point out that interpretive theories are really 'global', in the somewhat vague sense in which the word has come to be used. I shall here make fully explicit the nature of the 'globality' involved in my proposals.

Chomsky (1974-75 class lectures) has recently proposed that semantic interpretation is determined from surface structure augmented with 'traces' that mark positions from which things have been moved (see Fiengo (1974) for discussion of traces). Liberman (1974) has shown some interesting things that can be done within such a framework. Should the technical details of this approach prove forthcoming in a satisfactory manner, the provisions I make for globality will be unnecessary. They may, however, be eliminated with no consequences for the structure of the theory. Hence the present developments are compatible both with a traditional interpretivist outlook and with Chomsky's more recent ideas.

A more serious criticism is that interpretive rules are typically made up *ad hoc* for English, coming from no antecedently determined metatheory. There is therefore no clear distinction between the language-particular and the language-universal, and claims to have constrained linguistic theory by depriving the syntax of some power are evacuated by giving a wild card to the rules of interpretation. This charge is not really fair. Jackendoff writes, for example (Jackendoff 1973, p. 380):

> "This is not to say that the rules of semantic interpretation are universal, any more than the base or transformations are. It is clear, for example, that focus and presupposition are not realized with the same syntactic and phonological devices in all languages, and that reflexivization does not universally obey the constraints of English. What is claimed, rather, is that any device used to mark focus and presupposition, be it stress, syntactic position, or a focus morpheme, will be interpreted at the surface structure, conditioning

>a rule which performs the same operations upon the semantic
>interpretation; whatever the structural conditions on
>reflexivization, if there is reflexivization in a language,
>they will be operative at the end of cycles, conditioning
>a rule making an entry in the table of coreference. Similarly,
>one might guess that certain aspects of the environment for
>pronominalization and reflexivization are universal; it might
>turn out that there are only a small number of possible options
>available."

In spite of this, it still must be admitted that interpretive semantics smudges the distinction between language-particular grammar and universal metatheory outside of the syntactic component: there is no serious attempt to distinguish formulations of interpretive rules from the devices that apply them. Neither can it be said that 'generative semanticists' have done well with the problem. They have frequently made assertions that 'global rules' are better than 'indexing devices', but have not made much progress on putting satisfactory constraints on either.

In the following pages, I will set up a language-universal system for imposing certain extra-constituent structure relations, which I shall call 'global relations', on the phrase-markers in transformational derivations. Although most of the details of the system will be determined on the basis of English, the work on relative clauses in chapter 1 provides some basis for postulating the universality of the system proposed. The system will determine the constituent structure relations of relative clauses and their heads and their relative constituents. Although many problems will remain of how languages refer to these relations in the statement of rules, the result will still be a more substantially constrained approach to the phenomena than any that I am aware of. I emphasize again that it is the fact that the mechanisms are proposed as language universals that renders them metatheoretical provisions rather than *ad hoc* descriptions.

There is finally the question raised by McCawley (1973) of what the objects created by interpretivist rules of

'semantic interpretation' have to do with semantics, as
the term is used by logicians interested in natural language, philosophers of certain persuasions, and, increasingly,
linguists. I explicitly take the position that the global
relations I postulate are syntactic, rather than semantic,
objects. They would of course, play a rule in semantic
interpretation: for example, in systems of the form explored in Cooper and Parsons (1974), where rules are given
for translating constituent structures into logical formulae, the global relations I develop here would tell one
how to assign variables to NP and to variable-binding
operators. I presume that the contribution of the global
relations to semantic interpretation would be specifiable
universally for natural language.

2.3.1 *Node Indexing*: Global phenomena (such as the multi-level semantic interpretation typical of all but the most
recent interpretive theories) require the introduction
into syntax of some scheme of node indexing to keep track
of the 'corresponding nodes' relation. Lakoff (1971) takes
global phenomena as a warrant for sweeping reformulations
in the theory of grammar. Setting aside the technical difficulties with his proposals (see Soames (1974)), I do not
think that such drastic reformulations are called for.
The phenomena that are solid (and involve matters internal
to the derivation -- the dependencies of derivations on
extra-derivational and even extra-linguistic matters being
a different order of problem) can be dealt with by means of
various localized alterations in the theory, in the style
of Jackendoff. I shall therefore set up the corresponding
nodes relation so as to make minimum, virtually null,
changes in the theory of grammar.

I shall say that a phrase-marker is a well-formed terminal labelled bracketing in the sense of Peters and Ritchie
(1973) (thereby discarding the original usage of the term
as referring to a set of strings meeting certain conditions
designed to guarantee that it determine a tree). That is,
a phrase-marker is a string of terminal symbols and labelled brackets in which each bracket matches with a bracket

that has the same label. I furthermore stipulate that in indexed phrase-marker is like a phrase-marker but has the additional feature that each right bracket bears a positive integer as a superscript. Finally, a regularly indexed phrase-marker is an indexed phrase-marker in which the first right bracket has superscript 1, and second 2, and so forth.

It is clear that there is only one way of applying indices to a phrase-marker so as to get a regularly indexed phrase-marker. Therefore, instead of starting out a transformational derivation with a phrase-marker produced by the base, we can start it with the regularly indexed phrase-marker corresponding to one produced by the base (the rules of which could not supply the indices at all without being context sensitive). (108) is then a simplified regularly indexed deep structure for *John admires Mary*:

(108) $[_S[_{NP}[_N \ John]_N^1]_{NP}^2[_{Aux}[_T \ Pres]_T^3]_{Aux}^4[_{VP}[_V \ admire]_V^5$
$[_{NP}[_N \ Mary]_N^6]_{NP}^7]_{VP}^8]_S^9$

It remains to provide conventions for the preservation of node-indices under transformations.

I believe that the elementaries may be constrained to Deletion, Chomsky adjunction and Substitution. Deletion poses no problem. For the other two, I propose the obvious: the node created by Chomsky adjunction bears the node index (along with all the category features) of the node adjoined to, while in Substitution the node substituted for disappears entirely, along with its index, and is replaced by the substituting node, along with its index. I will give an example involving Substitution.

Bresnan (1972) proposed that passive sentences had underlyingly empty subjects, with the NP in the agent phrase (the logical subject) generated in that position in deep structure. Assuming this, a somewhat simplified deep structure for *John is admired by Mary* might be (109a), with (109b) being the structure derived from (109a) by Object Preposing:

(109) a. $[_S[_{NP}*]^1_{NP}[_{Aux}[_T Pres]^2_T]^3_{Aux}[_{VP}[_{Pass} \text{ be en}]^4_{Pass}$

$[_V \text{ admire}]^5_V[_{NP}[_N \text{ Mary}]^6_N]^7_{NP}[_{PP}[_P \text{ by}]^8_P$

$[_{NP}[_N \text{ John}]^9_N]^{10}_{NP}]^{11}_{PP}]^{12}_{VP}]^{13}_S$

b. $[_S[_{NP}[_N \text{ Mary}]^6_N]^7_{NP}[_{Aux}[_T Pres]^2_T]^3_{Aux}[_{VP}[_{Pass} \text{ be en}$

$]^4_{Pass}[_V \text{ admire}]^5_V[_{PP}[_P \text{ by}]^8_P[_{NP}[_N \text{ John}]^9_N]^{10}_{NP}]^{11}_{PP}$

$]^{12}_{VP}]^{13}_S$

'*' is a special terminal hypothesized by Fiengo (1974) to be insertable by convention under any phrase node in the base. A derivation that reaches the surface with surviving '*' is ungrammatical. Hence Object preposing must apply to (109a), there being no other applicable rule that could erase the '*' (Fiengo supposes that there is a rule of agent postposing that applies in Passives, putting the subject into the *-filled NP of a *by*-phrase, but this is an independent matter).

Fiengo also proposes that when a constituent is moved, the symbol 't' is left in the position from which the constituent is extracted. 't' is said to be 'bound' by the moved constituent, and if a derivation reaches the surface with a 't' (trace) which commands and precedes that which binds it, then the derivation blocks. Agent postposing thus may yield a structure exactly like (109a) with '*' replaced by 't', to which Object preposing must apply to erase the trace.

We might formalise Fiengo's proposal by recasting the deletion elementary so as to replace each maximal deleted constituent with '$[_L t]^n_L$' where L is the label of that constituent and n is its index. Carrying this out in a framework in which variables are deleted is rather messy. In Fiengo's framework, the Deletion elementary is restricted to constituents, and furthermore to constituents which the transformation doing the deletion replicates elsewhere by Substitution or Chomsky adjunction.

With traces left by movement in the manner specified

above, Object preposing would derive (110) from (109a):

(110) $[_S[_{NP}[_N \textit{Mary}]_N^6]_{NP}^7[_{Aux}[_T \textit{Pres}]_T^2]_{Aux}^3[_{VP}[_{Pass} \textit{be en}]_{Pass}^4[_V \textit{admire}]_V^5[_{NP}t]_{NP}^7[_{PP}[_P \textit{by}]_P^8[_{NP}[_N \textit{John}]_N^9]_{NP}^{10}]_{PP}^{11}]_{VP}^{12}]_S^{13}$

There is a final problem connected with the rule of Right Node Raising and other potential rules applying to coordinate structures. Some of these rules perhaps have the effect of fusing two constituents into one. What relation does the index of *John* in *Bill admires, and Susan detests, John* have to do with the indices of the two occurrences of *John* in *Bill admires John and Susan detests John*? It is not clear to me what sort of operations effect Right Node Raising, so any decision here is somewhat premature, but I will venture the guess that it is the final node of the last conjunct that is raised, with the final nodes of the others being deleted. Hence the raised *John* will have the index of the underlying second occurrence of *John*.

If we now associate with a constituent structure a relation specified in the form of some sort of table composed of node-indices, we can apply transformations to the constituent structure, and the table will continue to induce the relations we desire over the constituent structures derived by the transformations. We can thus represent those properties and relations which seem to be globally present in the derivation without any significant disruption in the theory of grammar.

One might in fact claim that a node-indexing scheme was implicit in the *Aspects* theory of grammar, and even in that of *Syntactic Structures*. For in the *Aspects* framework the structural description of a sentence is a pair (∅,   ), where ∅ is a surface structure and   is its deep structure. One of the tasks of the structural description is to indicate the underlying grammatical relations between the constituents of the surface structure. It is difficult to imagine how the structural description could accomplish this without the aid of a node-indexing scheme.

I will illustrate the technique with an over-simplified

treatment of coreference. Generate a regularly indexed deep structure, take it to surface structure with the transformational component, and then set up a table of coreference as a set of ordered pairs of node-indices meeting the following conditions:

(111) a. each index that appears in the table indexes an NP node in the surface structure
b. the table determines an equivalence relation
c. if (x, y) is in the table, and the node indexed by x precedes and commands the node indexed by y, then the node indexed by y is a pronoun

Condition (111c) is derived from unpublished work by Howard Lasnik. A well-formed sentence structure is then a triple (Φ, Ψ, C), where Ψ is a regularly indexed deep structure provided by the base, Φ is derived from Ψ by the transformational component, and C is a table of coreference assigned to Ψ by (111). The sentence structure can clearly determine a semantic interpretation in the desired manner.

The treatment above is of course only illustrative: it does not treat of reflexivization, for example. But the technique is obviously applicable to more sophisticated proposals, such as those of Jackendoff (1972).

There is no essential difference between this kind of treatment and one in which the relevant properties and relations are inscribed directly into the phrase-markers, as by the 'coreference index' proposal of *Aspects*. I believe, however, that the present approach is somewhat more perspicuous to the mind.

It is obvious that we must specify exactly what sorts of tables are allowed in universal grammar, and how they may be tied to syntactic structure. Without such specifications, a mechanism such as the one I have proposed is merely an arbitrary indexing device, allowing such absurd consequences as those pointed out by Cole (1973).

2.3.2 *The Head-COMP Relation*: We have seen various reasons for believing that there is some sort of relation subsisting between a relative or comparative clause and its head.

There is first of all the fact that these clauses have their heads in construction with them, even though they may be separated by an unbounded stretch of material. Next, we may observe the *er...than.../as...as...* dependencies and the mirror-image constraint in the English comparative system, or the requirement in the Indic languages discussed in chapter 1 that the head of an anticipatory relative be definite. We may also observe such paradigms as (112) (based on Vergnaud (1974:90-93):

(112) a. The woman started sewing and the man started reading who had been shouting at each other.
b. A woman started sewing and a man started reading who had been shouting at each other.
c. *The woman started sewing and a man started reading who had been shouting at each other.
d. *A woman started sewing and the man started reading who had been shouting at each other.

Something has to squeeze these determiners into a ball in order to enforce the requirement that they be the same.

There are essentially two ways in which one might go about setting up such a system. We might say that there was a direct relation subsisting between the head and its 'equivalent' constituent in the dependent clause. We may represent this situation with the diagram (113):

(113) ...A...[$_{\bar{S}}$ COMP...B...]...

The $\bar{S}$ that is the relative or comparative clause (and thereby its COMP) is uniquely identified because it is the maximal constituent dominating the 'target' (dependent) constituent but not the head.

Unfortunately, many of the properties of comparatives are replicated by result clauses and infinitive complements of *too*; *so...that...* and *too...for...* present the same selection problem as to *er...than...* and *as...as...* . We may furthermore see that these constructions also obey the mirror-image constraint:

(114) a. So many more people than I invited that I couldn't count them came to the party.

b. *So many more people that I couldn't count them than
I invited came to the party.
c. So many more people than I invited came to the party
that I couldn't count them.
d. *So many more people that I couldn't count them came
to the party than I invited.
e. So many more people came to the party than I invited
that I couldn't count them.
f. *So many more people came to the party that I couldn't
count them than I invited.

(115) a. Too many more people than I invited for us to count
came to the party.
b. *Too many more people for us to count than I invited
came to the party.
c. Too many more people than I invited came to the
party for us to count.
d. *Too many more people for us to count came to the
party than I invited.
e. Too many more people came to the party than I
invited for us to count.
f. *Too many more people came to the party for us
to count than I invited.

We therefore need a relation that holds between the clause and its head.

Since the morphology of the COMP and the morphology of the Det of the head are interdependent, I will represent the relation as holding between the Det of the head and the COMP of the clause, and call the relation the Head-COMP relation.

Questions with *wh*-words are in many ways analogous to relative clauses. But since questions lack heads, we could not use a head-target constituent relation to identify the target constituents of a question in the fashion of (113). Rather, there must be a relation (usually formalized as co-indexing) between the COMP of the question and its target constituent. Let this relation be called the COMP-target relationship. If we assume that it subsists in relative clauses as well as in interrogatives, we may replace (113) with (116):

(116) ...A...[$_{\bar{S}}$ COMP...B...]...

(113) and (116) are pretty much the most economical way to represent the necessary relations for relative and comparative clauses, and when we look at more clause types, (116) turns out to require the fewest sorts of primitive relations. In this subsection, I will develop the axioms for the Head-COMP relation, and in the next those for the COMP-target relation.

We have seen that a COMP can have a whole set of heads. Hence we want the Head-COMP table (referred to henceforth as H) to consist of a set of n-tuples $(x, y_1, \ldots, y_n)$ where x is the index of a COMP node and $y_1, \ldots, y_n$ are the indices of Det nodes. We will want an axiom to enforce the requirement that the heads are in construction with, but not contained by, the $\bar{S}$ of the COMP. This is achieved by (117b) below. We may secondly observe that a Det can be head for only one COMP, and I will also suppose that for each COMP there is only one entry. This is accomplished by (117c). I thus give the following principles governing the assignment of a Head-COMP table to an indexed phrase-marker:

(117) For an indexed phrase-marker ϕ, H is a well-formed Head-COMP table only if

$$H = \{(x_1, y_{1,1}, \ldots, y_{1,m_1}),$$
$$\vdots$$
$$(x_n, y_{n,1}, \ldots, y_{n,m_n})\}$$

where

(a) for $i = 1, \ldots, n$, x_i is the index of a COMP in ϕ and for $j = 1, \ldots, m_j$, y_i, j is the index of a Det in ϕ.

(b) if $(x, y_1, \ldots, y_m) \, \varepsilon \, H$, then the nodes indexed by $y_1, \ldots, y_m$ are not dominated by the node immediately dominating the node indexed by x, but they are dominated by the node immediately dominating that node.

(c) H mentions no index twice.

(117) captures the major structural conditions. To actually rule sentences out, however, we need an additional mechanism to enforce some requirements of consistency.

Edmonds (1970), Chomsky (1973) and Vergnaud (1974) have proposed analyses in which COMP is treated as an increasingly complex node, expanding into a wide variety of things. I shall develop this further by supposing that there is a 'place' in COMP wherein are placed the features of the determiners that the COMP may take as head. Whether this 'place' should be treated as a constituent or as a new kind of feature I do not really know. I shall take the latter course. I shall represent it as a symbol $[\pm F_1 \ldots \pm F_k]_D$, where the $\pm F_i$ are the features over which consistency is enforced. This symbol may be treated as a component of the label of the COMP brackets. By requiring the $[\ldots]_D$ symbol to be featurally nondistinct from those of the determiners of the heads, we require these determiners to all have the same composition, and furthermore permit that composition to determine the formative used to spell the COMP. This solves the problem of the *er...than.../as...as...* selectional dependencies.

We may also observe that some clauses, such as English comparatives, or ordinary English relatives, require heads, while others, such as ordinary Navajo relatives, do not. We thus may suppose that there is in COMP a universal feature [±Hd]. A COMP that is [+Hd] must have a head; one that is [-Hd] does not have a head. I propose that the $[\ldots]_D$ symbol is present regardless of whether or not there is a head.

Formally, we may capture these requirements as follows:

(118) If ϕ is a phrase marker, and H is a well formed Head-COMP table for ϕ, then

(a) if x is the index of a [+COMP +Hd] node in , then there are $y_1, \ldots, y_m$ such that $(x, y_1, \ldots, y_m)$ is an element of H

(b) if $(x, y_1, \ldots, y_m)$ is an element of H then the node indexed by x is [+Hd [...]$_D$], where '[...]' is nondistinct from the node indexed by each y_i, $i = 1, \ldots, m$.

Finally, we must propose a feature system. I shall first distinguish nominal determiners from QP determiners by having the former be [+ND -QD] and the latter [-ND +QD]. Amongst the nominal determiners, *the* is of course [+Def] while *a*, etc., is [-Def]. Amongst the QP determiners *er* and *as* will be [+Cm -Rs] and *too* and *so* will be [-Cm +Rs]. (Cm for 'comparative', Rs for 'resultative'). Finally, *er* will be [+≠], and *as* will be [-≠], while *too* will be [+Ex] and *so* will be [-Ex]. My choices here are somewhat arbitrary, serving merely to distinguish from each other the formatives involved, and to impose upon them an intuitively reasonable classification. At present, I would not suppose that these features are at all the correct ones. I do believe, however, that the correct features should be taken as belonging to some language-universal feature framework. Much more work in various languages would be required to acquire a real understanding of the kind of feature system necessary.

We can now see that we need merely specify that *than* goes into a [+COMP +Hd [-ND +QD +Cm +Rs + ≠]$_D$] node in order to state the fundamental facts of its distribution. The other complementizers may be dealt with in a precisely comparable fashion. The feature +R introduced in Chapter 1 to distinguish the complementizers of relative clauses may be taken to be a symbol for [+ND -QD ...]$_D$.

We are now in a position to rule out some sentences. I shall first consider an example in which a comparative clause occurs in an S together with a QP that has the appropriate determiner, but the clause is not in construction with the QP:

(119)

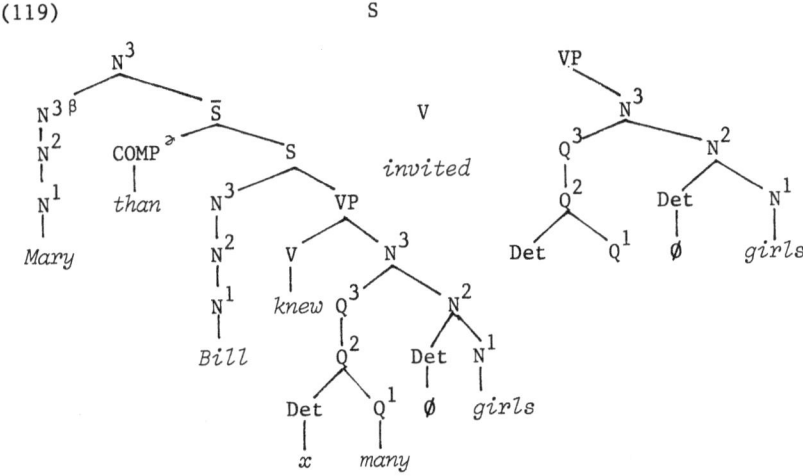

I have left out various inessential nodes, and given only certain crucial node-indices in the form of Greek-letter superscripts.

By the lexicon, ₂ must be [+COMP +Hd]. But then, by (118a), there must be $(x, y_1, \ldots, y_n) \in H$ such that $x = $ ₂, and by (117a) the nodes indexed by $y_1, \ldots, y_n$ must be [+Det]. But by (117b), they must be in β, and there are no such nodes in β. Therefore the structure has no Head-COMP table that satisfies the required conditions, and the sentence *Mary [than Bill know girls] invited more girls is ruled out. QED.

Another example, in which the constituent structures are O.K. but the determiners and complementizers do not agree properly, is (120):

(120)

[Tree diagram:
S branches to N³ and VP
N³ branches to N³γ and S̄
N³γ branches to Q³ and N²
Q³ branches to Q² and Det N¹ (with ∅ girls)
Q² branches to Det β and Q¹
Det β → er; Q¹ → many
N² → Det N¹ → ∅ girls
S̄ branches to COMP ə and S
S branches to N³ and VP
N³ → N² → N¹ → I
VP branches to V and N³
V → invited
N³ branches to Q³ and N²
Q³ → Q² → Det Q¹; Det → x, Q¹ → many
N² → Det N¹ → ∅ girls
VP: V came, PP
PP → P to, N³
N³ → N² → Det the, N¹ party]

By the lexicon, ə will be $[+\text{COMP} +\text{Hd} [-\text{ND} +\text{QD} +\text{Cm} -\text{Rs} -\neq]_D]$.
But by (118a), there must be $(\text{ə}, y_1, \ldots, y_m) \in H$, where
$y_1, \ldots, y_m$ index determiners within γ. β is the only
candidate. But β is $[-\text{ND} +\text{QD} +\text{Cm} -\text{Rs} +\neq]$, so it disagrees
with γ, and therefore condition (118b) cannot be met.
Hence the sentence *more girls as I invited came to the
party has no well formed Head-COMP table and is therefore
ungrammatical.

Now let us consider the mirror-image constraint. (121)
is a typical acceptable structure and (122) is a typical
violation:

(121) As many er many people than I invited as you

predicted came to the party.

(122) *As many er many people as you predicted than I

invited came to the party.

There are sufficiently many other string-tangling phenomena
in syntax to make a formulation of the constraint premature
(or trivial). I merely observe that the Head-COMP relation
provides the strings to tangle.

Multiple headed comparatives and result clauses are
compatible with the principles (117-118). They enforce the
requirement that the determiners all be the same. That this

is correct is evidenced by (123):

(123) a. Fewer people moved more cinder blocks this time than ever before.
b. As many people moved as many cinder blocks this time as ever before.
c. *As many people moved more cinder blocks this time as/than ever before.

Note the inexplicable *as few people moved as many cinder blocks this time as ever before. This somewhat casts into doubt the significance of (123).

More interesting cases of the consistency requirement being enforced are those involving relatives, since here, there is no overt formative in the COMP that is selected on the basis of what appears in the determiners of the head. Relative clauses also give some evidence with regard to what features the consistency requirement is to be enforced over. (124) is grammatical:

(124) One man came in and three women went out who were related.

Yet the Det of *one man* is [+Sg] and that of *three women* is [-Sg]. This shows that ±Sg is not specified in $[...]_D$.

This leads to an immediate prediction: because ±Def appears in $[...]_D$, there will be languages in which there are complementizers that require definite heads, and because ±Sg is not in $[...]_D$ there will not be languages in which there are complementizers that require singular heads. As far as I know, both of these predictions are borne out. In Navajo (sections 1.1.2.1, 1.1.3.6), the complementizer *ígíí/ę́ę́* is only used to form definite descriptions, whether in the internal head, pre-relative or extraposed relative construction. We may thus specify *ígíí/ę́ę́* in the lexicon as being [+COMP [+ND -QD +Def]$_D$] leaving it unspecified with respect to ±Hd (the features that specifies whether there is a head or not). English contains a near miss to the claim that no languages have complementizers that select a certain number on their heads in the form of the paucal relative clause (section 1.1.2.2).

The reader may well be suspicious about one of the properties of (117): (117a) involves a crucial mention of the category 'Det'. Our suspicions deepen when we note that there are words such as *sufficient/sufficiently*, that are clearly A, and *enough*, which the $*Q^0\ A^0$ Filter shows to be a Q (*tall enough*, **enough tall*; *different enough, enough different*), that take *for* (and maybe sometimes *that*) complements, just as does *too*.

Reflecting on this problem leads us to an important revision in (117-118). Why not say that the COMP is connected not to a Det, but to a [-COMP] node bearing a $[...]_D$ feature.[7] The consistency requirement is then merely that the contents of the two $[...]_D$ features be identical (or perhaps nondistinct).

Making this move, we can form a unified reformulation of (117, 118), combining (117a) and (118b):

(125) For an indexed phrase-marker ϕ, H is a well-formed Head-COMP table only if

$$H = (x_1, y_{1,1}, \ldots, y_{1,m_1}),$$
$$\vdots$$
$$(x_n, y_{n,1}, \ldots, y_{n,m_n})$$

where

(a) for $i = 1, \ldots, n$, x_i is the index of a [+COMP +Hd $[...]_D$] node in ϕ and for $1 \leq j \leq m_i$, $y_{i,j}$ is the index of a [-COMP [---]$_D$] node such that ... is identical to ---

(b) if $(x, y_1, \ldots, y_m) \varepsilon H$, then the nodes indexed by $y_1, \ldots, y_m$ are not dominated by the node immediately dominating the node indexed by x, but they are dominated by the node immediately dominating that node

(c) no index is mentioned twice in H

(e) if x is the index of a [+COMP +Hd] node
in ϕ, then there are $y_1, \ldots, y_m$ such
that $(x, y_1, \ldots, y_m) \varepsilon H$

We may classify a node that is a $[\ldots]_D$ symbol as [+D], and one that lacks one as [-D]. [+D] is then the feature borne by those elements that participate in the determiner complement system, be they determiners or not. 'D' may be thought of as something that is either absent, or present in a variety of forms (but not, of course, being absent in a variety of forms).

At what level of the derivation does (125) hold? one possibility is that it holds only at surface structure. In this case, our elimination of the 'Det' specification was well advised, for *er* Shift surely removes the Det node from over *er*. Under our new treatment, however, it need only be assured that *er* Shift moves the $[\ldots]_D$ specification onto the Q: *more* can then be treated like *enough*.

If semantic interpretation can be determined entirely off of surface structure, then we can effect a grand simplification of the theory by simply eliminating the indices, and building H out of occurrences of substrings in the labelled bracketing that is the surface structure. There is another interesting possibility, however, which is to claim that (125) holds for H throughout a derivation. One would generate an indexed deep structure, supply a Head-COMP table, check to see if (125) was satisfied, and then in the derivation recheck after each rule has applied. (125) would then serve to prohibit a wide variety of derivational shenanigans.

I have sought to explain some phenomena by means of the hypothesis that there is in COMP something, I shall call it a complex feature, that recapitulates the determiner of the head, or, more accurately, the determiner-like aspect of the head. When there is no head, this complex feature performs the function that the head's determiner would perform. We are saying, then, that it is in some sense essential for the relative clause to have a determiner, and that it is the same as the determiner of the head, if there is any. This is not a new idea in linguistics, being one of the central proposals in Benveniste's classic (1975) article on the relative clause.

2.3.3 *The COMP-Target Relation:* To complete the picture, it remains to set up the relation that holds between COMP and the target constituents. This relation can be set up as a table T of sequences, similar to H, the head-COMP table, but obeying somewhat different conditions. From the existence of multiple *wh* word questions and relative clauses, we can see the necessity for a COMP to have several targets. But clearly, a target is related to only one COMP. There is the further requirement that the target(s) be contained within the $\bar{S}$ of the COMP.

These principles may be given a preliminary form as (125):

(126) For an indexed phrase marker ϕ, T is a well-formed COMP-Target table only if

$$T = (x_1, y_{1,1}, \ldots, y_{1,m_1}),$$
$$\vdots$$
$$(x_n, y_{n,1}, \ldots, y_{n,m_n})$$

where

(a) for $i = 1, \ldots, n$, x_n indexes a COMP in ϕ
for $j = 1, \ldots, n_m$, $y_{i,j}$ indexes a Det in ϕ

(b) If $(x, y_1, \ldots, y_m) \in T$, then the node immediately dominating the node indexed by x dominates the nodes indexed by $y_1, \ldots, y_m$

(c) no index is mentioned twice in T.

(126) is obviously parallel to (117).

(126) is by itself insufficient. We need something comparable to (118) to permit the lexical entries of formatives to specify that the formative is a relative pronoun, an interrogative, or whatever. We find, furthermore, something analogous to a consistency requirement: in the great

majority of languages, the relative pronoun is different in form from the interrogative. Hence the relative/interrogative pronoun choice is varying with the R/Q choice in the complementizer. I thus posit a complex feature 'W', which may contain the specification '+Q' for 'interrogative', and '-Q' for relative. A relative complementizer will have the feature composition [+COMP [-Q]$_W$], an interrogative complementizer (for a *wh* word question) will have the composition [+COMP [+Q]$_W$], a relative pronoun will be [-COMP [-Q]$_W$] and an interrogative will be [-COMP [+Q]$_W$].

We can thus formulate (127), parallel to (125):

(127) For an indexed phrase marker ϕ, T is a well-formed COMP-Target table only if

$$T = \begin{pmatrix} (x_1, y_{1,1}, \ldots, y_{1,m_1}), \\ \vdots \\ (x_n, y_{n,1}, \ldots, y_{n,m_n}) \end{pmatrix}$$

where

(a) for $i = 1, \ldots, n$, x_n indexes a [+COMP [...]$_W$] node and for $j = 1, \ldots, m_n$, $y_{i,j}$ indexes a [-COMP [---]$_W$] node such that ... is the same as ---.

(b) If $(x, y_1, \ldots, y_m) \in T$, then for $i = 1, \ldots, m$, the node immediately dominating the node indexed by x dominates the node indexed by y_i.

(c) no index is mentioned twice in T

(d) If z indexes a node that is [[...]$_W$], then there are $x, y_1, \ldots, y_m$ such that $(x, y_1, \ldots, y_m) \in T$ and either $z = x$ or for some i, $1 \leq i \leq m$, $z = y_i$.

I leave open the full range of contents of the $[\ldots]_W$ complex feature.

We can now specify the features we have used in the lexical entries for various pronouns so as to characterize their uses. English *wh*, for example, is [-COMP +W]. Modern Greek *o opíos* (a relative pronoun that cannot be used as an interrogative) is $[\text{-COMP } [\text{-Q}]_W]$.

We may deal with multiple headed constructions on the basis of the observation that multiple headed relative clauses either have several antecedents for one relative pronoun, or one antecedent for each relative pronoun. We do not find analogues to the teratologism (128):

(128) *A man$_i$ killed a woman$_j$ and a boy$_h$ kissed a girl$_k$ which males$_{i,h}$ were in love with which$_{j,k}$ females.

The following principle may therefore be proposed:

(129) If ϕ is an indexed phrase marker with Head-COMP table H and COMP-Target table T, then if $(x, y_1, \ldots, y_n) \in H$ and $(x, z_1, \ldots, z_m) \in T$ either $m = 1$ or $m = n$.

(129) enforces the restriction that in a relative clause with several *wh* words, each has its own head.

There are many ways in which one could continue to tighten up the system so as to capture well-known constraints. The 'strong crossover principle' that Crow (section 1.2.1.1) reveals to apply to *wh*-marking is an obvious candidate, and so is Chomsky's (1973) constraint that a *wh* word that is in a COMP is interpreted as bound by that COMP. I shall restrict myself to getting the system to recognize the major constituent structure types.

We may clearly discern three important kinds of relative clauses: the anticipatory and trailing relatives, the pre-, post- and extraposed relatives, and the headless relatives. I shall assume here that the pre- and post-relatives are all underlyingly what they are on the surface, hence rejecting the extraction analysis. (Observe that under the extraction analysis, the situation would arise in which the surface structure head and NP$_{rel}$ would have the same node index: thus the various *the's* in the well-formedness relations for the tables would suffer from presupposition failure. I can see no problem in replacing all these *the's* with *a's*). Comparative clauses fall into the first two families. I shall call the first family the adjoined clauses, the second the headed embedded, and the last the headless, as suggested in section 1.1.3.

We wish to explain the fact that typically, *wh* words and complementizers are usable in one, but not all of the three types of clauses. We further see in the indefinite comparative reason to believe that NP_{rel} and NP_{hd} share some complex feature.

I shall suppose that NP_{rel} shares the $[...]_D$ feature of its controlling COMP. This may be enforced by the following stipulation:

(130) If ϕ is a phrase marker with a well-formed COMP-Target relation T, and if for $(x, y_1, ..., y_m)$ ε T and for $i = 1, ..., m$, then the node indexed by x agrees with the node indexed by y_i on the composition of $[...]_D$.

I then suppose the various positional environments to impose a feature on the $[...]_D$ of the COMP of the relative clause. By (130), these specifications are also enforced in NP_{rel} and NP_{hd}, and so can influence the form of determiners, etc.

The three families may be distinguished with the features ±Ad and ±At. Anticipatory and trailing relatives are [+Ad -At]. Clauses generated by a rule of the form X → X $\bar{S}$ or X → $\bar{S}$ X are [-Ad +At]. Finally, clauses generated by X → $\bar{S}$ (headless clauses) are [-Ad -At]. Putting this in symbols, we get (131):

(131) If a [+COMP [-Q]$_W$]node is immediately dominated by
   (a) an $\bar{S}$ immediately dominated by $\bar{S}$, then it is also [[+Ad -At]$_D$].
   (b) an $\bar{S}$ immediately dominated by an X and sister to an X (where X is a category variable), then it is also [[-Ad +At]$_D$]

(c) an $\bar{S}$ immediately dominated by X and sister
to nothing, then it is also $[[-Ad\ -At]_D]$.

We may now distinguish some words by their featural specifications. Relative *which* is specified as $[-COMP\ [-Q]_W$ $[+ND\ -QD\ -Ad\ +A]_D]$. *the er* is $[-COMP\ [-ND\ +QD\ +Ad\ -At]_D]$. Bresnan's 'x' determiner is $[-COMP\ [-Q]_W\ [-ND\ +QD\ -Ad\ +At]_D]$.

Before closing the section and the chapter, I will describe briefly some principles that would assist a language learner in sorting out these types on the basis of minimal evidence. First, consider the extraposed versus the trailing clauses. Trailing clauses characteristically can appear in anticipatory position, but there is no matrix initial position for extraposed clauses. Note that this is also the case for afterthought clauses. If we suppose that intonation patterns suffice to distinguish afterthought from extraposed clauses, then we can discern the trailing clauses to be the non-afterthought clauses that never appear matrix initially. I suspect that intonation would also serve to distinguish extraposed from trailing clauses, which suggests that these positional facts are not really relevant to language-learning.

We have also observed a general principle that in a clause introduced by an $X \to X\ \bar{S}$ or $S \to \bar{S}\ X$ rule, which I shall also call an attached relative, NP_{rel} must usually be a pronoun, with Japanese being an apparent exception to this. We may establish a principle that includes Japanese under a non-extraction analysis (see section 1.3.1) by stipulating that in an attached relative structure NP_{rel} be anaphoric to NP_{hd} in the sense of Wasow (1972). It is a basic principle of anaphora that if NP A is anaphoric to NP B, then A must be more general than B. In the typical anticipatory relative, NP_{rel} is less general (i.e., is an NP like *wh-horse*), while NP_{hd} is just a pronoun. Hence the typical anticipatory relative cannot be misanalysed as a pre-relative without leading to violations of universal conditions.

There is a final consequence that we can extract from the anaphoricity condition. Vergnaud (1974) observes a constraint that a pronoun cannot be anaphoric to a containing NP. Hence (132) are ungrammatical:

(132) a. *The fact$_i$ that it$_i$ was discovered is amazing.

b. *Pictures$_i$ of collectors of them$_i$ are on the wall.

This condition, together with the condition that NP_{rel} of an attached relative clauses be anaphoric to NP_{hd} requires that an embedded relative attached to an NP be introduced by NP → NP $\bar{S}$: for NOM → NOM $\bar{S}$, and N → N $\bar{S}$ would not provide for NP_{rel} an NP_{hd} that did not dominate it. Hence solely on the basis of examples like *the boy who died*, etc., we are forced to get the NP → NP $\bar{S}$ rule, which provides the constituent structure needed for the examples like *the boy and the girl who were engaged*.

The system of relations would thus appear to permit one to formulate principles that contribute in a demonstrable way towards making relative clause construction in principle learnable.

FOOTNOTES TO CHAPTER 2

1. Much of the material in this chapter is based on this article, which I shall henceforth refer to as merely 'Bresnan'. I am heavily indebted to Joan Bresnan and Mark Liberman for discussions of many of the subjects treated here.

2. I am indebted to Dorothy Siegel for uttering this example, and to Mark Liberman for pointing out that she had.

BIBLIOGRAPHY

Anderson, S.R: in preparation, 'Ergativity and Linguistic Structure.'

Anderson, S.R. and P. Kiparksy, (eds.): 1973, A Festschrift for Morris Halle, Holt, Rinehart and Winston.

Andrews, A.D.: 1974, 'One(s) Deletion in the Comparative Clause,' in NELS V, 246-255.

Ashton, E.O.: 1944, Swahili Grammar, London: Green & Co..

Bach. Emmon: 1965, 'On Some Recurrent Types of Transformations,' in C. W. Kreidler (ed.), Sixteenth Annual Round Table Meeting on Linguistics and Language Studies, Georgetown University Monograph Series on Languages and Linguistics 18.

Baker, C.L.: 1965, Indirect Questions in English, unpublished Ph.D. dissertation, Indiana University.

Baker, C.L.: 1970, 'Notes on the Description of English Questions: the Role of an Abstract Question Morpheme,' Foundations of Language 6, 197-219.

Benveniste, Émile: 1957, 'La Phrase Relative, Problème de Syntax Générale,' in Problèmes de Linguistique Générale, Paris: Galimard.

Bergsland, Knut: 1965, 'A Grammatical Outline of the Eskimo Language of West Greenland,' ms., Oslo.

Bowers, John: 1970, 'Adjectives and Adverbs in English,' distributed by the Indiana University Linguistics Club.

Brame, M.K.: 1968, 'A New Analysis of the Relative Clause: Evidence for an Interpretive Theory,' ms., MIT.

Bresnan, J.W.: 1970, 'On Complementizers: Towards a Syntactic Theory of Complement Types,' <u>Foundations of Language</u> 6, 297-321.

Bresnan, J.W.: 1972, <u>The Theory of Complementation in English Syntax</u>, unpublished Ph.D. dissertation, MIT.

Bresnan, J.W.: 1973, 'Syntax of the Comparative Clause Construction in English,' <u>Linguistic Inquiry</u> 4, 275-344.

Bresnan, J.W.: 1974a, 'On the Position of Certain Clause Particles in Phrase Structure,' <u>Linguistic Inquiry</u> 5, 614-619.

Bresnan, J.W.: 1974b, 'Comparative Deletion and Constraints on Transformations,' <u>Linguistic Analysis</u> 1, 25-74. Actually appeared in 1975.

Browne, Wayles: 1970, 'More on Definite Markers: Interrogatives in Persian,' <u>Linguistic Inquiry</u> 1, 259-263.

Carslon, G.N. and L.W. Martin: 1974, 'Relative Clauses and Resumptive Pronouns,' ms., University of Iowa.

Chomsky, N.A.: 1957, <u>Syntactic Structures</u>, The Hague: Mouton.

Chomsky, N.A.: 1965, <u>Aspects of the Theory of Syntax</u>, Cambridge, MA: MIT Press.

Chomsky, N.A.: 1970, 'Remarks on Nominalization,' in Peters and Rosenbaum (eds.).

Chomksy, N.A.: 1973, 'Conditions on Transformations,' in Anderson and Kiparsky (eds.).

Cooper, Robin and Terence Parsons: 1974, 'Montague Grammar, Generative Semantics and Interpretive Semantics,' published in Partee, B.H. (ed.) (1976), <u>Montague Grammar</u>, Academic Press.

Cole, Peter: 1973, 'Global Grammar and Index Grammar,' <u>Studies in the Linguistic Sciences</u> 3:1, University of Illinois.

Donaldson, Susan: 1971, 'Movement in Restrictive Relative Clauses in Hindi,' <u>Studies in the Linguistic Sciences</u> 1:2, University of Illinois.

East African Swahili Committee: 1955-58, <u>Studies in Swahili Dialect</u>, Kampala: Maberere College.

Emonds, J.E.: 1970, <u>Root and Structure Preserving Transformations</u>, unpublished Ph.D. dissertation, MIT. Distributed by the Indiana University Linguistics Club. Revised version published in 1976 as <u>A Transformational Approach to English Syntax</u>, Academic Press.

Fiengo, R.W.: 1974, <u>Semantic Conditions on Surface Structure</u>, unpublished Ph.D. dissertation, MIT. Revised version published in 1980 as <u>Surface Structure: the Intersection of Autonomous Components</u>, Harvard University Press.

Geis, M.L.: 1970, <u>Adverbial Subordinate Clauses in English</u>, unpublished Ph.D. dissertation, MIT.

Ginsburg, Seymour and Parbara Partee: 1969, 'A Mathematical Model for Transformational Grammars,' <u>Information and Control</u> 16, 297-334.

Gorbet, L.F.: 1974, <u>Relativization and Complementation in Diegueno: Noun Phrases as Nouns</u>, unpublished Ph.D. dissertation, UCSD.

Hale, K.H.: 1970, 'Relative Clauses in Some Non-Indo-European Languages,' Paper presented at NELS V, Cambridge, MA. Warlpiri data published in Hale (1976).

Hale, K.H.: 1976, 'The Adjoined Relative Clause in Australia,' in R.M.W. Dixon (ed.), <u>Grammatical Categories in Australian Languages</u>, Canberra: Australian Institute of Aboriginal Studies.

Hankamer, Jorge: 1971, <u>Constraints on Deletion in Syntax</u>, unpublished Ph.D. dissertation, Yale University. Published in 1979 by Garland Press.

Hankamer, Jorge: 1974, 'On Wh Indexing,' in <u>NELS V</u>, 61-76.

Hintikka, Jaakko: 1974, 'Quantifiers vs. Quantification Theory,' <u>Linguistic Inquiry</u> 5, 153-178.

Jackendoff, R.S.: 1972, <u>Semantic Interpretation in Generative Grammar</u>, Cambridge, MA: MIT Press.

Jackendoff, R.S.: 1973, 'The Base Rules for Prepositions,' in Anderson and Kiparsky (eds.).

Jacobs, Roderick, and Peter Rosenbaum, (eds.): 1970, <u>Readings In English Transformational Grammar</u>, Waltham, MA: Ginn and Co..

Jeanne, Laverne: 1974, 'The Relative Clause in Hopi,' ms., MIT.

Junghare, I.Y.: undated, 'Restrictive Relative Clauses in Marathi,' ms., University of Minnesota.

Kaufman, E.S.: 1974, 'Navajo Spatial Enclitics: A Case for Unbounded Movement,' <u>Linguistic Inquiry</u> 5, 507-534.

Keenan, E.L.: 1972, 'On Semantically Based Grammar,' <u>Linguistic Inquiry</u> 3, 412-462.

Keenan, E.L. and Bernard Comrie: 1972, 'NP Accessibility and Universal Grammar,' ms.. Published as Keenan and Comrie (1977).

Keenan, E.L. and Bernard Comrie: 1977, 'Noun Phrase Accessiblity and Universal Grammar,' Linguistic Inquiry 8, 63-99.

Kleinschmidt, S.: 1851, Grammatik der Grönlandischen Sprache, Hildesheim: Georg Olms Verlags Buchhandlung.

Klokeid, T.J.: 1970, 'Research on Mabuiag,' ms., MIT.

Kuno, Susumu: 1971, 'The Position of Locatives in Existential Sentences,' Linguistic Inquiry 2, 333-378.

Kuno, Susumu: 1973, The Structure of the Japanese Language, Cambridge, MA: MIT Press.

Kuno, Susumu: 1974, 'The Position of Relative Clauses and Conjunctions,' Linguistic Inquiry 5, 117-136.

Kuno, Susumu and J.J. Robinson: 1972, 'Multiple Wh Questions,' Linguistic Inquiry 3, 463-488.

Kuroda, S.-Y.: 1969, 'English Relativization and Certain Related Problems,' in Reibel and Schane (eds.).

Lakoff, G.P.: 1969, 'On Generative Semantics,' in D.D. Steinberg and Jacobovits, L.A. (eds.), Semantics, Cambridge, England: Cambridge University Press.

Lakoff, G.P.: 1974, 'Syntactic Amalgams,' in CLS 10, 321-344.

Lalou, Marcelle: 1950, Manuel Elementaire de Tibetain Classique, Paris: Imprimerie Nationale.

Lambton, A.K.S.: 1967, Persian Grammar, Cambridge, England: Cambridge University Press.

Lewis, G.L.: 1953, Teach Yourself Turkish, London: English Universities Press.

Lewis, G.L.: 1967, *Turkish Grammar*, London: Oxford University Press.

Liberman, Mark: 1974, 'On Conditioning the Rule of Subject Aux Inversion,' in *NELS V*, 77-91.

Lockwood, W.B.: 1964, *An Introduction to Modern Faroese*, Copenhagen: Munksgaard.

Loogman, Alfons: 1965, *Swahili Grammar and Syntax*, Pittsburg, PA: Duquesne University Press.

Lowie, R.H.: 1941, *The Crow Language*, Berkely and Los Angelese, CA: University of California Press.

Malisdorf, Zafrira: 1974, 'Relative Clauses in Hebrew,' ms., CUNY, New York.

Martin, L.W.: 1972, *Apposative and Restrictive Relative Clauses in English*, unpublished Ph.D. dissertation, University of Texas at Austin.

McCawley, J.D.: 1972, 'Japanese Relative Clauses,' in Peranteau, Levi and Phares (eds.).

McCawley, J.D.: 1973, 'External NPs versus Annotated Deep Structure,' *Linguistic Inquiry* 4, 221-240.

Meinhof, Karl: 1909, *Lehrbuch der Nama-Sprache*, Berlin: Druck und Verlag um Georg Reimer.

Montague, Richard: 1974, *Formal Philosophy*, New Haven, Connecticut: Yale University Press. Edited by Richard Thomason.

Peranteau, P.M, J.N. Levi and G.C. Phares, (eds.): 1972, *The Chicago Witch Hunt*, Chicago, IL: Chicago Linguistic Society.

Perkins, Ellavina: 1975, 'Extrapostion of Relative Clauses in Navajo ,' *Diné Bizaad Nánil'įįh* (The Navajo Language Review) **2**, Number 2.

Perlmutter, D.M.: 1970, 'On the Article in English,' in
M. Bierwisch and K.E. Heidolph (eds.), Progress in
Linguistics, The Hague: Mouton.

Perlmutter, D.M.: 1971, Deep and Surface Structure
Constraints in Syntax, Holt, Rinehart and Winston.

Perlmutter, D.M.: 1972, 'Evidence for Shadow Pronouns in
French Relativization,' in Peranteau, Levi and Phares
(eds.).

Perlmutter, D.M. and J.R. Ross: 1970, 'Relative Clauses
with Split Antecedents,' Linguistic Inquiry 1, 350.

Peters, Stanley: 1972, 'The Projection Problem: How is a
Grammar to be Selected,' in Peters, Stanley (ed.),
Goals of Linguistic Theory, Englewood Cliffs, NJ:
Prentice-Hall.

Peters, Stanley and R.W. Ritchie: 1973, 'On the Generative
Power of Transformational Grammars,' Information
Sciences 6, 49-83.

Platero, P.P.: 1974, 'The Navajo Relative Clause,'
International Journal of American Linguistics 40,
202-246.

Platero, P.R. and K.H. Hale: 1974, 'Aspects of Navajo
Anaphora, Relativization and Pronominalization,' Diné
Bizaad Náníl'įįh (The Navajo Language Review) 1, 9-25.

Postal, P.M.: 1971, Cross Over Phenomena, Holt, Rinehart
and Winston.

Postal, P.M.: 1972, 'A Global Constraint on
Pronominalization,' Linguistic Inquiry 3, 35-60.

Postal, P.M.: 1974, 'On Certain Ambiguities,' Linguistic
Inquiry 5, 325-366.

Reibel, D.A. and S.A. Schane, (eds.): 1969, *Modern Studies in English*, Englewood Cliffs, NJ: Prentice-Hall.

Ross, J.R.: 1967, *Constraints on Variables in Syntax*, unpublished Ph.D. dissertation, MIT. Distributed by the Indiana University Linguistics Club.

Ross, J.R.: 1974, 'More on -*er* Globality,' *Foundations of Language* 12, 269-270.

Sapir, Edward: 1963, 'Abnormal Speech Forms in Nootka,' in D.G. Mandelbaum (ed.), *Collected Writings of Edward Sapir*, Berkely and Los Angeles, CA: University of California Press.

Satyanarayana, P. and K.V. Subbarao: 1973, 'Are Rightward Movement Rules Upward Bounded?,' *Studies in the Linguistic Sciences* 3, 183-192, University of Illinois.

Schultz-Lorentzen, C.W.: 1945, 'A Grammar of the West Greenlandic Language,' *Meddelelser om Grönland* 129, Copenhagen.

Selirk, Elisabeth: 1970, 'On the Determiner System of Noun Phrases and Adjective Phrases,' ms., MIT. Revised version published as Selkirk (1977).

Selkirk, Elisabeth: 1977, 'Some Remarks on Noun Phrase Structure,' in P. Culicover, T. Wasow and A. Akmajian (eds.), *Formal Syntax*, Academic Press.

Siegel, Dorothy: 1974, *Topics in English Morphology*, unpublished Ph.D. dissertation, MIT.

Soames, Scott: 1974, 'Rule Orderings, Obligatory Transformations, and Derivational Constraints,' *Theoretical Linguistics* 1, 116-138.

Southworth, F.C. and N.B. Kavadi: 1973, *Spoken Marathi*, Philadelphia, PA: University of Pennsylvania Press.

Stockwell, R., P. Schachter and B. Partee: 1973, The Major Syntactic Structures of English, Holt, Rinehart and Winston.

Thiersch, Craig: 1973, 'The Harder They Come, The Harder They Fall,' ms., MIT.

Underhill, Robert: 1972, 'Turkish Participles,' Linguistic Inquiry 3, 87-100.

Vergnaud, J.R.: 1974, French Relative Clauses, unpublished Ph.D. dissertation, MIT.

Wackernagel, Jacob: 1930, Altindische Grammatik, Göttingen: Vandenhoed und Ruprecht.

Wasow, Thomas: 1972, Anaphoric Relations in English, unpublished Ph.D. dissertation, MIT.

Wilson, W.A.: 1963, 'Relative Constructions in Dagbani,' Journal of West African Languages 1, 133-144.

For Product Safety Concerns and Information please contact our EU
representative GPSR@taylorandfrancis.com
Taylor & Francis Verlag GmbH, Kaufingerstraße 24, 80331 München, Germany

www.ingramcontent.com/pod-product-compliance
Lightning Source LLC
Chambersburg PA
CBHW070401240426
43661CB00056B/2486